Electronic Alarm and Security Systems

A Technician's Guide

Recent books by Delton T. Horn

Amplifiers, Waveform Generators, and Other Low-Cost IC Projects
Basic Electronics Theory —4th Edition
Build Your Own Home Security System
Build Your Own Low-Cost Signal Generator
Electronic Projects to Control Your Home Environment
Ready-to-Build Telephone Enhancements

Electronic Alarm and Security Systems

A Technician's Guide

Delton T. Horn

TAB Books
Division of McGraw-Hill, Inc.

New York   San Francisco   Washington, D.C.   Auckland   Bogotá
Caracas   Lisbon   London   Madrid   Mexico City   Milan
Montreal   New Delhi   San Juan   Singapore
Sydney   Tokyo   Toronto

©1995 by **McGraw-Hill, Inc.**
Published by TAB Books, an imprint of McGraw-Hill, Inc.

Printed in the United States of America. All rights reserved. The publisher takes no responsibility for the use of any materials or methods described in this book, nor for the products thereof.

pbk   1 2 3 4 5 6 7 8 9   FGR/FGR   9 9 8 7 6 5
hc   1 2 3 4 5 6 7 8 9   FGR/FGR   9 9 8 7 6 5

Library of Congress Cataloging-in-Publication Data
Horn, Delton T.
     Electronic alarm and security systems : a technician's guide / by
Delton T. Horn
     Includes index.
     ISBN 0-07-030529-3 (P)   ISBN 0-07-030528-5 (H)
     1. Dwellings—Security measures. 2. Electronic security systems.
I. Title.
TH9745.D85H672   1995
643'.16—dc20   95-11434
                                                          CIP

Acquisitions editor: Roland Phelps
Editorial team: B.J. Peterson, Book Editor
                Susan W. Kagey, Managing Editor
                Joanne Slike, Executive Editor
                Jodi L. Tyler, Indexer
Production team: Katherine G. Brown, Director
                Wanda S. Ditch, Desktop Operator
                Alan Bookmiller, Computer Artist
Design team: Jaclyn J. Boone, Designer   0305293
                Katherine Stefanski, Associate Designer   EL1

Contents

Introduction

Crime is unfortunately a significant factor in modern life, making security a major concern. There is a big market for security and alarm systems. Except for the simplest (and less effective) systems, someone must install the alarm system, which usually involves some degree of customized design. The regrettable need for alarm systems creates an excellent opportunity for reliable, trustworthy electronics technicians with good mechanical skills and attention to detail.

This book covers the basic principles of designing, installing, and maintaining home alarm systems to suit virtually any circumstances and special needs. This book is not a book of specific circuits but a set of guidelines for using almost any security circuits you might encounter. Security circuits are available from many sources these days. Professional alarm system installers often contract with a particular manufacturer who will provide the necessary circuits, but the installer must put the circuits together into the most effective and functional system possible.

The emphasis in this book is on home security systems, simply because home systems are the most likely markets for the average technician's skills. Commercial alarm systems for stores, warehouses, or factories will almost always be installed by well-established companies with long and impressive track records. The only way for someone new to this field to obtain such a track record is to start small with home systems, and possibly a few small business installations.

Another advantage to the home market is there are a lot more potential home customers than large commercial customers. A home alarm system will almost always be a smaller job than a commercial installation, so you can take on more assignments in a given time and have fewer assets tied up in your supply inventory, equipment, and payroll for assistants.

This business is an ideal one for starting small (as few as two people can handle most standard home installations), yet it is excellent potential for growth, if you do good work reliably and are able to build and maintain your customers' trust in you. Trust is a vital element in the security field.

The first chapter might be a review for many readers, though some readers might be more unfamiliar with the area. This chapter briefly explains the basic principles of any alarm system and discusses most common types of sensors used in such systems.

Chapter 2 discusses some issues that you need to consider in the very important preplanning stage. Planning for these issues can save a lot of time and money in any alarm system. By considering and solving potential problems ahead of time, you can design and install a more effective, more reliable, and less expensive system. The system will suit the specific requirements of the home to be protected and can be completed faster if you plan ahead.

It is often forgotten that the home (or other building to be protected) is itself a major part of the security system. Chapter 3 examines some ways the design and structural details of the home can interact with an alarm system, providing strengths and special weaknesses that require extra protection.

Chapter 4 covers the installation procedures of an alarm system in the home. The chapter includes special attention to techniques for heading off problems before they ever get a chance to occur. In addition to covering the main installation, this chapter also considers important finishing touches. It also deals with the most important yet frequently forgotten element of any home security system: your customers, the legitimate residents of the protected home.

Chapters 5, 6, and 7 help you broaden the usefulness of a security system by covering fire, gas, and flooding hazards with your security system.

Any system requires some degree of maintenance to continue operating reliably and at peak performance. Although most home alarm systems require very little active maintenance, you shouldn't ignore the issue completely. Some tips on regular maintenance of a home alarm system are covered in Chapter 8.

Sooner or later any system can be expected to develop problems and fail partially or completely to fulfill its intended operation. Alarm systems designers will be called back to repair systems they have installed—and sometimes systems installed by others as well. Troubleshooting and repairing home alarm systems are the subjects of Chapter 9. Troubleshooting any but the simplest alarm systems can be difficult and tedious without a well thought-out plan of attack. This chapter will demonstrate how to eliminate many of the possibilities quickly before you even turn on any of your test equipment.

Like everything else these days, there have been a lot of high-tech developments in the security field. Most were designed with protecting industrial complexes, not homes, in mind. The tenth chapter explores what modern electronics can do in alarm systems. Chapter 10 also explores the question of what is or is not appropriate for a home alarm system. Although many gadgets are exciting and fun, often more reliable security can be achieved by keeping the system relatively simple. In some cases, a computer-based alarm system is a good and valuable idea, but often it is simply wasteful and increases the number of things that can go wrong. Rather than foolishly jumping for the latest nifty gadget available, you as a reputable home alarm system installer should discuss the advantages and disadvantages of such enhancements with the customer and consider whether or not they offer any real advantage to meet the customer's needs.

Without dealing with specific circuitry, this book provides an extensive look at all major areas of installing, maintaining, and troubleshooting home alarm systems. The focus of this book is on the professional alarm system installer, but electronics hobbyists and do-it-yourself homeowners and apartment dwellers will find much of value here as well. The only real difference, after all, is that the do-it-yourself system installer is his or her own customer.

1

Basic elements of an alarm system

In principle, an alarm system is simple. It is nothing more than a series of switches that can activate some output device, usually though not necessarily an audible siren or bell or something similar. All but the simplest of alarm systems also feature special control circuits, such as timers. The switching devices used in alarm systems are specialized sensors, which often are sophisticated and complex.

The greatest challenge in designing and installing an alarm system is choosing and placing the sensors used to maximize the protection offered by the system. Because a large number of sensor switches are normally used, the control circuitry required is more involved than the basic conceptual description of an alarm system might suggest.

There are actually many different types of alarm systems, defined by just what condition the sensors are designed to "look" for. This book is concerned with security systems, which implies that the alarm systems are designed to monitor an environment and provide a warning if certain emergency conditions are detected.

Burglar or intrusion alarms are the most obvious and common type, and unless otherwise mentioned in the text, it is the alarm system that will be assumed throughout most of this book. Except for the specific sensors used, almost all of what is said here about burglar alarm systems also will apply to other types of emergency alarm systems, such as fire/smoke detectors, flooding alarms, gas leak detectors, and so forth. Virtually any environmental condition that can be electronically detected can be used to trigger an alarm system. In fact, the alarm types can often be combined in a single system. For example, many deluxe burglar alarm systems also include heat sensors or smoke detectors to offer security against fire as well as an actual intrusion. The control circuitry doesn't care what the use is. In many cases, however, it is a good idea to keep the sensor types electrically separate so they sound different alarms. With this scheme, occupants of the protected area can immediately identify the type of emergency by the sound of the alarm, and take appropriate protective actions.

The focus in this book is on home security systems. Most of the information can easily be adapted for use in a small business, such as small offices or stores, but the special requirements of industrial security systems is not covered here.

The three sections of an alarm system

Almost any practical alarm system consists of three basic sections. Assume you are dealing with a burglar alarm for the time being, but realize that almost any alarm system will follow the same basic pattern.

First, a *sensor* or sensors (first section) detects the presence of an intruder, activating the *control circuitry* (second section), and sounding the output alarm or some other *indication device* (third section). This process is shown in the schematic of Fig. 1-1. Notice that in its basic principles, the alarm system is no different from any standard electronics system. Some input signal (*sensor stage*) is operated on in some way (*control stage*), producing a different but related output signal (*alarm sounder stage*). The principles are very simple, but in practice the specific details can get complex.

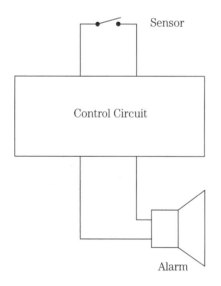

1-1
A practical alarm system has three basic sections: sensor, control circuit, and output alarm.

In some cases, one or more of these stages might be so simplified that it might be difficult to even notice in a system or circuit, but it is difficult to imagine a practical alarm system that does not include all three stages in some form.

Generally speaking, the sensor section of an alarm system is nothing more than a bunch of switches, perhaps in glorified disguises, but no different electrically than any familiar slide or push-button switch. A few specialized sensors operate over a continuous range, rather than in a discrete on/off switching manner. Such continuous-range sensors are, by far, the exception rather than the rule. In most cases, when they are used in an alarm system, they are used with a comparator circuit, which produces a switch-like on/off, yes/no output when the detected condition exceeds some specific preset trigger level. In effect, the continuous-range sensor combined with its comparator stage functions like a switch with an adjustable sensitivity.

Specific types of sensors are discussed in more detail in this chapter.

The output section of an alarm system also is pretty simple. When the monitored condition is detected, an appropriate voltage is applied to a sound-producing circuit (such as an oscillator and loudspeaker) or device (such as a bell or a buzzer). When the control section puts out this voltage, the alarm sounds; otherwise it is silent.

(Some alarm systems might produce a visual or other output signal in addition to—or instead of—an audible alarm, but this arrangement is the exception rather than the rule, and the basic principle is pretty much the same in any case.)

For any but the simplest (and most easily defeated) alarm systems, the control section is the most complex electronically. Ultimately, it can be considered just an automated signal switching circuit. You could call this the "brain" of the alarm system.

The alarm system's control circuitry activates and deactivates the system, and (when activated) monitors the sensor(s), determining from moment to moment whether or not to sound the output alarm device. Many different types of circuits are used to control alarm systems, but all are essentially switching circuits of one type or another. Most practical alarm systems use either relays or *SCRs* (silicon-controlled rectifiers) or occasionally (especially in sophisticated systems) digital gate circuits to perform the main switching functions. Occasionally other types of switching devices might be used, but the basic principle remains the same. When an intrusion (or other monitored emergency situation) is detected by the sensor(s), the control circuit sounds the output alarm device.

Most practical alarm-system control circuits also incorporate timing circuits and other special features to give the system some degree of intelligence. Such special features are discussed where appropriate throughout this book. In very sophisticated alarm systems, the control circuit might actually be a full computer.

Sensor basics

Most, though not all, sensors used in alarm systems are essentially specialized switches, no different electrically than any standard switch familiar to any electronics technician.

Like an ordinary slide or toggle switch, a sensor might be either open or closed, with no in-between values to introduce ambiguity into the system. You could consider such a sensor to be a crude binary digital circuit. Its output must always be either HIGH or LOW, with no other possibilities.

In most cases, alarm sensors function like momentary-action switches. It will automatically revert to its normal detecting state as soon as it is released, in effect resetting itself. Of course, like standard momentary-action switches, an alarm sensor can be designed as either *NO* (normally open) or *NC* (normally closed), depending on the specific requirements of the intended application. It is important to select the right sensors for a functional and practical alarm system.

The natural question arises: which is better, a normally open sensor or a normally closed sensor? In the abstract, the question is not answerable. It all depends on the specific details of your intended application. In some cases, normally open sensors would be the best choice; in others, normally closed sensors will be called for. Generally, either type can be used, although one type might require more complex support circuitry than the other in a specific application.

In *intrusion detection* (burglar alarm) systems, normally closed sensors will usually (though certainly not always) provide greater security than comparable normally open switching. To understand why this is so, consider the very simple alarm circuit shown in Fig. 1-2(A). The sensor in this circuit is a normally open switching device. When the sensor switch is closed, the alarm will be sounded. An open sensor switch indicates to the system that all is safely secure. An intruder entering the protected area will set off the sensor, closing the switch and sounding the alarm. But what if the intruder knows the alarm system is there? It would be very easy for the intruder to cut the wire between the normally open sensor and the control circuit, as shown in Fig. 1-2(B). The control circuitry will not notice this break, because electrically it looks just like an open sensor switch—the normal, secure condition. Now if the actual sensor switch is closed, it will be ignored by the control circuitry, which still sees an open circuit. In effect, the sensor switch is hard-wired permanently open, and the intruder has defeated the alarm system, with very little effort or technical know-how.

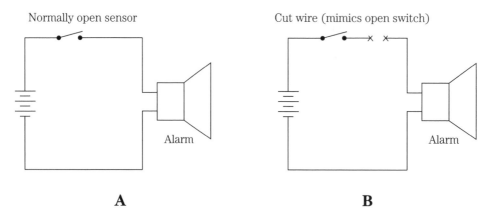

Normally open sensor

Cut wire (mimics open switch)

Alarm

Alarm

A

B

1-2 In most burglar alarm systems, normally open sensors tend to be more vulnerable to tampering than comparable normally closed sensors. A typical normally open circuit (A). Breaking the circuit neutralizes the normally open sensor (B).

Now consider the same situation in an alarm system that uses normally closed sensors, as shown in Fig. 1-3(A). When an intruder enters the protected area, the sensor switch is opened, and the alarm sounds. If an intruder attempts to cut one of the connecting wires, as shown in Fig. 1-3(B), the control circuit will simply assume the opened circuit means the sensor has been activated, detecting an intrusion, and sounding the alarm.

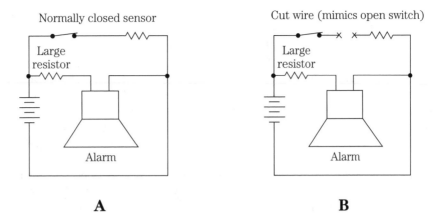

A **B**

1-3 In a burglar alarm system, normally closed sensors will usually offer greater security than comparable normally open switching. A typical normally closed circuit (A). Breaking the circuit triggers the alarm, just as if the normally closed sensor was tripped (B).

This example is a very simple one, assuming a very crude burglar alarm system. If the intruder doesn't have access to the connecting wires, it probably won't make much practical difference whether you use normally open or normally closed sensors. Many practical alarm systems incorporate both types of sensor switches. Some types of sensing naturally takes a normally open form, and others just naturally work as normally closed switching. You will encounter examples of both types in the discussion of specific sensor devices. This simple example illustrates an important point in the design of alarm systems. The possibility of interference to the system must be anticipated and protected against. The best approach, of course, is simply to make such tampering physically impossible, but such perfection can rarely be achieved in real-world systems. Throughout, this book considers (and attempts to show you how to counteract) potential sabotage.

Of course, *continuous-range* sensors do exist, as well as *yes/no* switching sensors. For example, a photoresistor exhibits a resistance directly proportional to the intensity of the light striking its sensing surface, and a thermistor varies its resistance with the sensed ambient temperature. Although such continuous-range sensors have many important applications in modern electronics, their use in security systems is limited, especially for systems dedicated to intrusion detection. As with any general rule of thumb, there are occasional and sometimes even important exceptions.

Even when a continuous-range sensor is used in an alarm system, such as a thermistor in a heat-activated fire alarm, it is usually combined with a comparator, to make it act like a switch after all. When the sensed parameter exceeds some specific preset limit, comparator output goes HIGH (otherwise it is LOW). In this case the comparator circuit is the "switch," which is either "open" or "closed" depending on the output value of the sensor. The output of the comparator is either "on" or "off," with nothing in between.

In a very few cases, you can use multiple comparator stages to switch different functions at different sensor trip points; the principle is the same, only multiplied. This arrangement is not often very useful in practical alarm systems, however. The very nature of alarm systems tends to call for clear-cut, simple yes/no sensor reactions.

In circuit diagrams for alarm systems, it is common (though not universal) to show all switching sensors (especially unknown sensors that can be of almost any type) as if they were just standard push-button switches. Electrically, they are the same thing anyway. The circuit doesn't care about the mechanics of how the switch is opened and closed, and that is the only significant difference between most types of switching sensors.

A number of specialized switch sensors have been developed specifically for alarm systems. Mechanically, standard momentary push-button switches are not going to be very useful in most alarm system applications. You could leave out a note that says, "Dear Intruder, please press this button," but it's unlikely to do much good. An alarm system calls for switches that will be mechanically tripped more or less automatically by the intruder, who is left with no choice in the matter. Ideally, the intruder should not even be aware that a specific sensor switch is there at all until it is too late and the alarm has been triggered. Of course, an intruder who knows where all the sensor switches are would have a big advantage in attempting to disable the alarm system, and you will want to keep them hidden.

Many of the specialized switching devices used in alarm systems also are used in such applications as automation and remote control. In the next few pages, take a quick look at a few of the more common and useful of these specialized switching devices. Some of them you might already be familiar with, and others might seem exotic at first. They're all just plain switches in various guises.

Magnetic reed switch

One of the most popular switch used in burglar alarm systems is the *magnetic reed switch*. This device can conveniently and inexpensively monitor a door or window and trigger the alarm circuit when the door or window is opened. The primary application of a magnetic reed switch is to determine electrically whether an object is moved away from some other object or from a specific position near a wall.

A magnetic reed switch consists of two physically separate sections. As Fig. 1-4 shows, these two sections don't really look like much in themselves. The sections appear to be just two plastic enclosed rectangular blocks with ear extensions for mounting screws. One of the pieces has contacts for two (rarely more than two) wires to be connected. These wires lead off to the alarm system control circuitry. The other section has no wires or electrical contacts. It is not electrically connected to anything.

It is usually preferable to use recessed mountings for magnetic reed switches whenever possible. The reasons for this are explained in following paragraphs. For convenience of this discussion, assume the sections are surface mounted.

The wireless half of the magnetic reed switch contains a small permanent magnet and nothing else. The other (wired) section contains the actual switching unit, a lightweight, magnetically operated reed switch. This switch can be connected to the

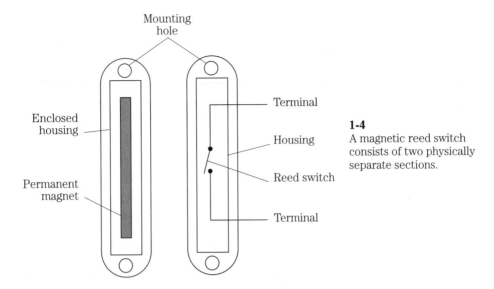

Mounting
hole

Terminal

Enclosed
housing

Housing

1-4
A magnetic reed switch
consists of two physically
separate sections.

Reed switch

Permanent
magnet

Terminal

alarm circuit (or any other type of circuit, for that matter) just like any ordinary switch. With very, very few exceptions, most magnetic reed switches are of the *SPST* (single-pole, single-throw) type. The switches are momentary-action switches. Both *NO* (normally open) and *NC* (normally closed) versions are readily available. The choice depends on the requirements of the intended application.

The *slider* of the magnetic reed switch is a magnetically sensitive reed. It is hermetically sealed in a plastic housing. When there is a sufficient magnetic field in the vicinity of this reed, it will change its physical position somewhat, activating the switch. When the magnetic field is removed (or reduced in intensity below a critical threshold level), the switch is deactivated, and the reed springs back to its normal position.

In a normally open magnetic reed switch, the reed is normally positioned so it does not make contact with the other terminal. In the presence of a sufficient magnetic field, the reed moves to touch the other switching terminal, closing the connection and permitting current to flow through the switch. When the magnetic field is removed, the connection is reopened, as the reed moves back to its normal, deactivated position. Of course, a normally closed magnetic reed switch operates in exactly the opposite way.

In operation, the wired switching unit is mounted at a fixed location, and the magnet unit is mounted on the object to be monitored. This arrangement permits the magnetic reed switch to sense the position of the monitored object. Is it close enough to the fixed reference position (the switching unit) or isn't it? For example, to monitor a door, the magnet (the section with no wires) would be mounted directly on the door, and the switch unit (the part with wires) would be mounted on the door frame. When the door is closed, the two sections will be as close to one another as possible, as shown in Fig. 1-5(A). This closeness will permit the maximum magnetic field to activate the reed within the switching unit. When the door is opened, as shown in Fig. 1-5(B), the magnet is physically moved away from the switching unit, so the magnetic field seen by the reed is reduced until the switch is deactivated.

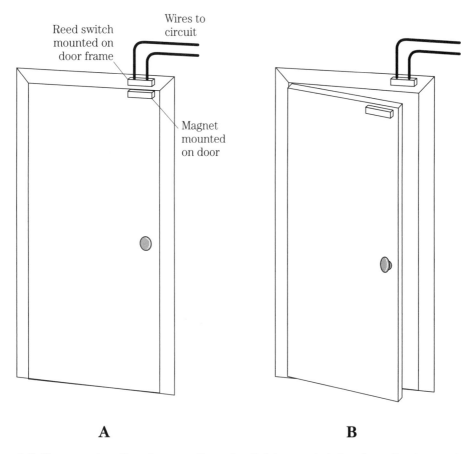

1-5 The magnet section of a magnetic reed switch is mounted directly on the door, and the switch section is mounted on the stationary door frame. When the door is closed, the two sections will be physically close to each other (A). When the door is opened, the magnet is physically moved away from the switch section (B).

Obviously, both sections of the magnetic reed switch must be mounted so an intruder cannot unscrew their mountings and move them. In most cases, this is just a matter of mounting the switch on the inside of the door or window you don't want an intruder to pass through.

For a professional installation job, it is strongly recommended that all magnetic reed switches be recessed, rather than surface mounted. This mounting is shown in Fig. 1-6. It not only makes it more difficult for any intruder to attempt to interfere with them, but it also looks a lot more attractive. Such aesthetic matters are of considerable importance in most home installations. Recessed magnetic reed switches are more difficult and time consuming to mount, but the benefits in appearance and added security make it well worth the effort.

Whenever you are mounting magnetic reed switches, take great care in all measurements and positioning of components. If the two sections of the magnetic reed switch don't align correctly, the switch will not work reliably, if at all.

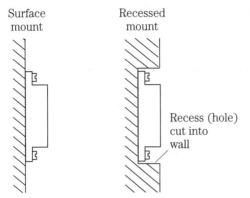

Surface mount

Recessed mount

Recess (hole) cut into wall

1-6
For the most professional installation, recess magnetic reed switches rather than surface mount.

Alignment is fairly easy in a surface-mounted installation. Line up the two sections by sight and jiggle slightly to adjust their position before tightening down the mounting screws. In a recessed installation it's a bit more complicated than that. First drill holes to recess each section. Each section must fit snugly in its recess, and they must line up perfectly the first time. There's no way to jiggle the sections to correct for any errors or misjudgments. The only way to do the job is take very precise and careful measurements before you pick up the drill or any other mounting tools.

Special aligning tools are available to help you with installation. Such specialized tools are certainly helpful, but not essential. If you don't have one, the correct procedure is to mount the magnet (no wires) section first. Once you've mounted this section, place a steel thumbtack at the end of the magnet. The magnet will hold a steel tack in place. Now, carefully and slowly (so you don't knock the tack out of place) close the door or window. The point of the tack will make a slight hole at the correct mounting location for the wired switch section. This hole will be very small and shallow. It might be easier to see if you first put some colored chalk on the point of the tack. Just stick the tack into a piece of chalk.

If you are mounting a magnetic reed switch on a metal door or window, the metal frame can interfere with the magnetic field, and effectively weakening it. To prevent weakening, use a plastic separator (insulator) between each section of the magnetic reed switch and the metal it is mounted on. If only one section is mounted on metal, only one plastic separator is required.

Magnetic reed switches can sometimes seem sensitive to the weather, especially in extreme or very changeable climates. Weather changes can often cause swelling or warping of a door or window (especially if made of wood). Even a relatively small change could move the reed switch too far from the magnet section. The distance could cause erratic operation or a false alarm if the magnet is weak. The magnets in magnetic reed switches are identified by a specification known as the *gap rating*. The gap rating is a measure of how wide a gap between the sections is required for the magnetic field to release the reed switch to its normal, deactivated position. For the best results, choose a magnetic reed switch with the highest gap rating available. It might cost a little more, but you get what you pay for.

Even some experienced technicians have been known to get a little confused about normally open and normally closed operation in such applications. Assume you are working with a normally open magnetic reed switch mounted on a door as described previously. When the door is open, the two sections of the magnetic reed switch are physically separated from each other, so the magnetic field from the permanent magnet does not reach the reed within the switch section, at least not with any significant intensity. This means the reed is in its normal deactivated position, so the switch contacts are open. When the door is closed, the magnet section is brought into close proximity with the switch section, so the magnetic field moves the reed to its activated position, closing the switch. The action of a normally open magnetic reed switch is shown in Fig. 1-7.

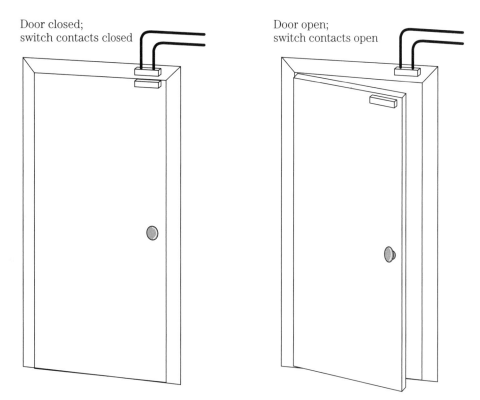

Door closed;
switch contacts closed

Door open;
switch contacts open

1-7 When the door is open, the reed section of a normally open magnetic reed switch is in its normal deactivated position, so the switch contacts are open. Closing the door closes the switch contacts.

A normally closed magnetic reed switch works in exactly the opposite way, as shown in Fig. 1-8. In this case, when the door is open and the magnetic field cannot reach the reed in the switch unit, the reed will be in its normal deactivated state, closing the contacts of the switch. Closing the door brings the magnet section near the switch section, activating the reed to open the switch contacts.

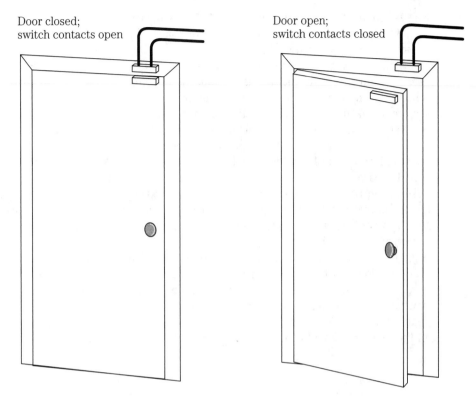

Door closed;
switch contacts open

Door open;
switch contacts closed

1-8 A normally closed magnetic reed switch works in exactly the opposite way as a normally open device.

Refer to Table 1-1 for a summary of the operation of magnetic reed switches in alarm systems that protect doors.

**Table 1-1. The operation of a
magnetic reed switch depends on
whether it is normally open or normally closed.**

Door condition	Alarm response	NO switch	NC switch
Open	Activated (alarm sounds)	Open	Closed
Shut	Normal (alarm silent)	Closed	Open

Operation can get a little confusing. In an intrusion alarm system, the control circuit should respond as if it were looking at a normally closed switch, because in this application, the door is supposed to stay closed. Closed is its "normal" condition.

The alarm system must react to the (presumedly) unusual condition of the door being opened, opening the switch. So a normally open magnetic reed switch should be used in a normally closed alarm system.

To make matters worse, some manufacturers of magnetic reed switches, knowing that their products are frequently used in alarm systems, "helpfully" designate the switch condition when the magnetic field is present (switch activated) as the "normal" state, even though this designation is not technically correct. This reverse labelling can sometimes be more convenient and obvious to the inexperienced do-it-yourself hobbyist. The fact that the expressions *normally open* and *normally closed* are standardized and in widespread use in electronics makes the reverse labelling a bad idea and potentially far more confusing. Always read the manufacturer's description of any magnetic reed switch with extra care. If you have any doubt, test a sample switch with your ohmmeter to definitely identify the true normal state. Even professional installers have made problems for themselves by installing the wrong type switch.

A magnetic reed switch also can be used to guard a window, as shown in Fig. 1-9. This application isn't too different from the way a magnetic reed switch is used on a door. Again the magnet section (no wires) is mounted on the movable part of the window pane, and the actual reed switch section (wired) is mounted on the fixed window pane. If the window is opened past a specific point (depending on the positioning of the switch elements), the alarm will be set off, just as when a protected

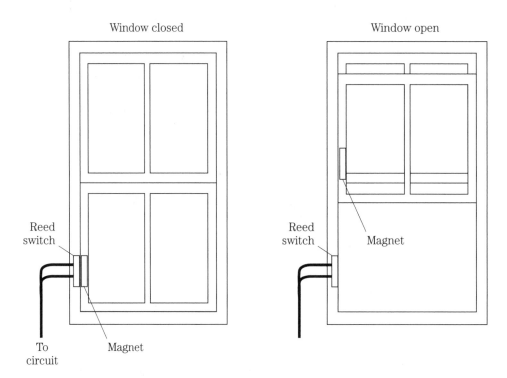

1-9 A magnetic reed switch also can be used to protect a window from intrusion.

door is opened. You might have to do some experimentation to get the switch positioning just right.

One potential problem is that you might sometimes want the window opened slightly to let air into the protected area. You often might want the intruder alarm system active while people are home, especially at night. Many people like fresh air and would be unhappy with an alarm system that makes them feel like closed-in prisoners in their own homes. One potential compromise solution is shown in Fig. 1-10. Here are two magnetic sections (one for a closed window and one for an open window). There is just one reed switch on the fixed window pane. If you want the window open, line up the lower magnet section with the reed switch. For good security, the window generally should not be opened more than about six inches. If you want the window closed, the reed switch will be lined up with the upper magnetic section.

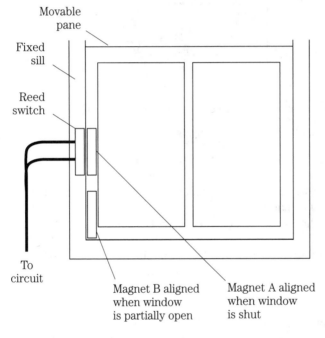

Movable pane

Fixed sill

Reed switch

To circuit

Magnet B aligned when window is partially open

Magnet A aligned when window is shut

1-10
By using two magnetic sections of a magnetic reed switch, but just one reed switch on the fixed window pane, the window can be either left closed or in a slightly opened position.

This arrangement is simple enough, but like most simple solutions, it might create problems of its own. The user must be aware that the window cannot be moved from one position to the other while the alarm control circuitry is activated, or the alarm will be sounded. The system has no way of knowing you're just closing the window. The sensor switch has been triggered, and that looks like an intrusion to the alarm system. More sophisticated solution to the window problem is covered in this book.

A magnetic reed switch also can be used to protect a movable object from theft under certain conditions. This idea is illustrated in Fig. 1-11. For purposes of illustration, assume the object to be protected is a crate (but it can be almost any inanimate object). The magnet (no wires) section is mounted on the crate, and the reed switch (wired) section is mounted on the wall or some other immovable object,

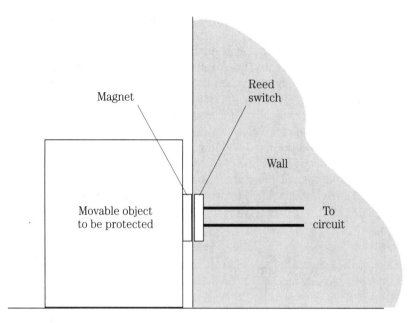

1-11 A magnetic reed switch also can be used to detect the removal of a movable object from a predetermined position.

where you want the protected crate to stay. The two sections of the magnetic reed switch must be positioned carefully, so they are as close to each other as possible. As long as the crate is left undisturbed, the magnet will hold the reed switch in its activated position (seen as the normal, untriggered condition by the alarm system). Moving the crate will break the magnetic field, releasing the reed switch, and activating the alarm circuitry.

With a little creativity and imagination, you can make the magnetic reed switch a versatile and powerful tool in your alarm system installers arsenal.

Mercury tilt switch

Another specialized switching device that is useful in alarm systems is the *mercury switch*. This device also is sometimes known as a *tilt* switch, because it is closed by being tilted at an angle. It is a very simple movement detector that can be affixed to almost movable object.

Mercury tilt switches are always of the SPST, normally open type.

The basic construction of a typical mercury switch is shown in Fig. 1-12. It is a simple sealed glass tube, containing a globule of mercury and two electrical contacts. These internal contacts are brought out to external leads for connection to the control circuitry. When the tube is tilted so the globule of mercury simultaneously touches both contacts, an electrical connection is made, and the switch is closed. If, however, the tube is tilted at any angle that leaves either one (or both) of the internal electrodes uncovered by the mercury, there is no electrical connection, and the mercury switch is opened.

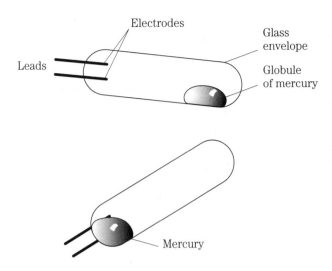

1-12
A mercury switch consists of a simple sealed glass tube, containing a globule of mercury and two electrical contacts.

Mercury switches can be used to detect relatively small physical movements easily, although they generally require very careful and precise initial placement.

The mercury switch has fairly limited applications because it is a wired switch that must be movable to function. But in certain cases, this device can be extremely useful to the designer or installer of an alarm system. It is especially useful for protecting equipment that might be highly attractive to thieves, but are not normally moved about during ordinary operation (such as computers, television sets, and home stereo systems).

Other disadvantages of the mercury switch are that it is relatively large and somewhat fragile (it is made of glass).

A very careful thief with a steady hand might be able to move the protected object in such a way that the alarm is not set off, especially if the thief can see the mercury switch and watch how closely the globule of mercury is coming to the electrodes. For this reason, it is a good idea to use two or more mercury switches mounted at differing angles to make it difficult, if not impossible, to move the object without activating at least one of the mercury switches. Of course, such multiple protection will require even greater care and precision in mounting the mercury switches and setting up the initial, normal positioning. A small error here will result in frequent false alarms or even the alarm going off immediately as soon as the control circuit is turned on.

Vibration switch

Closely related to the mercury switch is the vibration switch. This device is a sophisticated device, which just looks like an impressive little box with a pair of wires coming out of it. It generally isn't necessary for the technician to be too concerned with just what goes on within the vibration switch unit. Just treat it like a "black box." Actually there are several different internal designs in use, but they might all be considered interchangeable and functionally identical for discussion purposes. A vibration switch is almost always of the SPST, normally open type.

When the vibration switch is just sitting there with no movement, the internal switch contacts remain open, and nothing happens. Any physical movement or disturbance above a critical threshold level sets off vibrations that activate the switch, closing its internal contacts. Better-quality vibration switches have an adjustment control that permits you to fine-tune the device *sensitivity*. *Sensitivity* is a measure of just how much vibration is required to activate the switch. This feature is a very useful one that can help minimize irritating false alarms, which are almost always problems with any type of motion detector. (These problems are discussed in depth in this book.)

In addition to being prone to false triggering, the chief disadvantages of vibration switches are the size and cost. Typically a vibration switch will be at least $6 \times 2 \times 2$ inches, if not larger. This device is very bulky compared to most other types of switches commonly used in modern electronics work. Vibration switches also are fairly expensive. Very few sell for under $20 apiece, other than in special sales and surplus deals. You could probably buy close to a dozen mercury switches for the price of one vibration unit, but the vibration switch will be easier to use and won't require such precise placement. Because it can detect vibrations at any angle, the vibration switch also will tend to be more reliable and effective in theft protection than a simple mercury switch.

Snap-action switch

In some alarm applications, a *snap-action* switch might be useful in detecting a relatively small motion. A typical snap-action switch is shown in Fig. 1-13. It is a standard push-button switch with a relatively long, but very lightweight, lever over the actual push button. The extreme end of this lever is positioned to touch the object you wish to sense or monitor. Even a very small, light pressure against the lever is sufficient to activate the switch. When the lever is moved, even slightly, the switch is activated.

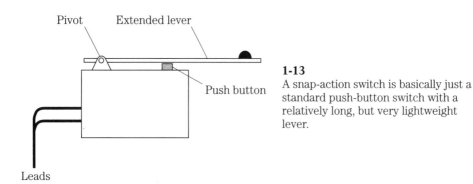

1-13
A snap-action switch is basically just a standard push-button switch with a relatively long, but very lightweight lever.

Most snap-action switches are momentary-action switches, but a few are of the push-on/push-off latching type. Momentary-action snap-action switches are available in either normally open or normally closed versions. Most of these devices are SPST switches. More complex snap-action switches—such as *SPDT* (single-pole, double-throw) or *DPDT* (double-pole, double-throw)—are available for special applications.

The unique feature of a snap-action switch, of course, is its extension arm lever, which transfers (and magnifies) a small motion from one place (the protected object) to another (the actual switch). Snap-action switches are available with many different mechanical lever arrangements to suit various applications and circumstances. The choice is determined by the physical requirements of the task. The same basic principles apply in each case.

Several separate snap-action switches can be used together to detect different possible positions of a single object.

Snap-action switches, like many specialized sensor devices, are only suitable for certain specialized applications and aren't too easily adapted to other purposes. Because they are designed to be activated by very small amounts of pressure, they are fragile, and can be damaged or broken if abused or roughly handled. Especially in very small snap-action switches, the lever can be very thin, and therefore it can be easily bent or broken. Obviously, any practical installation (especially in a security system) must take this inherent fragility into account and protect as much as possible against unnecessary damage. Certainly an intruder should not be able to defeat an alarm system simply by breaking a lightweight switch or lever. For use in alarm systems, it is a good idea to position a snap-action switch so its lever holds its button in the activated condition except when an intrusion occurs, moving the lever so it releases the push button and triggers the alarm.

Roller switch

Another specialized sensor useful in some alarm system installations is known as the *roller* or *compression* switch. A roller switch incorporates a small rolling ball built into the body of the switch, which makes contact with a window or door as it closes. Mechanically, it is vaguely similar to a mouse used with a personal computer. As the ball is depressed, it breaks (or makes) the contact. Unfortunately, the mechanism in this type of switch is prone to trouble and poor reliability due to dust and grime that can collect inside the relatively open mechanism.

A similar device is the push-button or *compression* switch. With this sensor, closing the door or window pushes a plunger in, making or breaking electrical contact. Once again, this switch can all too easily collect dirt inside its relatively open mechanism, causing the sensor to malfunction.

Although well suited to certain applications, roller switches and compression switches probably shouldn't be selected if some other sensor will do the job as well. Both these types of sensors are much more subject to unreliability due to warping of the monitored door or window than are magnetic reed switches. This consideration is particularly important in areas with widely varying climatic conditions.

Pull-trap switch

Some alarm systems use a device known as a *pull-trap* or *pull* switch. This sensor is activated by pulling out a pin or tab. There are several types of pull traps currently available.

One type of pull trap features two sets of metallic balls within the switch body. Each set of balls has a metal tab between them, a conductive cord connects the tabs.

If this cord is cut, the electrical connection is opened. This sensor is a normally closed sensor.

Another type of pull trap acts as a normally open sensor. In this version, two internal metallic balls are positioned to oppose each other through spring tension. Wires from alarm system are connected to each ball, and there is an insulating tab between the two balls. The pull trap is positioned so an attempted intrusion pulls this tab out. This action permits the two balls to come together and make electrical contact, activating the alarm. The structure of such a device is shown in Fig. 1- 14.

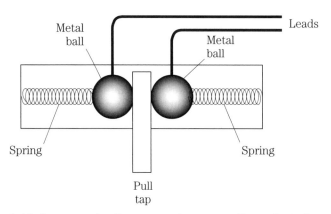

1-14 One type of pull trap contains two small metallic balls, positioned opposite each other through spring tension, with an insulating tab between the two balls. Removing the tab permits the two balls to come together and make electrical contact, activating the alarm.

Yet another type of pull trap switch uses a spring-loaded contact. If the pull cord of this device is cut or broken, the spring will trip the circuit.

Pull traps can be good choices for protecting metal doors, especially if they are not frequently used by the legitimate occupants of the home. Many basement or garage doors are metallic. A magnetic reed switch would not work well with a metal door because the steel base would interfere with the magnetic field. Pull traps also are useful for protecting property such as a parked boat or motorcycle.

The greatest disadvantage of pull traps in home security systems is one of aesthetics. Because the occupants of the home have to live with such detail, appearance is important. The pull cord is easily visible in almost any practical installation of a pull trap, and it's not very attractive. Therefore, pull traps are best used in rarely frequented locations where appearance is not a significant concern. Some examples include basements, attics, garages, and storage sheds. Actually, pull traps are not widely used in home security systems, primarily because of the appearance issue. These devices are much more popular in commercial, industrial installations.

Pressure switch

Many burglar alarm systems today use pressure switches (often called *pressure mats*). A *pressure* switch is a relatively large (in two dimensions), flat package that is usually strategically placed under a rug or mat, generally near an entryway. When an intruder steps on the pressure switch, the switch closes and activates the alarm. A simplified diagram of such a device is shown in Fig. 1-15.

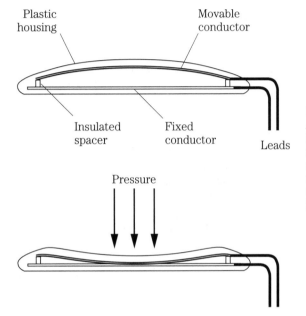

1-15
A pressure switch is a relatively large flat package. When the switch is stepped on, or otherwise compressed, it closes an internal momentary contact switch, making electrical contact between its two leads.

Careful placement of a pressure switch is necessary, or it won't offer any real protection at all. It must be concealed to be effective. Any intruder who can see one would have to be pretty stupid not to simply step over or around it. By carefully hiding the pressure mat, you might trick an intruder into stepping on it (by strategic placement), and catch the intruder by surprise.

Although a pressure switch is large compared to most other types of switches, it is still only a few inches square. This means the area it can actively protect is small. The pressure switch must be placed very carefully to maximize the chance of an intruder stepping on it. Because these devices are relatively expensive, it is rarely practical to try to cover a large area with multiple pressure switches.

A pressure switch also can be placed under a movable object to be protected. In this case, the alarm system control circuitry should be designed to the switch (by its weight) holding it closed. If someone picks up or otherwise moves the object, the pressure switch will open its contacts, and the alarm should sound.

Pressures switches are almost always of the momentary-action SPST type. These switches usually have normally open switching contacts, although a few normally closed pressure switches might be available from some manufacturers.

Foil tape

A useful item for some burglar alarm systems is foil tape. Currently, this seems to be falling out of popularity, but in some cases it might be the best and most economical solution to security protection.

Foil tape is a narrow strip of adhesive-backed tape, much like ordinary cellophane tape. Instead of cellophane, the foil tape is made of a conductive metallic foil. Its primary use is in protecting windows against breakage. It also can be used as a security seal in some specialized cases.

As discussed previously, a magnetic reed switch can protect a window from unauthorized opening. But by breaking the glass out of a window, a burglar might be able to get inside without actually opening the window. Statistics show that this method of entry is not too common for home break-ins. An intruder is more likely to break a window, then reach in to unlock it and open it. But especially with a large window, such as a picture window, someone might try to get in that way. It is more of a problem in stores with large display windows, but it can be a real concern in some home systems as well.

Foil tape is usually affixed around the perimeter of the window, something like the arrangement shown in Fig. 1-16. It is not necessary to cover most of the window area. Usually when a window is broken, cracks will carry throughout the pane. Skilled use of a glass cutter can neatly remove a section from the center of a window, but this is an unlikely possibility, and you certainly don't want to cover the majority of a window with foil tape. It would be unattractive, and the window wouldn't be much good as a window. The occupants couldn't see out, and it wouldn't let in much light.

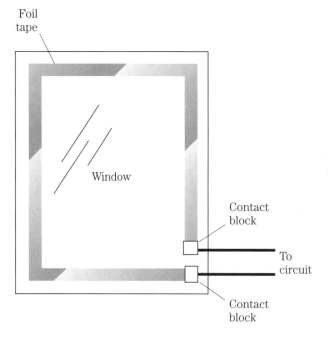

1-16
Foil tape is usually affixed around the perimeter of the window.

Even just going around the perimeter of a window with foil tape looks unattractive to most people, which is one reason why foil tape is declining in popularity in home alarm systems. (It is still widely used in commercial security systems, however.)

Notice that the foil tape is placed on the window in one continuous strip. The continuity is essential. If necessary, multiple strips of foil tape can be used, but they must be carefully overlapped so there is good electrical contact between them. To the alarm system control circuitry, the separate overlapped pieces of foil tape appear to be a continuous strip. Still, the connection won't be quite as good as a single continuous strip, so it is very important to use as few separate pieces of tape as possible.

A small contact block is placed at either end of the completed foil tape strip, once it has been affixed to the window pane. (Again many people think these contact blocks look klunky and unattractive in a home environment.) The contact block is just a little mechanical device that makes secure electrical contact with the conductive foil tape and permits connection to a wire to the alarm system control circuitry.

Ordinarily, the foil tape provides a continuous current path from one contact block to the other. To the alarm control circuit, the foil tape is a normally closed switch.

If an intruder breaks the window, the odds are very good that some portion of the foil tape around the parameter of the pane also will be split by a crack. Just one small crack in the tape is all that is needed to open "the switch," and activate the alarm, just like any other normally closed sensor switch.

In addition to the inherent limitations mentioned, foil tape can be a problem because it is very thin and therefore fragile. Very small breaks could cause annoying false alarms. I encountered such a problem in a commercial installation when I worked for a retail store years ago. I frequently got a call in the middle of the night telling me the store alarm had gone off. I'd get out there and discover that all was secure. It finally turned out that there was a hairline crack in the foil tape on the front window. As the temperature changed at night, the glass would expand and contract slightly, just enough to make or break an electrical connection across the crack in the tape. This problem, and ways to locate and prevent is discussed in other chapters on troubleshooting.

Glass break detector

Glass break detectors are popular currently. A glass break detector is an acoustically sensitive device, tuned to respond to the frequencies that occur in the sound of breaking glass. Unfortunately, the same frequencies can occur in other sounds, resulting in potential false alarms. Moreover, the exact frequency composition of the sound might vary, depending on just how the glass is broken, so a glass break detector might not always function reliably.

A glass break detector is usually mounted on the frame of a large stationary window. A picture window is a common choice. A small acoustic sensor (or sometimes a vibrational sensor) is held against the glass. In some cases it is adhesively fastened to the glass, with a suction cup, or special tape. If the glass is broken, the detector (theoretically) responds to the sound and triggers the alarm system.

Another variation of a glass break detector is mounted on a wall inside the protected room. It also detects the sound of breaking glass. This type particularly might have reliability problems. The type with a sensor right against the window can have fairly low sensitivity to minimize false alarms from other sounds. Because of the close proximity, not much force will make the breaking of the window more than sufficient to trigger the sensor. The wall-mounted type must be able to respond to somewhat weaker sounds, because of the distance between the sensor and the glass. Unfortunately, no currently available sensor can truly distinguish between actual breaking glass and similar sounds. Many sounds that wouldn't sound much like breaking glass at all to a human might confuse an electronic sensor if the sound has a similar frequency spectrum. Obviously, this device is inherently prone to false alarms. The only recourse is to lower the sensitivity of the sensor, in which case, it might not respond if the glass actually is broken, especially by a careful intruder. Glass break detectors are best used in unoccupied locations, such as commercial installations at night, where other falsely triggering sounds are unlikely.

Although a glass break detector has some emotional appeal to a lot of people and sounds like such a good idea, it's usually not necessary for an adequate home security system. Statistics show that burglars rarely break a window and crawl in through the broken glass. More commonly, an intruder might break a glass window just to reach in and unlock a window or door to open it for entrance. Other types of sensors can protect against this with greater reliability and less chance of false alarm problems.

Other sensors

Other, often more obscure, specialized sensor switches also are available and might be suitable for use in home alarm systems under some circumstances. The alarm system designer/installer should be creative in finding ways to use various unusual switching devices that might be available, especially when a security system has unusual requirements. Any switching device will probably be suitable only for a few particular locations throughout the alarm system coverage. A good alarm system will incorporate many different types of sensors to maximize the overall total protection and security.

Active and passive alarm systems

Security alarm systems can be divided into two basic categories, which are often termed *active* and *passive*. With very few exceptions, an active system is more suitable to a commercial installation than to a home installation, although in some cases certain active features can add to the security offered in a home system, especially if the home is likely to be unoccupied frequently or for extended periods of time.

As a very simple definition, a passive alarm system is activated by a mechanical switch. It assumes an intrusion attempt when a protected door or window is opened. Such a system can be activated while the family is at home. Their activities within the home are unrestricted by the alarm system. Family members can essentially ignore the system as they go about their business in the home (although the system must be deactivated if anyone wants to leave or enter the premises without setting off the alarm.)

An active security system electronically "looks" for the actual intruder. Some type of motion detection is involved. Most such systems use infrared beams and detectors, although a few work off existing visible light, using standard photosensors.

A typical active system will emit its own beam signal. Infrared light or ultrasonic waves are generally preferred, because they are not directly detectable by humans. When this generated beam strikes an object, it is reflected back to a sensor. In some systems, the beam is broken by an object passing between the beam emitter and the sensor/detector. It doesn't matter how large or small the object is, as long as it is large enough to interfere with the beam path (and that doesn't take much size at all). Objects that remain motionless are ignored by the system, but anything that moves will cause a change in the beam pattern detected by the sensor. This difference activates the alarm circuitry. Any moving object is assumed to be an intruder, and will set off the alarm. Obviously, no one (including children and pets) can be within the protected area while the system is activated, or the alarm will be triggered. If the system is activated while the family is home (for example, at night), certain rooms or areas must be avoided by everyone. Forgetting and wandering into a protected area will cause a false alarm. The system has no way of distinguishing between people (or animals) who are legitimately present and actual intruders.

In many cases, active alarm systems have set off false alarms from such things as moving drapes and (with a few designs) even moving shadows from outside a window. Clearly, false alarms are much more of a problem with an active security system than with a passive system, although they can plague either type.

Some active alarm systems have carefully calibrated sensitivity that will permit them to more or less reliably ignore small pets. But the lower the sensitivity, the greater the chance that a smart, careful intruder could fool the system. Ultrasonically based systems can create additional problems in households with pets. Although the ultrasonic tones are inaudibly to humans, they might be clearly audible and irritating, perhaps even painful, to common pets like dogs and cats. At best this could affect your pet's temperament. It could lead to some medical problems as well.

Such active motion-detection systems are best suited for protecting relatively large unoccupied areas. The systems are ideal for commercial locations such as warehouses and stores during off hours. In a home, their use is far more limiting, and can make the occupants feel like prisoners in their home. This prison atmosphere is hardly the desired goal for installing a security system. It is likely to make the people in the home feel more fearful than secure.

Active devices like this can be useful in a home security system if there will be frequent or extended periods when no one is at home. The active portions of the system should be set up as a secondary, independent subsystem. That is, you should be able to activate just the main, passive system without the active devices, or the full system (both passive and active devices). Such a flexible system is not hard to design and install, and in a sense it does offer the best of both worlds.

For most home installations, a predominantly passive security system will be the most appropriate choice. A passive alarm system will be far more reliable and result in far fewer false alarms than an active system. Many lay persons would assume that an active system would provide greater security than a passive system, but the exact opposite is true. A passive alarm system with no active elements will offer far greater security overall than an active alarm system with no passive elements. Active motion detectors should only serve as back-up in addition to full passive protection.

If a customer questions this, point out that a passive alarm system functions before the intruder gets into the protected area. It guards the entrances. An active system, on the other hand, only comes into play once the intruder is already inside the protected area. Obviously, the best security would be an attempt to keep the intruder from ever getting inside at all. The active back-up is just extra insurance in case an intruder somehow manages to get past the first (passive) layer of protection.

The control circuitry for an active security system is a bit more expensive than for a comparable passive sensor system; however, this difference is more than offset by the added difficulty and expense involved in the installation of the passive system. A passive alarm requires the mounting of appropriate sensors on each and every individual entryway (doors and windows) and any special protection points (pressure mats, etc.), and physical wires must be run from each of the sensors to the control circuitry. Of course, its appearance is an issue (as it usually is in a home environment), the installation job is increased accordingly. But the extra effort is more than worth it. The hard-wired passive system will do a better job than an easily installed active system.

You should discourage your customers from opting for one of the many self-contained modular alarm systems now being marketed. Modular systems are often advertised on TV and in magazines. The big selling points of these devices are their low cost and easy installation. Yes, they do tend to be inexpensive, and installation usually involves little more than taking the unit out of the box and plugging it in. Some customers might feel that you are arguing against these units in the interest of making greater profits for yourself. But it's actually a case of getting what you pay for. These cheap modular units don't do a very good job of securing a home.

These modular alarm units are usually active motion detectors of some type. Most are ac (alternating current) powered. Some also offer a back-up battery, but this is certainly the exception rather than the rule. In addition to the usual limitations and problems of active alarm systems (as described in preceding paragraphs), these modular units are rarely even particularly good active alarm systems. A good motion-detector circuit is not cheap, and these units are designed primarily for low cost. Because of their super-simple approach, sensitivity can be a significant problem. Either they are so overly sensitive that almost anything (or seemingly nothing in many cases) can set them off with lots of false alarms. At the other extreme, the sensitivity might be so low that an intruder would practically have to start break-dancing to trigger the alarm.

Because the entire unit is small and fully self-contained, the actual alarm sounding device also is small, and not very loud as alarms go. It can alert somebody in a nearby room in the same building but that's about it. It would probably be completely useless when no one was at home. Even if neighbors could hear it, any burglar with the slightest bit of intelligence could quickly find the power cord and unplug it, silencing the alarm. The neighbors are sure to conclude the brief burst of noise was just a false alarm, if they give it any thought at all.

The range of these modular alarm units also is limited compared to full, active motion detectors. At best they can protect only a very limited area. A few modular units are designed to permit some external expansion connections, but such units are rare. After all, one of the chief selling points is "no installation units," and for technophobes, plugging in an expansion unit counts as "installation," which they might wish to avoid.

Still, these modular alarm systems are so low in cost and easy to use, they might be considered useful as limited protection under certain circumstances. For example, someone who travels frequently, might want to set one up in their motel room to discourage anyone from stealing their luggage while they're out of the room. Someone in a nearby room is sure to hear the alarm, and investigate or call the front desk (if only to complain about the noise). But these quick-and-dirty modular systems are inadequate to provide any meaningful security as a permanent home installation. Cheap as they are, it's almost like throwing money away.

Limitations of passive alarm systems

Although passive alarm systems are generally preferable in a home security system, they are not perfect. Certain inherent limitations to the passive approach must be kept in mind.

One of the most obvious disadvantages to the end user is actually an advantage to the professional alarm installer—that is, such systems need actual installation, unlike active systems that often only need to be set up and plugged in. Usually in a passive alarm system, the various sensors must be physically wired to the control circuitry. Obviously enough, this leads to installation expense and effort. The greater security provided by the passive system make this extra cost and effort well worthwhile.

In a home, the installation process is further complicated by the simple fact that all of the wires and sensors must be mounted to be as unobtrusive and attractive as possible.

The end user must help the passive alarm system along to some degree. Although the required effort is minimal, it might be considered as a disadvantage by some. For example, all of the protected doors and windows in the home must be closed before the system can be activated. If any door or window is left open, the alarm will be set off immediately. This precaution really isn't much of a hardship. Closing all doors and windows before leaving home or going to bed at night is clearly something that should be done anyway, even with no alarm system in the home. Leaving doors or windows open is just an invitation to burglars to come on in and help themselves. In a way, this disadvantage of a passive alarm system might actually be more of an advantage. The system doesn't let the homeowner forget to secure the home in this most basic of ways.

A more genuine problem is that of getting fresh air in the home while no one is home. It is unpleasant to come home to stuffy, possibly musty house. An alarm system should not make life more unpleasant. One simple solution is already discussed in the section on magnetic reed switch sensors in this chapter. Simply add a second set of magnets to selected windows throughout the home. The second magnet should make contact with the reed switch when the window is in a slightly open position. Don't let the window be opened too far. The open position should leave a gap of no more than 6 inches, so no one can get in without opening the window farther (and triggering the alarm). This opening is ample to provide sufficient air flow to prevent the home from getting stuffy, closed-up air.

Another built-in disadvantage of a passive alarm system is that each person having legitimate reason to enter the home unaccompanied has to carry an extra key or remember a code to arm and disarm the alarm system. In a multiperson household, especially with large families, an entry code will probably be less fuss and bother than multiple copies of a key, which can more easily be lost or stolen. By all means, keep the code simple and easy for family members to remember. It should be something obvious to legitimate family members, but not to anyone else.

Commercially monitored alarm systems

When many people think of a full-featured alarm system, they think of a commercially monitored alarm system. Such systems are more or less the Cadillacs of the field. This high quality means they are expensive and are much more than what is required to meet the average consumer's need. In many cases they are selected more for snob appeal and keeping up with the Joneses than any really practical reason.

When this alarm system is triggered, a message is automatically sent out to the monitoring company, who confirms the validity of the alarm and calls the authorities or sends out their own guards to check your premises. Knowing that your system is being protectively watched can be comforting, but does it really add to your actual security?

In most homes, sounding a local alarm (and perhaps turning on lights, etc.) is sufficient. This action will probably scare off the intruder and alert anyone who is legitimately in the home. If no one is at home, the loud alarm is likely to prompt neighbors to call the police. Their call might be made helpfully, or they might just call to complain about the noise. For your security purposes, it doesn't make much difference. Either way the police are notified that something is going on in your home, and they need to investigate immediately.

Especially in an apartment complex or in an area with closely spaced homes, it's no real problem to install an alarm that is loud enough to get the job done. For homes in remote areas, it is possible that a local alarm sounding might not be heard by anyone when it goes off. In this case a commercially monitored alarm system is a viable and desirable choice.

False alarms can be a problem with any alarm system. A monitoring company is not going to call the police or send out their own personnel until they've determined that it is probably not a false alarm. The verification procedure can be a real nuisance, especially in homes with small children. When the alarm system is triggered, the monitoring company will telephone the customer's home. If it is a false alarm, the customer should give a special code word (which should be kept secret, only on a need-to-know basis). If no one answers the phone, or if the person answering the phone does not give the correct code word, the monitoring company will assume it is a legitimate alarm and will then call the police or send out its own guards.

Except for the telephone link to the monitoring company, the actual alarm system is pretty much the same as any comparable hard-wired alarm system. The system hardware will almost always be installed by the monitoring company. The company will rarely accept a previously installed alarm system that does not meet their own usual standards.

Some deluxe alarm systems are similar to the commercially monitored systems, but a monitoring company is not kept under contract. Instead, the system's telephone link automatically dials the number for the police and plays a prerecorded tape giving the address and summoning help. This device could save some critical time. However, it is important to realize that false alarms is a very serious problem here. In many areas the police now charge for investigating what turns out to be a false alarm. Some people might be offended by this. After all, they pay taxes, and feel they should receive police protection without paying extra for it. Such false alarm charges really are fair and reasonable when you consider the limited resources of most police departments. While officers are checking out your false alarm, another crime might be in progress without an officer available. And some systems are very prone to frequent false alarms. In a densely populated area, a number of such systems could keep the police very busy just checking out false alarms.

Often the police will tend to give such automated alarm calls a low priority, because they've gotten so many false alarms from them. It's like the boy who cried wolf. Nuisance false alarms might cause a genuine alarm to be ignored.

Unless there are special circumstances involved, this alarm system is not recommended. An alarm installer should be prepared to explain to customers why it's not the good idea it sounds like at first.

More security, not more fear

A good alarm system does not make one feel like a prisoner in one's own home. If it does, the system is not doing its job well. An alarm system should make the customer feel more secure, not more paranoid and afraid.

The amount of protection should be reasonable in proportion to the risk and the value protected. Of course, the value of the lives of your loved ones can't be calculated. Beyond reasonable precautions, too much protection can be counter-productive. If too heavy an alarm system is used, any occupants of the home will lead lives of constant fear and restriction. Instead of feeling more secure, they will feel like helpless prisoners. In a sense, this would make their lives worth less.

Certainly, poor people's lives are worth as much as rich people's. But rich people are more likely to have a burglar in the first place, because they have more of value to steal. It makes sense to consider how much alarm protection is needed based on material goods. It would clearly be ridiculous to install a $3000 alarm system to protect $500 worth of valuables. Adequate protection can be achieved for far less.

Some alarm installers might be inclined to oversell their systems for the highest profit. But this practice does not make good business sense. An oppressive, overdone alarm system will result in dissatisfied customers. Because this is a business that depends heavily on trust, word-of-mouth recommendations can play an important, if not decisive role in how long the installer stays in business.

It is vital for any independent alarm installer to have a good reputation. Customers must trust your honesty and must believe that you won't go out of business when their system needs servicing or develops problems due to installation errors. Many customers might be concerned that you (or one of your assistants) might actually burglarize their home after installing the system. After all, who is better equipped to defeat the system? You must take care to reassure your customers of your honesty and that of your employees. A dress code of some type might be advisable. It won't help the customer trust you if your assistants look like they were just released from prison or part of a street gang. You don't need formal uniforms or spotlessly clean attire—installation can get you dirty quite quickly. But reasonable neatness counts for a lot. Humorous slogans on Tee shirts could backfire if they raise any doubts in the minds of your customers. Remember, different people have different senses of humor, and some people have little sense of humor at all—especially when it comes to their security systems.

2
Planning an alarm system

Planning all the details of an alarm system before beginning any aspect of the physical installation is never a waste of time. It should not even be considered optional. More often than not, planning makes all the difference between success and failure. Certainly an adequately planned system will be more efficient and less expensive overall than one that is designed as it is installed in almost a hit-or-miss fashion, addressing problems as they come up instead of anticipating and preventing them ahead of time.

Conceptually, an alarm system is not at all complicated. It's just a straightforward matter of a series of switches and a few incidental circuits, such as timers. On a different level, designing and installing a good alarm system is complex, because there are so many details involved. Careful advance planning of an alarm system is essential.

Every practical alarm system is different. Different homes are designed differently, and individual needs vary. Therefore, no book like this can responsibly give a universal system design, or simple step-by-step directions for designing a useful alarm system. Fortunately, there are a number of useful tips on how to design a system to meet the specific requirements of the situation you are facing.

There is much variation, but the basic material costs of a typical full-featured home-security system will run about $500. This cost is just the cost of the physical materials. No installation charges are included. Fully installed alarm systems usually run about $1500 to $2500. Even with labor costs for yourself and a partner, and the costs of advertising and maintaining an office, a decent if unexceptional profit margin can easily be achieved if you work efficiently. Naturally you want to avoid wasting time and the need for call backs. Call backs are probably the biggest problem that can drive an alarm system installation business under. To stay in business, you must head off potential call-back situations before they occur. The only way to do that is by carefully planning before the actual physical installation of the system. Planning is not wasted time, nor is it an option. It is probably the most vital part of the job of installing an alarm system.

For most projects, you will need to hire at least one assistant or take on a partner. With very few exceptions, it will take at least two people to install a decent alarm system properly. If nothing else, you are dealing with relatively long lengths of wire from the various sensors to the central control circuitry. Unless you're willing to run back and forth very frequently, an assistant at the opposite end of the wire will be very desirable and worthwhile. In fact, you will often find that someone needs to be at both ends of a wire at once to get the job done right, or even to get it done at all.

An inexpensive set of walkie-talkies will make communication with your assistant more convenient during the installation. A second assistant also can come in handy on larger jobs.

Don't scrimp on labor or materials. Scrimping will inevitably show in your finished work and is likely to result in frequent costly (to you) and time-consuming call backs and customer dissatisfaction. In all consumer businesses, word-of-mouth recommendations are important, but for alarm system installation, good word-of-mouth publicity is almost essential. People want somebody they can trust to install their security systems, for obvious reasons. Almost every potential customer will want to ask their friends and neighbors if they've used your services and if they recommend you. You definitely won't be doing yourself or your business any favors by cutting corners. You will probably have to accept a smaller profit margin when you begin to ensure any profits at all later on. Don't let your business fail because you were too cheap to hire sufficient help or to buy materials of adequate quality.

For reasons discussed in this book, assume that the alarm system you are working with is primarily of the passive type.

One of the most important tricks of the trade for customer satisfaction is to mount all of the system wires and sensors as unobtrusively and attractively as possible. Remember, this is someone's home. They have to live with the system. An ugly, excessively prominent installation will almost certainly result in serious customer dissatisfaction. You might lose the contract in the middle of the job. At best you won't get positive word-of-mouth advertising. In an industrial installation, such aesthetics will not be as important, but most people go to some effort and expense to decorate their home to suit their tastes. Clumsily mounted sensors and exposed wires aren't likely to go with the general decor. They'll almost certainly stick out like the proverbial sore thumb.

Essential features for a home alarm system

Certain factors are virtually essential in any worthwhile home security system. Trying to economize by leaving out any of these features is foolish at best because it will limit, if not eliminate, the protective value of the entire system.

A home alarm system needs to be as invisible to the legitimate occupants of the home as possible. This invisibility doesn't mean they don't know its there, of course, or even that they don't know the details of how it works. They (at least the adults in the house) should know these things. But they should be able to ignore the alarm system as they go about their daily life. Naturally, they will need to make some adjustments. The system won't provide any security at all if they don't arm it and disarm it when appropriate. All protected doors and windows must be shut before they can activate the system, which should be done any time the house is being left unoccupied (even for just a moment or two). But these things are easy enough to get used to. They will quickly become a matter of habit.

But it is very important that the family doesn't feel like prisoners in their own home. The imprisoned feeling is why active systems are undesirable when anyone is home. Family members should feel free to enter any room they choose, without setting off an alarm. They should have to take any special actions or precautions to make a midnight trip to the bathroom or the refrigerator. The alarm system should guard against a possible intruder getting in, not against family members going about their lives.

Especially in households with young children, it's simply not reasonable to expect everyone to remember "Don't go in there," or "Don't touch that." In a well-designed security system, no one in the family will have to worry about such things at all.

Ultimately, the function of a security system really is to provide security, which is an emotional state. The family knows the alarm system is "on the job," and feels a little safer. Ideally it will never really be needed, but its nice to have it there, just in case. Family members don't have to worry so much about the possibility of a prowler or burglar. But if the alarm system is intrusive and inconvenient, it is a constant reminder of such a risk, and some family members might even feel less secure than before the system was installed. This feeling destroys much of the value of a security system in a very real (but often ignored) sense.

Clearly the legitimate occupants of the house need some way to arm and disarm the system as they come and go. This process should be as simple and convenient as possible but as inconvenient as possible to any intruder. Usually this task is accomplished with either a key-operated lock switch or a code entered on a keypad, similar to that of a pocket calculator. Arming and disarming systems is discussed in more detail in this chapter.

In addition to a simple but reasonably secure method of arming and disarming the alarm system, a set of status lights or indicators should be included in any good security design. This indicator panel should be near the arming switch. At a bare minimum, it should include an *LED* (light-emitting diode) or other indication device that tells you at a glance whether the system is activated or not. It would be even better to use two indicator lamps for this purpose. One light (preferably red) is lit when the system is armed, and the other (preferably green) lights up when the system is in its deactivated state. One of these two indicators should be lit at any given time (assuming power is applied to the system). This information might seem redundant, but LEDs are very inexpensive and don't take up much space on a control panel. With the intentional redundancy, there is greater reliability and less chance of error. This way you know the status of the system, even if there is a defective or burned-out lamp or LED. It's a very inexpensive way to build confidence in the system.

Additional indicator lamps also would be helpful, especially in a moderate to large system with any degree of complexity. A good idea is an indicator lamp that lights up if any of the protected doors or windows are open while the system is deactivated. This feature might seem a little odd at first—it should be okay to open the doors or windows while the system is deactivated, shouldn't it? Of course it's all right, but it can be very helpful to have some convenient way of knowing if anything is not secured (open) before arming the system. Assume there is no such indicator, and you happen to forget one open window in another part of the house. When the alarm system is armed, the alarm will immediately go off because of the activated sensor on the forgotten window. No serious harm would be done in such a case, but it is an unnecessary false alarm and could be jarring on the nerves. It also could disturb and annoy the neighbors.

In more sophisticated systems, especially in a large house with many rooms, several such open-door or open-window indicators could be used to make it easier to determine just where the problem is located, so you don't have to check through the entire house. For example, one indicator might be used for the living room, one for the kitchen, and one for each bedroom. A simplified schematic of the house can even be drawn on the control panel to make the system as easy as possible to use. A typical example is shown in Fig. 2-1.

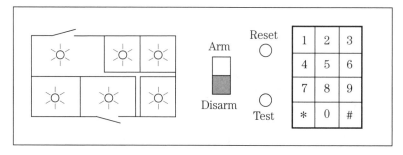

2-1 A simplified schematic of the house can be drawn directly on the control panel.

In addition, the same indicators could be used by occupants of the house in a real alarm situation while someone is at home, say at night. Someone in the family would merely have to glance at the control panel to know approximately where in the house the presumed intruder might be. This information could be very valuable. It could even save lives under some circumstances.

Such open-door or open-window indicators could be added to almost any multi-room alarm system with minimum added expense or installation difficulty, but it could be a big convenience, which your customers are sure to appreciate.

Many of the inexpensive modular alarm systems on the market use just battery power. This idea is not really a good one. Batteries eventually run down and lose power, even just sitting on a shelf. In accordance with Murphy's law they have a nasty habit of going bad just when they're most needed. An alarm system without operating power is not going to provide any practical security at all. The manufacturers of such equipment customarily advise users to check the batteries periodically. But human nature being what it is, this advice is all too often forgotten or neglected. Even with regular battery checking, there could be an unexpected battery failure at a critical moment, just because of simple unlucky timing. For instance, an intrusion could occur the day before the regularly scheduled battery check that would have revealed that battery power had gotten too low to do the job properly.

On the other hand, a number of other modular alarm systems use just ac power, and this could be an even worse idea. With a few of the most inexpensive designs, there is nothing to stop an intruder from simply reaching out and pulling the plug, rendering the system utterly useless. There certainly wouldn't be much security in such a case.

Even without an obvious and easily accessible power cord (which most commercial alarm systems do avoid, for obvious reasons), many ac-powered alarm systems have been shut down by an intruder cutting the power line to the house, or even getting to the fuse box and throwing the home's master power switch. In many areas, external power meters (used by the electric company for billing purposes) can be yanked out with little real difficulty, although there is some serious risk of a major shock hazard. But then, burglary is a pretty dangerous business, and many burglars would be willing to take the risk. With the power meter removed, the power line circuit is broken, and the house will receive no ac power. Obviously an alarm system that relies solely on ac power would be helpless and useless.

A power brownout or blackout, from whatever cause, also would disable a solely ac-powered alarm system. Many burglars are ready to jump at such convenient opportunities whenever they occur. In some regions, a heavy thunderstorm could do burglars a big favor in this way. Prospective burglars would just have to listen to the news on the radio and wait for a report on an area-wide power outage nearby, then go to the affected area, and go to work.

So an alarm system that is powered by batteries is unreliable (under certain circumstances), and so is one that uses ac power (under other circumstances). What other option is there? Simple—use both types of power.

These days there is really no excuse for anyone to bother with any alarm system that does not use ac power with battery back-up (although there are still many such systems still on the market and in use). It's the only system power that offers a reasonable degree of security. Normally the system operates off ordinary, inexpensive and convenient ac house current. In most systems, the power drain will be negligible, except when the alarm has actually been triggered in response to a detected security problem. When the system is merely armed and on guard, it uses just minimal power, and would not create a noticeable increase in the average home electric bill, even if it was left activated all the time. At the same time, the back-up batteries are being continuously trickle-charged to ensure that they will be at full power when and if they are needed.

If ac power is interrupted for any reason, the system detects this and immediately switches itself to battery power. When the ac power is restored, the system automatically goes back to its normal (ac-powered) mode of operation. Unless the ac power happens to be off for a very long time, permitting the batteries to be drained (in most systems a period of several months would be required for this), there will be no break in the security coverage of the system. It is really the best of both worlds. Such ac power with battery back-up should be considered an absolutely essential feature of any worthwhile alarm system. The only possible exception might be if a security system was needed in some rural area without any ac power available.

Another essential feature for a home alarm system that is too often neglected is a shutoff timer for the alarm, siren, or bell. There is no reason whatsoever for permitting the alarm to sound indefinitely. If the intruder is not scared off or caught in the act in the first few minutes after the alarm starts to sound, odds are exceedingly slim that continuing to sound the alarm will accomplish anything at all beyond wasting power and annoying the neighbors. In almost all cases, an alarm shutoff after ten to fifteen minutes would be sufficient. Actually even this is a very long time to sound an alarm. If the alarm hasn't achieved results after that much time, it's reasonable to assume it's not going to achieve any results at all. Certainly there would never be any reason to set the shutoff timer for anything more than 20 to 30 minutes, as an absolute maximum. Sounding an alarm longer than that could actually increase the chances for additional burglaries in your home and for your immediate neighbors. If another burglar (or even the same one hiding nearby) notices the alarm has been sounding a while without response, it would be very reasonable for the burglar to assume the premises can be reentered without much risk of being interrupted or caught. The intruder certainly wouldn't have to worry about the possibility of setting off an alarm. A burglar also might consider it pretty safe to hit one or more of your neighbors' homes as well. So what if they happen to have an alarm system too? Yours is already making enough noise, odds are that a second alarm would hardly be noticed. Even if it was, if no one responded to the first alarm, it's unlikely that anyone would respond to a second.

There's another very good reason to include a shutoff timer in any home alarm system. In most cities the police are permitted to enter an unoccupied home to silence a continuously sounding alarm, even if it means breaking in. (The alarm might have been set off by a false-alarm condition, of course.) If any of your property gets damaged in the process, you probably won't have any legal recourse. After all, your alarm was disturbing the peace (not to mention increasing the risk of burglary for your neighbors), which is against the law. The good of the community prevails.

Recently there was a nationally covered news story that well illustrated these points. In the spring of 1994, a doctor armed his alarm system and went on vacation in Europe. While he was gone, a power failure caused a false alarm, and his system did not have a shutoff timer. Because of a loophole in the local ordinances, the police couldn't enter the premises to turn it off without authorization, and no one knew where to reach the home owner. The alarm continued to torment the neighbors for six full days before the homeowner could be reached and arrangements could be made to turn the system off. The doctor probably found himself facing some heavy lawsuits and possibly minor criminal charges. Inadvertently or not, he literally tortured a good number of people for several days. Also, there was absolutely no excuse for his cruel negligence. A minimal quick-and-dirty timer circuit can be built for just a couple of dollars. It would not add appreciably to the design of any home alarm system. (Of course, many additional features could be added if more sophisticated and expensive timer circuitry is used.)

At least a minimal shutoff timer should be considered an absolute must for any home alarm system. The alarm system cannot be considered complete without it.

Except in the simplest and least expensive alarm systems, the timer circuit should be at least sophisticated enough to reset and rearm itself after the automated shut down procedure, or the home will be left unprotected until someone comes home and resets the system. A smart burglar could deliberately set off the alarm and immediately retreat, then come back an hour or so later to ransack the now unprotected home. If the system automatically resets and rearms itself, this burglar's trick will not work.

Unfortunately, any such automatic reset function is inherently limited. If a door or window has been left open (and you can hardly count on a fleeing intruder being courteous enough to resecure the premises), the system will not be able to reset itself. If it did reset, it would just set off the alarm again immediately, defeating the vital purpose of the shut down timer. The system must therefore have some method of checking that all sensors are in their normal condition before resetting itself. If not, the system should shut down entirely. (It would be a good idea to keep any fire alarm sensors on an independent circuit that is not shut down.) The result is effectively the same as having no reset function at all. But it's the best that can be done under most circumstances. The reset function will be most useful after false alarms or alarms due to sound or optical sensors rather than entryway switches.

Probably the simplest way to set up such a shut down function would be to add a secondary timer, with a short time period—no more than a minute or two. This timer is activated when the system attempts to reset itself. If the alarm is retriggered before this timer times out, the system assumes something is unsecured and shuts down rather than sounding repeated false alarms.

Another approach would be to monitor the signals sent to the localized indicators on the control panel (discussed in this section). A simple digital gating circuit could determine if there is a HIGH signal on any of the indicator lines, indicating one or more unsecure sensors, and disable the reset function.

In very sophisticated computer-controlled alarm systems, the computer can easily be programmed to look for any unsecure sensors before beginning the automatic reset procedure. If the computer is reasonably powerful and versatile enough in its programming, it could even ignore one unsecure sensor after resetting the system, while keeping the rest of the system active. This security still isn't perfect, but it's a lot better than the all-or-nothing choices available in simpler alarm systems.

Some people might attempt to excuse not using an automatic shutoff timer in a home alarm system by claiming that a continuously sounding alarm will let the homeowner know there was a violation of the security system when returning home. But this excuse is flimsy and foolish. It would be easy enough to add a latched indicator LED (or something similar) to the system control panel. This LED lights up if the alarm is triggered, and is latched on. It is not affected by the automatic system reset, but must be manually reset at the control panel. This feature might add about a dollar or two to the total system parts cost.

Advanced alarm systems, especially those incorporating computer control, might even store more detailed information, such as how many times the alarm was triggered since the last manual reset, what sensors were involved, and possibly even the time(s) of the security violation(s).

Adding a fire alarm

When setting up a home security alarm system, it is almost always worthwhile to include a built-in fire alarm while you're at it. This alarm is usually a minimal and simple addition. In most cases it won't take much more than a few extra sensors added to the main alarm system. In more sophisticated systems, there might be minor additions to the control circuitry as well. Such additions are surely easy to justify. Fire is always a very real, though too-often neglected risk.

Yes, many communities today do require the installation of smoke alarms in most homes. This regulation is better than nothing, but it might not be enough to prevent a tragedy. For one thing, virtually all standard smoke alarms use battery power only. They use battery power because so many home fires are electrical in origin, so ac power is particularly unreliable and ill-advised for this application. In fact a few early ac-powered smoke alarms were actually discovered to cause some fires. Batteries are safer, but they can't always be counted on. Again, human nature being what it is, many people (perhaps most) do not check their smoke alarm batteries as often as they should, if they ever test them at all. A dead battery means the smoke alarm will do nothing in the event of a fire.

Even worse, many people take the battery out of a smoke alarm from time to time and might fail to remember to put it back in. Sometimes this might be for a foolish reason, like borrowing the battery from the smoke alarm for use in some other (probably frivolous) piece of equipment. More often though, the battery will be taken out of a smoke alarm because it's usually the only way to shut it off if there is a false alarm.

False alarms from smoke alarms actually occur with surprising frequency, especially if the smoke alarm is poorly placed in the home. Many people (including a number of authorities who really should know better) insist a smoke alarm should be installed in or near the kitchen because fires are particularly likely to start there. Bad idea. The kitchen is really the very worst place to mount a smoke alarm, especially if there is only the one smoke alarm in the home. The people who recommend this foolish location forget that ordinary cooking generally produces smoke.

Ordinary smoke alarms are generally pretty good and have saved hundreds of lives. They are useful, but they are not really enough to do the job reliably all by themselves. Under some circumstances a smoke alarm might not detect certain types of fires in time, if at all. Not all fires produce much smoke, at least in their early stages. A lack of smoke often happens with electrical fires, which are among the most common causes of fires in homes. An electrical fire might burn within the building walls for a long time without any detectable smoke reaching the smoke alarm sensor until the fire breaks through the wall, often in a massive burst, the fire already in full force. In some cases, the smoke alarm might sound just a few seconds before it is consumed by the fire.

So, in light of all this, when installing a home security alarm system, it makes very good sense to add a few heat sensors in critical locations throughout the house, for better protection against fires as well as against human intruders.

Higher-rated temperature sensors should be used in attics. During the summer months in many areas, a temperature of 140°F might not be unusual in an uninsulated attic. Obviously you don't want the alarm to go off just because it's particularly hot weather today. A sensor rated for at least 190°F should be used in attics. Most other locations throughout the home should use sensors that respond to lower temperatures to make sure a fire is detected as soon as possible. Slow, simmering fires might not put out much heat for some time. A trip point of 130 to 150°F is a reasonable choice for heat sensors in any occupied area. It definitely shouldn't get that hot in another room, such as a bedroom, unless something was very wrong and justifies sounding of the alarm.

It is critical to remember that these temperature sensors should be used in addition to, not instead of, standard smoke detectors. Neither type will detect all fires. Some fires will produce plenty of smoke before they get hot enough to trigger a temperature sensor (especially if its some distance away from the fire), and other fires produce very little detectable smoke until they've already progressed to a very dangerous point.

It might be a good idea to use a separate, different-sounding alarm device for the fire-alarm portion of the security system. If the alarm goes off in the middle of the night, it makes a big difference whether the problem is an intruder or a fire. Very different responses would be required from the occupants of the house, so different alarm sounds will let everyone know immediately what the problem is. Knowing the problem allows people to do what they should to protect themselves and the rest of the family. For more information on fire and smoke alarms, see chapter 5.

Arming and disarming the system

Experts in the alarm field often debate heatedly whether the alarm system's arm/disarm station should be inside or outside the house. As in many such debated topics, there are good arguments to be made for either choice.

An external switch is obviously most convenient for most people. After all, they have to get their key out to unlock the door anyway. They can easily deal with the alarm system at the same time and place. The alarm arm/disarm switch, being openly visible, might even act as a deterrent to some potential burglars of the casual, opportunistic type. It announces that an alarm system is in use. It is especially effective if an LED or other LED indicates that the system is armed. The LED also can be helpful for absent-minded homeowners. "Did I turn the alarm system on or not?" On the other hand, if you forget to arm the system when you leave the house, the potential burglar knows it's pretty safe to break into your home. You might as well lay out a mat that says "Welcome Burglars!"

Of course the switch must be secured in some way. There'd not be much point in using a standard push button that anyone could pick.

A key switch can be a handy choice for disarming the system. In theory no one can turn off the system without the key, and the homeowner already has the key ring out to unlock the door anyway. Unfortunately, most lock switches don't provide nearly as much security as you might suspect. Some inexpensive brands use keys that are almost interchangeable. If a burglar buys a similar lock, the odds are good that her or his key will work as well as yours. Even worse, most commonly available lock switches simply aren't very good locks. Many types of lock switches can be easily picked in less than a minute by an amateur with a stiff wire. Such a poor lock wouldn't even slow down an experienced burglar.

Another (minor) problem with lock switches is that every member of the family will probably need a copy of the key. Also, keys can be easily lost, especially by kids (including teenagers) but many adults as well. Someone might be left sitting out on the front step for a while, waiting for another family member to come home. Not a disaster, of course, but surely an irritating nuisance.

If you use a lock switch, make sure it is a very high quality lock. The lock should be at least as good as the one on your door, if not even better. Your entire security system depends on it. But keep some reasonable perspective. Really, there is no such thing as a truly unpickable lock. If someone is sufficiently determined, they can find a way past any lock. After all, isn't that just what safe crackers do? How much of a lock will be enough to be more trouble than it's worth for someone to break into your home? Most burglars will probably be discouraged easily, and they'll go away to find an unprotected house in the neighborhood.

The other standard approach for external arming and disarming an alarm system is to use a keypad, like that of a common electronic calculator. To disarm the alarm system, you enter a specific code, in the proper sequence, and preferably within a definite time limit. This system, if well designed, can be a lot tougher to defeat.

The decoding circuitry should have a timer function of some sort. A patient intruder shouldn't be permitted to experiment with various combinations until getting lucky. Many systems today permit three incorrect attempts before locking out the keypad for several minutes before a new attempt can be made. Assuming just numerical entries, a three digit code could have any of 1000 possible combinations (000 to 999). A four-digit code has 10,000 possibilities, and a five-digit code has 100,000 possibilities. For a home system there's no point in using codes longer than five digits. The increase in security would be minimal, and it would be harder for the legitimate occupants of the house to remember the code.

The keypad should not be locked out after the first incorrect attempt. This precaution will only inconvenience and annoy legitimate family members. It's easy to hit the wrong button, especially when you're in a hurry, or thinking about someone else. Such strictness would not add noticeably to the security of the system, it would just be a damned nuisance. But someone who doesn't get the code entered correctly after three tries is probably just guessing, and it's a good idea not to let them keep trying.

Select the code for ease of memory if possible. If the members of the household have to check a slip of paper for the code every time they want to enter or leave the house, they will probably find it a major inconvenience. Also, a written note identifying the security code, like a key can all too easily be lost or stolen. It's even more likely with a small slip of paper. So the code must be easy to remember if it is to be practical. As mentioned, the code should be no more than five digits.

A code that has some meaning or special significance to the family would obviously be ideal. But don't be too obvious. Many people first think of using the address of the house they are trying to protect. That would probably be the first thing a burglar would try to get past the alarm system. Part of the home telephone number also is not a very good idea, at least unless you happen to have an unlisted number. A professional burglar is likely to do some research. It would be easy enough to get the family name from the mailbox and the street address, then just look up the number in the telephone book or call information. Many burglars do this anyway, even if there is no security system code to worry about. They will call the house they intend to rob first to make sure no one is home. For this reason, outgoing messages on telephone answering machines should say no one is available to take the call at the moment, not that no one is at home. Let any prospective burglar think there might be someone home taking a bath or a nap, or something else where they don't want to be disturbed by phone calls.

Even if you come up with a good, easily remembered code, it might be helpful to use it backwards, or inside out, unless someone might guess what significant number you might be using. For example, assume one of your kids was born in 1987, and you decide to use that as your code. Consider making it 7891 (backwards) or 9178 (inside out). This code will make it even tougher for someone to guess, even someone who knows the family well, but it won't be that much more difficult for family members to remember.

Never tell anyone what your alarm system disarming code is, unless that person is someone you trust and expect to be inside your house when you're not there. Sometimes you must tell someone outside the family the code, such as a house sitter during a family vacation trip. Even then be careful of when and where you tell the other person. Make sure no one else is eavesdropping. It might be a good idea to change the code when you return from your vacation, or even periodically as a general precaution.

Many people in the security field object to any disarming switch outside the premises at all. They feel it gives the potential burglar too much of an opportunity somehow to defeat the system from outside, without setting off the alarm. This objection is probably valid for lock switches because they are usually easy to pick or force. But a well-designed keypad wouldn't necessarily be a security risk. Those who oppose this position point out that a technically savvy intruder could force the keypad box or panel open and get to the circuitry, but this easy access is probably only available on a really stupid design. The active alarm system control circuitry should be in a safe place inside the house anyway, and the keypad decoding circuitry should be too. If an intruder opens the keypad housing, he or she shouldn't find anything but the key switches themselves, and the ends of their wires leading on inside the house through a small conduit. The wires to the keypad switches won't do the attempted burglar any more good than the sealed keypad. The intruder would still need to know the code to send the appropriate signals down the wires to the inaccessible decoding circuits.

However, in certain climates, it might not be a good idea to have an outdoor keypad unless it is very well sealed, not so much from a potential burglar, but from the natural elements. Rain and other weather conditions could do damage so the system won't work properly. This probably won't reduce the security of the home—a burglar still couldn't get in without setting off the alarm, but legitimate family members who know the disarming code might have trouble getting in too. Besides potential damage from foul weather, kids playing pranks and vandalism also might be a problem. The trick is to mount the keypad box or wall panel where it is least likely to be damaged. This situation is not really a security risk, just the type of problems involved with any equipment that must be mounted outdoors.

There is one possible security risk to an outdoor keypad system. Someone with high-power binoculars could watch which keys you press and learn the code, even if you don't know anyone else is around. This problem also exists for ATMs (automatic teller machines). The solution is the same. Simply get into the habit of blocking the keypad with your body as much as possible while entering the code. Even with binoculars, no one can see around corners or through your body.

Ultimately, the decision of whether or not to use an outside disarming keypad comes down more to personal preference than any inherent security principle. The alternate to an outdoor arming/disarming switch is to place it inside the house. Some type of timer circuit now becomes absolutely mandatory, or the alarm system will not even be functional. Only one door (usually, though not necessarily the front door) should be connected to the time delay. Opening any other door or window should set off the alarm immediately. However, opening the front (or whichever) door while the system is armed will start the timer circuit's cycle. If the disarming switch is not thrown before this circuit times out, the alarm will be sounded. Typically, the time delay in such a system will be about 30 to 45 seconds. This delay might not seem like much, but it should be more than sufficient time for legitimate entry to the house. Anyone who doubts this should actually time the procedure with a stop watch—30 to 45 seconds is actually a long time.

The control box with the disarming switch does not need to be deviously hidden, but it should be mounted in a place that is not obvious. It should not be in open view or right beside the door, or a burglar could find it too easily and perhaps disarm the system. Don't count too much on hiding it however. There are usually just so many practical hiding places, and a smart burglar might make a shrewd guess quickly. So, even with an indoor disarming switch, it is strongly advisable to use a lock switch or a coded keypad, as discussed for external use in the preceding paragraphs. With an indoor installation, the requirements aren't as stiff. Outside the aspiring burglar has plenty of time to examine the disarming switch mechanism, and perhaps find a way to open it or otherwise defeat it. In the indoor system, a short-term clock is running before the intruder even gets to see the switching device. A cheaper lock switch can be used here, because the burglar will have little time to attempt to pick it or break it. Similarly, a keypad decoding circuitry doesn't need to bother with a timed lockout after a few incorrect entries. The intruder will only have time for a few guesses before the alarm goes off anyway. In this setup, perfect security for the disarming switch is not required. The system only needs to slow the intruder a few critical seconds, then the alarm will go off, and the intruder will either be scared off or caught in the act.

There are some frequently ignored inherent security flaws with the time delay/indoor disarming switch approach. The main problem is that the intruder does get a chance to get inside the house. The necessary 30 to 45 second delay is sufficient for someone to legitimately enter and disarm the system, with a little extra time to spare (in case of the unexpected). By the same token, it could give a bold burglar plenty of time to run in, grab something of value and run out. The alarm will still sound, but by that time, the thief will already be making a getaway with some of your property. The thief using this technique might only get one item, but it is likely to be a very expensive one. The burglar would probably peek in a window and pick out the target ahead of time. The system time delay would be more than ample, especially because the intruder is unlikely to be concerned about the possibility of breaking something else that might be in the way.

As with everything else in life, there are advantages and disadvantages to any choice, which must be weighed and balanced before a decision can be made. An intelligent rule to cover all, or even most, practical situations just isn't possible. It is vital to remember that perfect security is not a reasonable goal in any home alarm system. It just can't be done. Compromises and choices must be made.

For systems with entrance/exit delay timers, there is often a visual or audible indication while the timer is running. This indication is usually in the form of low beeps from a small speaker, or a flashing LED that alerts anyone entering or leaving the house that the alarm will soon go off. This feature is another one of those security system features that is the subject of much debate that ultimately comes down more to personal preference than anything else.

Some object that such an indicator warns the burglar that the alarm system is there, but how much of a problem is that? There are many other clues that could let a smart burglar know that an alarm system is present. The short timing period doesn't really give the intruder time enough to do anything with the knowledge other than leave, which is the ideal result of any security system. Getting an intruder to leave before doing anything is much better than catching one in the act. A nervous intruder is likely to leave right away on finding out that an alarm system is in use.

Ultimately, the purpose of such an indicator is not for any intruders, but for the legitimate users of the system. It is a reminder that can help prevent a false alarm due to simple absentmindedness. Even the most forgetful person will be reminded that the alarm system must be turned off right away. Some people might find such an indicator annoying, and it might even make them nervous and pressured. Such people would be happier if the system didn't include a timer indicator, but for most people it could be a minor advantage or an irrelevance included just in case.

Closely related to an entrance timer indicator is an indicator for when the system is armed. This indicator will almost always be a visual device, typically a red LED, often flashing. Again, its primary purpose is to remind the legitimate residents of the home that the system must be disarmed before (or immediately after) entering. This is especially useful in multiperson homes. Someone coming home will be able to know right away if someone else has gone out and armed the system, or if they can just walk right in.

Such a system-armed indicator can serve as a minor intruder deterrent. All things being equal, a casual burglar will prefer to try a home that is not protected by an alarm system. If an alarm system is in use, it's not worth the risk. Professional burglars, however, are not usually so easily deterred. They usually know pretty much what they're after before they break into a home, and if it's worth the effort or risk or not. A professional will probably try to defeat an alarm system, so a system-armed indicator will just be an extra reminder for the burglar to stay alert. A professional burglar will probably assume the presence of an alarm system unless there is evidence that it doesn't exist or isn't armed, so there isn't much practical security risk from this indicator.

In many areas, casual burglaries tend to be the greater risk, so the slight deterrent effect of a system-armed indicator light can be a significant advantage. In fact, some people have installed a key switch that does nothing but flash a red LED as if an alarm system was present and armed. Certainly this is less expensive than an actual burglar alarm, and it might be reasonably effective in discouraging casual, impulse break-ins. But there is no back-up protection if the potential intruder doesn't fall for (or is aware of) the trick. Professional burglars will rarely be fooled so easily. Also, if a member of the family forgets to turn off the flashing light when entering the house, the fact that no alarm goes off could inform any potential intruder watching that there is really no alarm system after all.

A system-armed indicator light could be a security risk, however, if anyone in the family leaves the house unattended and forgets to arm the system. A prospective intruder will see the alarm system is off, and that's practically laying out a mat that says "Welcome Burglars!" No alarm system is going to do any good unless it is turned on and properly armed.

There is a similar debate about the use of door or window decals or stickers that say something to the effect of "Warning, these premises are protected by a such and such brand alarm system." Again, many people just buy a pack of decals for a couple bucks and don't bother with an alarm system at all. Professional burglars know this, and generally ignore such decals, but a casual burglar might be convinced not to take the chance.

Some critics fear that such a decal (or an indicator light) could act as an invitation to prospective burglars, in effect saying, "There is something worth stealing here." This fear probably isn't very reasonable. Professional burglars rarely break into homes at random. They will do research first and determine what is worth stealing before they begin the burglary, and casual burglars probably won't be willing to take the chance that the indicated alarm system is for real.

Using just the decals without an alarm system could be risky in some cases, but as an addition to a full security system, it won't hurt, though it probably won't do much active good either. Actually, the primary purpose of such decals is advertising for the alarm system manufacturer and/or the installation company. Visitors and neighbors will see the decal, which prominently features the brand or company name whenever they come to the door of the protected home.

In most cases, it wouldn't hurt, and might occasionally help a little if a system indicator (an arming light and/or warning decal) is in plain view. The disarming switch could be slightly concealed from obvious view, as long as it isn't inconveniently located. This precaution won't prevent a break-in, but it could slow even a technically knowledgeable intruder, perhaps long enough for the alarm to be set off.

All of the actual intrusion detector devices and sensors should be concealed as much as possible. Besides being unattractive in a home, openly visible sensors might give an intruder too much of an advantage. A smart intruder will be careful not to trip any sensor that can be seen. If the intruder knows where it is, it probably won't work. Also, a technically knowledgeable intruder might figure out a way to defeat or fool any sensor before they are set off. Overall, the best security is to let prospective intruders know there is an alarm system at work, but not the specific details of where it is or how it works.

Thinking like a burglar

In laying out a specific alarm system, it is necessary to try to think like a burglar. Of course, the obvious entrances to the home—doors and large ground floor windows—should be protected. Anyone could figure that much out, and smart burglars know it. They will try to come up with a less obvious method of entry, in the hopes of getting by the alarm system. It is the system designer's job to anticipate and guard against such creativity. Imagine that you are a burglar and are bound and determined to get into the specific home you are designing the system for. How would you try to get in?

Upper floor windows are too often ignored in alarm systems, on the assumption that they are safe by virtue of their height. But are they truly inaccessible? Are there any nearby trees or trestles that a burglar could climb to get to them? Could a burglar easily lean a ladder against the wall? If someone could get up to the window, it should be protected by sensors just like first floor windows. The one exception would be a small window that no one could fit through, such as certain bathroom windows. Don't however, assume that the only possible intruder will be a full-size adult, however. These days, some burglars use kids as their accomplices to help them get into homes, and unfortunately, many kids are turning to crime on their own. It's safe to leave such a window unprotected by the alarm system only if it's too small for anybody to get through. When in doubt, protect it anyway. An extra set of sensors is not going to add that much to the overall cost of the alarm system, and it's better to be safe than sorry.

Assuming an intruder does somehow manage to get past the outer layer of the system's protection, what route is he or she likely to follow through the home? Usually this means, where will he or she look for goodies to steal? Once you've roughly mapped out the most likely routes, what additional sensors (such as pressure mats and motion detectors) are most likely to catch a burglar in the act? The best locations are those where two or more of the hypothetical routes converge.

To start the actual design of the system, draw a rough map of the entire home. Don't worry about your lack of artistic ability. It doesn't have to look good. It's just to help you plan out the system. No one else has to see it. Clarity, not aesthetics, is the critical issue.

On your map, mark the points you've determined need to be protected with one or more sensors. (Don't forget to include the obvious doors and windows. Including the obvious might be easier to do than you'd expect if you're concentrating on looking for the unlikely.)

The locations for direct intrusion sensors (usually doors and windows, but less obvious access points also should be included) are marked on the map with small circles. Additional sensors, such as pressure mats or sound sensors might be added, if appropriate to the specific circumstances involved. In a small apartment installation like this, there isn't much need to draw these extra sensors in on the layout map. In a larger, more sophisticated installation, it would probably be helpful to show all sensors. These special sensors might be shown with a different symbol on the map, such as triangles for pressure maps, squares for anything else. Heat sensors and smoke detectors could be indicated with small stars.

A sample map for a small apartment is shown in Fig. 2-2. In most apartments, there are relatively few entrances to protect. The main areas of concern are the single door to the apartment and two windows, one to the living room and one to the bedroom. This building has a central cooling/heating system, so you must check the ducts and vents. Are they large enough for someone, even a child, to crawl through? If so, they should be protected by the alarm system. In the sample apartment, assume there are three vents. Two are high up on the wall and measure only 3 × 6 inches. It can be seen by shining a flashlight through the vent that the duct pipe leading to each vent continues back several feet at this narrow width, so don't worry about them. No one can even climb through the duct to get close enough to reach in through the vent. But the third vent is a main system vent, and has a grated wall plate over a duct that measures 2½ × 3 feet. A person of small to moderate build might get in that way. There might or might not be a way for anyone to get into the duct from the other end of the cooling/heating system, and you might not be able to get this information from the apartment management, (you're likely to get vague reassurances that it would be "impossible" or "very unlikely" without any specific evidence). When in doubt, the smart and safest approach is to assume access is possible. Add the necessary sensor(s) to protect this potential point of access with the alarm system. The sensors in this example should protect against the removal of the vented cover plate over the large duct.

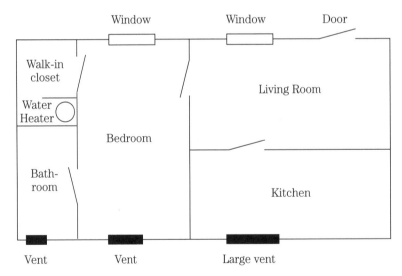

2-2 This is a sample layout map of a small apartment.

Assume that no specialized devices such as pressure mats or motion detectors are called for in this installation. The only other thing you have to consider are fire detectors. A heat sensor and a smoke detector should always be included in the bedroom. By placing them near the door of the bedroom, these sensors should be enough to protect the entire apartment. Larger homes will require more sensors, however.

But look at the map a little more carefully. The water heater is in the back of the walk-in closet. This design is an odd design and is a bit risky. A water heater can be expected to operate at high temperatures, and people tend to use the back of closets for storage. Flammable materials might inadvertently end up too close to the hot water heater. If something went wrong, this seems like a particularly likely place for a fire to start in this apartment. It is advisable to add a second heat sensor in the closet. Don't mount it too close to the water heater, which is expected to get hot in normal usage. But the heat shouldn't be permitted to go very far. Use a sensitive thermometer to determine the approximate normal temperature, and select a heat sensor that will trip at an appropriately higher temperature. As a rule of thumb, the thermal trip point of the sensor should be about 175 to 225% of the measured normal temperature. An extra smoke detector isn't really necessary here. Smoke will quickly flow through the apartment and reach the smoke detector in the bedroom. Heat, however, might remain localized for a long time. By the time the bedroom sensor sees the excess heat, it might be too late and the fire is already out of control.

Mount an extra heat sensor (but not a smoke detector) near the kitchen stove, because this also is a potential source of fires. Again, the thermal trip point should be selected high enough that the alarm will not be falsely set off from the heat of ordinary cooking.

The map of this sample apartment is shown again in Fig. 2-3 with the main sensor locations shown. In such a simple installation, such a map is optional, but advisable. A map can help draw your attention to the overall picture and help you avoid overlooking details such as the closet water heater in the example. In a larger home, requiring a more detailed and sophisticated alarm system, such a map is essential. It would be a very foolish alarm system designer or installer who think that all details could be visualized and retained mentally. Maybe some people could, but maybe some important details could slip by. Why take the chance? A sensor map is a very

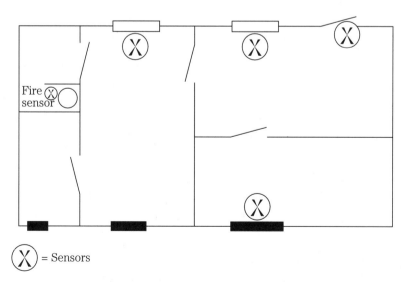

2-3 The sample map of Fig. 2-2 with the main sensor locations shown.

important part of the alarm system installation. You can see a more complex example in the following paragraphs, but first there are a few more comments to be made about some special conditions involved in protecting apartments with alarm systems.

In the current example, assume that this apartment has a door that opens directly to the outside. Some apartment buildings are designed so the apartments open out to a shared hallway. Often such apartment buildings offer some degree of security on their own, perhaps a security guard or maybe just a locked external door for the building. It's not a good idea to rely too much on the building security, however. It might not be enough. How good are the security guards? What are their qualifications for being hired? Often people who live in such a building will prop the outside door open so it doesn't lock, or they might hold the door open for a stranger, while coming or going. For that matter, burglars have to live somewhere too. If one lives in your building, the standard building security can't offer any noticeable protection. Treat the door (or doors) that open up to the shared hallway as if they were doors to outside. They should be protected by sensors just like any external doors. Also, don't forget that even an apartment in the most secure building around still probably has windows that might need to be protected against intrusion.

For people who happen to live in upper floor apartments (third floor or higher), most windows don't have to be protected by a security system, unless there happens to be something particularly valuable in the apartment that is likely to be a major attraction to burglary attempts. The extra effort required to get in such high windows is enough to discourage casual burglars, but a determined professional who is sufficiently motivated might make the effort and accept the risk of climbing the walls, using a scaffold, or using some other trick. This protection is not likely to be of much practical concern to most people, of course.

However, some windows in upper floor apartments in some buildings might be a lot more accessible than you realize. Any window near a fire escape can be reached from the ladder or landing by a reasonably agile intruder without much difficulty and needs to be protected by the alarm system as much as a ground-floor window.

Also watch out for situations like the one shown in Fig. 2-4. Here window A is in the apartment to be protected, but window B is in the shared hallway. Assuming a burglar has gotten into the building, it would be very easy to crawl out window B, walk along the ledge a few feet and crawl into window A to rob the apartment.

When you have any doubt about the possibility of someone getting in through an upper-floor window, the smart choice is to protect it with the alarm system. A couple extra sensors aren't going to increase that overall system cost significantly. It's better to be safe than sorry.

A more complicated alarm-system map is shown in Fig. 2-5. This house has two stories, so the map is in two sections. Obviously there are a lot more ways for a potential intruder to get into this house than the small apartment in the previous example.

Because you have to consider the potential accessibility of the second floor windows, an additional exterior map is shown in Fig. 2-6. Not much detail is needed in this map. All you are really concerned with is any convenient way for an intruder to reach any of the upstairs windows. Also look over the entire exterior of the house very carefully to spot any means of access that is not obvious. Walk around the

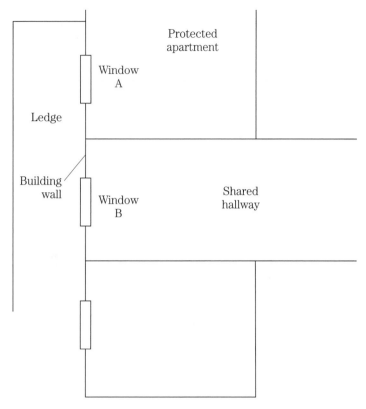

2-4 Watch out for situations where window A is in the apartment to be protected, but window B is in the shared hallway.

perimeter of the house several times to make sure you haven't missed anything. Of course, anything that you might find should be marked on your exterior map. If you are not using an exterior map, at least make notes of all possible access points you might discover. Do not trust your memory, no matter how good it usually is. Installing an alarm system involves many details. It's all too easy for something to get forgotten along the way. Write everything down, and check it off a list as it is actually taken care of in the installation process.

The front of this house faces a moderately busy street that is well lit. No trees are near the front of the house, and the design of the building is such that there doesn't appear to be any direct way to climb up to any of the front windows without difficulty. Yes, it could be done, if a burglar was sufficiently motivated, but assume the family living in this house has nice property but nothing unique or special that would serve as a special lure to thieves. Coupled with the high visibility of the front of the house in this example, you can reasonably assume the front windows on the second floor are inherently pretty secure as they already are.

On one side of the house is an attached garage, which is only one story. One small window looks out over the roof of the garage. This window, although it is small, might be large enough for a small or average-size intruder to crawl through, at least

2-5 This is a sample layout map of a two-story house.

with some agility. Because this window is easily accessible from the roof of the garage, protect it with the alarm system. There is nothing else that would be made more accessible by climbing onto the roof of the garage, so trying to add sensors to detect someone climbing up there would be unnecessary. It would be difficult to devise a system that would reliably detect the presence of an intruder on the roof. There are too many ways for someone to get up there at different points. About all you could do would be to lay out lots of weatherproofed pressure mats along the sur-

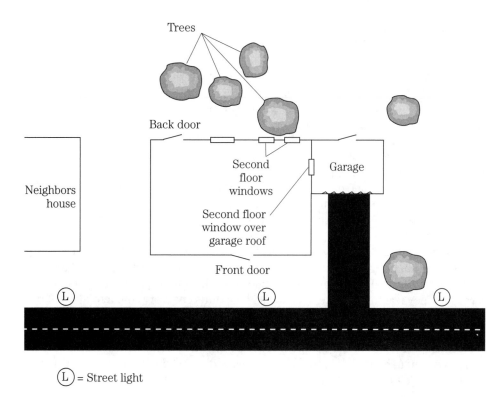

2-6 Exterior map of the home shown in Fig. 2-5.

face of the roof. In addition to being expensive, inconvenient and unreliable, this would almost certainly result in lots of false alarms from birds landing on the roof or cats jumping up there. Neighborhood kids might throw a ball or Frisbee onto the roof as well, and this would set off the alarm system as easily as an intruder's footstep. There is no point in resorting to ridiculous overkill in designing an alarm system. If the one accessible window is protected, the residents of the home don't have to worry very much about anyone climbing onto the roof of the garage. It would essentially be a dead end for a prospective burglar.

The side opposite the garage has two large windows on the second floor. No landscaping features block this side from the front. This side of the house also is clearly visible from the street, but being farther removed from the streetlights, someone might be able to hide in shadows. However, there is no ready way for someone to climb up to these windows. There are no trees on this side of the house, and the walls go straight up with no climbable protrusions. In a high crime area it might be a good idea to protect these windows at least minimally with the alarm system, to protect against someone with a not-too-visible ladder against the house. The front of the house is too well lit to make this a viable choice for a burglar of any intelligence. The decision is a judgment call in using sensors on these windows. There is no absolutely right answer. Generally the best approach would be to risk being too cautious rather than careless, but not go overboard. An extra magnetic reed switch on each of these windows wouldn't add noticeably to the overall cost of the alarm system, or much to the effort of installation. But any supplemental sensors, such as glass break detectors, or pressure mats in front of the window would probably be a waste for these two windows, even if they were used at other, more accessible windows throughout the house.

When you come around to the back of the house, however, you have more to worry about. The back yard is not visible from the street, and not much of the light from the street lamps will reach this far, not to mention the house blocking off most of it. Also, there are several trees in the back yard, and a couple of them are very close to some of the rear upper-floor windows. It wouldn't be difficult for someone to climb a tree to get to one of these windows. Except for the very small window in the bathroom, which no one could possibly crawl through, not even a small child, the windows on the rear side of the second floor of this house should be fully protected by the alarm system, just as if they were ground-floor windows.

There is a small chimney on top of this house, but even if an intruder could fit down it, the chimney leads only to the inside of a furnace in the basement. The chimney is not a practical or reasonable method of getting into this house. A moderate to large chimney leading to a fireplace would be a different story, and a number of burglars have gained entrance in this way.

There is a door from the kitchen to inside the attached garage. For simplicity of discussion, assume that the garage will not be included within the protection of the alarm system. (The issue of attached garages is discussed in more detail in chapter 3.) The door leading into the house should be treated by the alarm system exactly as if it was a full exterior door. If an intruder gets inside the garage (usually not a difficult feat to accomplish), there will be as much access to this door as any exterior door, with the added advantage of privacy to work on getting in. Inside the garage, an intruder would not risk being seen by neighbors. Many otherwise good alarm systems are rendered practically ineffective because the designer or installer (usually but not always an amateur) forgot about this "inside" door.

The house in the example also has a front door and a back door leading to a rear hallway. There is no outside cellar door. The basement is small and contains little other than the furnace and water heater. Because it was not intended for regular use, the architect of this house did not include any windows in the basement. The lack of basement windows simplifies the job for the alarm system designer and installer. There is no reasonable way to get into the basement from outside the house.

After careful consideration, you can't find any other ways a potential intruder could be expected to get inside the house. The interior maps of this example house are shown again in Fig. 2-7, with the potential points of entry that need protection with alarm system sensors marked.

The next step in the planning stage is where it is really necessary to start thinking like a burglar. Now, assume an intruder has somehow managed to get inside the house. No security system is foolproof. There is always some possibility that a smart burglar could somehow get past the first line of defense (the exterior entrance-way intrusion sensors). You don't have to worry about just how this could be done, you just need to assume it somehow can be done in an unforeseen way. A good alarm system will have a second line of defense inside the house. To catch an intruder at this

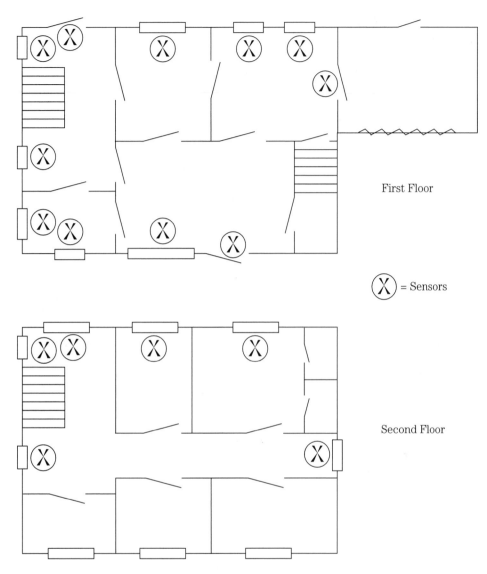

First Floor

$\left(\widehat{X}\right)$ = Sensors

Second Floor

2-7 The map of Fig. 2-5 with the main sensor locations shown.

stage, the system designer has to anticipate what a burglar might do or might go once inside the house, and "booby-trap" these likely spots with appropriate sensors.

If you were a thief, where would you go in a house you were robbing? What path(s) would you take through the house?

Assuming the intruder's motivation for breaking in is robbery, there aren't as many likely paths as you might first assume. Except for an incompetent, probably spontaneous burglary, there will probably be at least some degree of advance planning by the burglar. The thief knows more or less what he or she wants and should be able to make a good choice of where to look for it. For most homes, the most desirable items to steal are entertainment appliances (stereos, TVs, VCRs, etc.) and jewelry. Usually the entertainment appliances (at least the most valuable ones) will be in the living room or in a family room or den. There might be an inexpensive stereo or portable TV in one or more of the bedrooms, but those items will generally have less interest to a thief. Jewelry will usually be kept somewhere in the master bedroom. Therefore, normally assume that a thief will head as directly as possible for the living room (or family room or den) or the master bedroom. In most cases, a burglar will assume that time is at a premium and will take the most direct path as possible.

Select the most likely (most vulnerable or the most accessible) entry points on the interior map and trace out the path from each of these to the thief's assumed target. It might be helpful to use different colors for different target areas.

In this example, assume there is no valuable jewelry kept in this house, and no reason for anyone to think there might be. The home's entertainment center is in the living room, and that is where almost any thief is likely to go as soon as possible. Some of the most likely pathways throughout the house are shown in Fig. 2-8.

Now how can you catch the thief along one or more of these paths? What sensors can you use? Strategically placed pressure mats or sensors on selected interior doors are common possibilities. A motion detector also can be used.

Sensors to detect an attempt to move or unplug particularly valuable (desirable and easy to steal) equipment also can be used.

It is very important to make these second-line-of-defense sensors separately controllable from the main alarm system. People often like to turn on the alarm system while they are at home, because it can be dangerous to be caught unaware by an intruder, who might be armed. A burglar might think no one is at home or might not particularly care. So there can be very good reasons for turning on the exterior sensors while people are inside the house, but if the inside sensors also are activated, the family will be restricted in their movements and activities in their own home. No one should be made a prisoner of his or her own alarm system. The whole point is for the protected family to live their lives more freely and easily. The interior set of sensors should only be activated when no one is home.

All of the actual detection devices (sensors), interior or exterior, in any decent alarm system should be concealed as much as possible. One reason for this is aesthetic in nature. Most people don't want to live amidst a bunch of wires and ugly sensors. The effect is not very homey. Besides, concealed sensors will usually do a much, much better job. Don't give a smart intruder a chance to get around or defeat your sensors. The idea is to let an intruder know there is an alarm system in operation, but not the specific details of where and how it works.

By all means, hide the central control station. You definitely don't want an intruder to find it and possibly disable or destroy it. But there is no sense in going overboard on this. A determined burglar could probably find any hiding place if sufficiently motivated. Most locations will have just a few potential hiding places, and most people tend to make more or less the same choices. Usually the intruder will be looking for other desirable and easy-to-steal items. So as long as the alarm system control box isn't immediately obvious, she or he probably won't bother looking for it. The control box certainly shouldn't be so hidden that it is inaccessible or inconvenient to the legitimate occupants of the house.

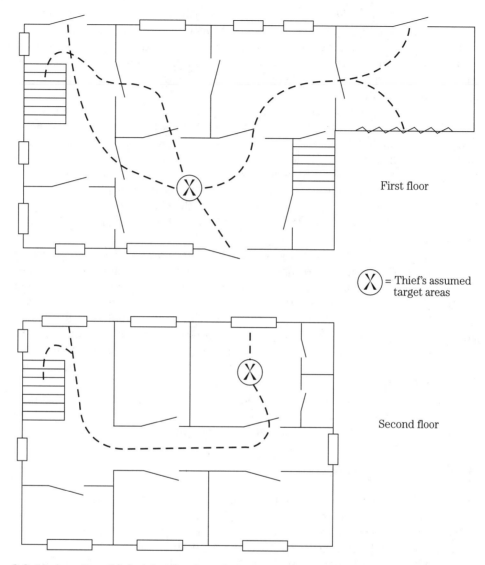

First floor

$\left(\!X\!\right)$ = Thief's assumed
target areas

Second floor

2-8 Likely paths a thief might take through the house shown in Fig. 2-5.

Lighting protection

In addition to sounding an audible alarm, it is a very good idea for the security system also to turn on lights automatically throughout the house when triggered, and perhaps even outdoor floodlights. With the lights turned on, an intruder will have less chance to hide and avoid getting caught, except by immediately fleeing the area. It also is more likely that the intruder will be seen and later identified by any witnesses in the area. It's difficult, if not impossible, to identify positively a figure in the dark.

If heavy lighting devices (especially floodlights) are used, be sure the current capability of the system output devices—relays, *SCRs* (silicon-controlled rectifiers), or whatever—can safely and reliably handle the load. When in doubt, go for some extra current-handling capability. Make sure everything in the system is adequately rated for the job it is expected to do, under any foreseeable conditions. Overrating by at least 15 to 25% is always advisable.

Because the system is already wired to lighting units, you might want to add some photosensitive controllers to operate outside lighting automatically. When it gets dark out, the lights go on, especially near major entrances to the home. The lights tend to discourage break-in attempts. Most burglars naturally prefer to work under the cloak of darkness, where they'll be less likely to be seen (and possibly recognized). If the area is well lit, a potential intruder is much more likely to be caught in the act, and most won't even try. (Some will take the chance, however. Other burglars might break the bulbs or otherwise disable the lighting units. So lighting by itself is scarcely an adequate security system.)

A related issue is the use of the so-called *security timer*. Many people use an automatic timer to turn lights on and off inside the house at specific times. The idea is to make it look like someone is at home. Unfortunately such lighting timers are not effective against experienced burglars, though they can discourage some casual thieves. The timers might have been more effective at one time, but today's criminals surely know about this trick. They know what to watch for. With most timers, the on/off pattern is too regular, especially if a burglar cases a house for a few nights before breaking in while the family is out of town. If the lights go on and off in the same pattern and at the same times night after night, automation is almost surely being used. You might as well put a sign out front that says, "Welcome burglars. No one is home." (Some top-line models introduce some degree of randomness, but their overall effectiveness as a security measure is still questionable at best.)

Panic buttons

A good added feature to consider for a home security system is a *panic button*. The panic button is one (or more than one) simple push-button switch conveniently located. If an intruder breaks in while someone is at home, pressing this button sets off the alarm, even if the system has not been armed. To turn the alarm back off, the system must be disarmed and reset at the central control station, just as if one of the automated sensors had triggered the alarm.

Placement of panic buttons is particularly critical in homes with young children who might be tempted to press the button out of curiosity or mischievousness. To avoid false alarms, the panic button should be mounted out of the reach of young children. To do any good, it must be within easy and convenient reach of adults or older children. It will probably never be needed, but if it is, it will probably be an emergency situation where every second counts. Quick access is essential.

A panic button is a simple and inexpensive addition to any alarm system, and it could save lives. Frankly, there is no good reason not to include this feature in any home alarm system. At worst, an intruder might force you to turn it off, but at least you've got more of a chance of summoning help. In most cases, it shouldn't make things worse. Of course, in a special situation where sounding the alarm might increase personal danger, you always have the option of not pushing the panic button. Remember, this is strictly a manual, not an automated device.

Design of central control-box circuits

The greatest difference between various brands and designs of home alarm systems is in the central control box. This box is essentially the "brains" of the system. Some alarm system central control boxes might appear to be extremely complex, but they are almost always made up of relatively simple circuit elements, repeated over and over. The central control box is simply a network of electronic switches used to route the control signals appropriately. A number of timer circuits also are likely to be included in all but the very simplest central control boxes.

Although it is beyond the scope of this book to examine the specifics of particular circuits, it is worthwhile to devote a few pages here to the design of alarm system central control boxes on the block-diagram level. Most central control boxes are built around the same basic design principles, though the exact circuitry used to accomplish the standard functions might vary considerably.

The basic building block of almost any alarm system central control box is an electronic switch circuit. This device or circuit opens or closes an electrical connection like a simple manual switch, except it does so automatically in response to an electrical control signal. There are many ways to achieve the electronic switching function. For the application, a *latching switch* is required. Once a latching switch is triggered by the control signal, it remains triggered, even if the control signal is removed. To deactivate or release the electronic switch, a separate reset control signal must be used. The reset signal might be automatic (from a timer or some similar control circuit), or manual (from a push button or other switch), depending on the function.

The simplest and most obvious electronic switch is the *relay*. A relay is an electromechanical device comprising two main parts; a coil and a magnetically operated reed switch. A relay is similar in principle to the magnetic reed switches used as sensors in alarm systems. When an appropriate signal passes through the relay coil, a magnetic field is generated around the relay, and this magnetic field activates the reed switch. The switch contacts of a relay might be either normally open, or normally closed, or both, with a double-throw function.

Of course, as soon as the activating control signal stops flowing through the relay coil, the magnetic field collapses and the reed switch is released. Special latching relays are available, which do hold their activated state even after the original control signal is removed. A separate release signal is required to return the switch contacts to their normal, unactivated state. Latching relays are relatively rare, and are often difficult to locate from parts suppliers. They also are more expensive than standard relays.

The effect of a latching relay can be achieved with a standard relay with a little external circuitry. Perhaps the simplest approach is shown in Fig. 2-9. Here a *DPDT* (double-pole, double-throw) relay is used in place of a *SPDT* (single-pole, double-

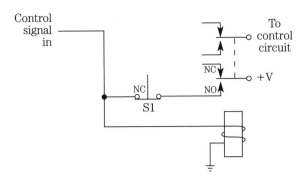

2-9
Double-pole, double-throw relay wired to simulate a latching relay.

throw) relay. The first set of switch contacts are used in the ordinary way to control whatever the relay is being used for. The second set of switch contacts are used for the latching function. At first, assume the relay is unactivated. All switch contacts are in their normal positions. When a control signal passes through the relay coil, all the reed switch contacts go to their activated positions. The controlled device or circuit is turned on (or off, as appropriate). At the same time, the second set of switch contacts close to complete a circuit that feeds a voltage back into the relay coil. If the original control signal is removed, this feedback voltage continues to pass through the coil, maintaining an active magnetic field. All the switch contacts in the relay remain in their activated state. This condition can be held indefinitely. To release the relay, the momentary action normally closed switch (S1) must be pressed. This action breaks the circuit. While this switch is open, no feedback signal can reach the coil. The magnetic field collapses, and the relay switch contacts are released to their normal, unactivated states. Releasing S1 does not restore the feedback voltage to the relay coil, because the circuit is now broken because the second set of relay switch contacts are open.

Of course, a second relay (or other electronic switch) can be used in place of the manual NC release switch assumed here. This relay permits automation of the release function, if that is appropriate to the specific application at hand.

Similar tricks can be used with other types of electronic switches to provide a latching function that might otherwise be difficult to implement.

Although relays make the basic concepts easy to understand, and generally require very simple circuitry, they are rarely used in modern alarm systems. For one thing, relays are relatively large and bulky, especially if they must carry any significant amount of current. Although the circuitry is simpler, relays are usually much more expensive than most other types of comparable electronic switches. As mentioned, latching relays tend to be particularly expensive and difficult to find. The main reason relays are rarely used today, however, is their lower general reliability. Relays are electromechanical devices with small moving parts that can jam or stick. Relays tend to fail much more often than a purely electronic switching circuit.

There are a number of options available in purely electronic switching. There are transistor switch circuits, like the one shown in Fig. 2-10.

SCRs, or silicon-controlled rectifiers (shown in Fig. 2-11) are well suited to this application. Ordinarily, a SCR blocks current flow from cathode to anode. When a

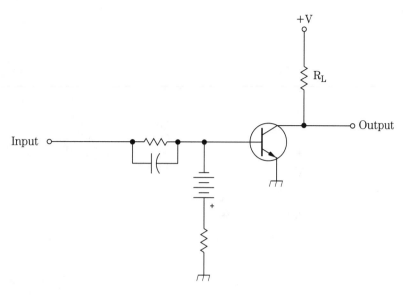

2-10 Transistors often are used for switching.

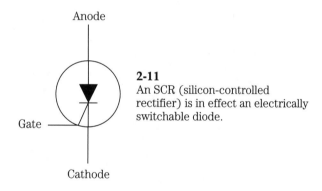

Anode

Gate

Cathode

2-11
An SCR (silicon-controlled rectifier) is in effect an electrically switchable diode.

sufficient control signal pulse is fed to the gate lead, the SCR is turned on, permitting current to flow from cathode (negative) to anode (positive). Like any standard rectifier, current flow in the opposite direction (from anode to cathode) is blocked. Only a brief pulse at the gate is required to switch on a SCR. Once it is turned on, it stays on, even if the control signal is removed from the gate. To turn off the SCR after it is triggered on, the input current must be reduced below a critical threshold level. The easiest way to do this is to briefly break the circuit and interrupt the current flow altogether. This action is shown in Fig. 2-12. As in the pseudolatching relay circuit discussed earlier, this can be a manual normally closed momentary action switch, or it can be a second electronic switch circuit.

Triacs (shown in Fig. 2-13) are similar to SCRs, but they permit current flow in both directions. In fact, a triac can be simulated by connecting a pair of SCRs back to back, as shown in Fig. 2-14.

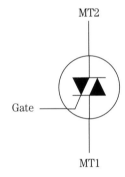

2-12
Break the circuit by opening the
normally closed switch to turn off
an SCR.

2-13
A triac is similar to an SCR, but permits
current flow in both directions.

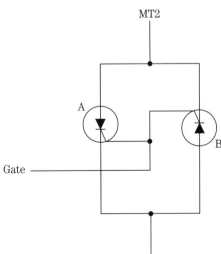

2-14
Simulated triac using a pair of
back-to-back SCRs.

Digital gates also can be used for electronic functions. With the increasing popularity and widespread use of digital circuitry, this is rapidly becoming the de facto norm in modern electronics work. It would not be appropriate to discuss digital gating in any depth here. This subject is well covered in a great many existing publications, and should be familiar to anyone working in any capacity in the electronics field today.

Any of these electronic switching devices and methods can be used in a wide variety of circuits ranging from the simple and straightforward to the very complex and sophisticated. In any case, the functional principles remain the same. So in a *block diagram*, represent any electronic switch device or circuit with a generalized block with four leads, as shown in Fig. 2-15. In addition to the obvious switch input and output, the third lead is a gate or control signal input. When an appropriate voltage or current appears on this lead, the electronic switch is activated. In most alarm system central control boxes, the electronic switches will need to be of the latching type, so the fourth lead is necessary. This lead is for the reset control signal. If the switch is activated, the appropriate signal on this line will deactivate the electronic switch, and the internal connections will revert to their normal states.

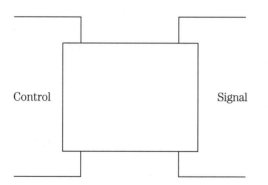

2-15
Any electronic switch can be generalized as a simple functional block with four leads.

In most cases, an electronic switch will perform a SPST function, so only two switch contacts are used. If a more complex switching function, such as SPDT (single-pole, double-pole), or DPDT (double-pole, double-pole) is implemented in the electronic switch circuit, additional switch input and output lines will be added to the block, as necessary.

Unless otherwise noted, assume all electronic switches throughout the following discussion will be SPST and normally open. This switch is the type of electronic switch circuit you most commonly encounter in a practical alarm system central control box.

In a home alarm system, the primary electronic switch(es) will be controlled by signals from the various sensors throughout the system. It is certainly easy enough to derive the control signal from the sensors. Recall that virtually all sensors used in home alarm systems are functionally just switches. They can complete or break a circuit carrying the required voltage or current signal. Fig. 2-16 shows how this works for normally open sensors.

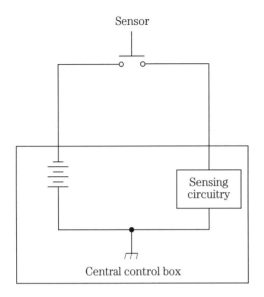

2-16
A normally open sensor easily can be adapted to create a suitable control signal.

Normally closed sensors are a little bit trickier. One approach to using NC sensors is shown in Fig. 2-17. Here resistor R1 has a much larger value than resistor R2. When the sensor switch is closed (its normal position), virtually all the signal is shunted through resistor R2 to ground. There is a much larger voltage drop across resistor R1. Very little voltage or current can reach the electronic switch, so it remains unactivated. But when the sensor switch is opened, resistor R2 is effectively removed from the circuit. All of the signal must pass through resistor R1, because it has nowhere else to go. Enough of the complete signal gets past this resistor to activate the electronic switch.

There are more sophisticated ways to use normally closed sensor switches, which waste less signal power. An inverter circuit, for example, can be used to re-

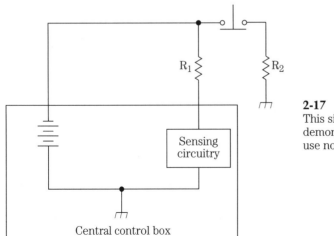

2-17
This simple circuit demonstrates a simple way to use normally closed sensors.

verse a LOW (0) voltage and a HIGH (triggering) voltage. A comparator circuit also can be used. The comparator is designed to produce a high voltage when its input voltage drops below some specific value. A circuit of this type is shown in Fig. 2-18. In this circuit, the comparator sees a relatively large input voltage when the sensor switch is closed (its normal state), so the output of the comparator is zero. But when the sensor switch is triggered, or opened, this voltage drops to zero, tripping the comparator to produce a high level output, which can activate the electronic switch.

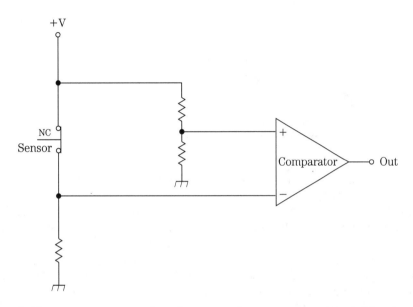

2-18 A comparator can adapt the output of a sensor to a more suitable control signal.

Digital gating also can be used to produce a HIGH signal when a normally closed sensor switch is opened. Other approaches also are possible, though less obvious and less commonly used.

The simplest possible central control box for an alarm system is simply a single electronic switch (of whatever type), as shown in Fig. 2-19. When an appropriate signal is received from one or more of the sensors, the electronic switch is activated, turning on the output alarm device. The alarm will continue to sound until the reset switch is manually operated. This would be a very crude alarm system, of course, lacking in any special features or versatility. But this basic circuit can easily be expanded into a very powerful system.

As mentioned, in a home of any size, the sensors should be grouped into semi-independent sections. An alarm system for a small apartment might have just a single electronic switch as shown here, but most alarm systems will give better results with multiple electronic switches. For example, a central control box circuit for three sensor sections is shown in Fig. 2-20. More sections can easily be added in exactly the same way. Limit the hypothetical system to just three sections here to keep

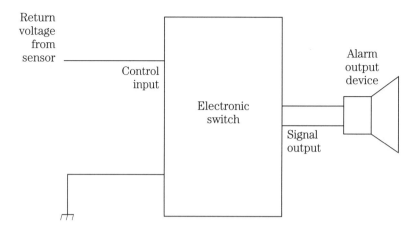

2-19 The simplest possible central control box is basically just a multiple-input electronic switching device of some sort.

the diagrams from getting too cluttered. Additional sections will simply be repetitions of what is shown here.

In this diagram, each sensor section controls its own electronic switch. The output of each electronic switch is split in two. One output controls a display device that indicates where the detected problem is on the front panel of the system's central control box. This device can be a simple LED, or a more complex and informative display. The other half of each electronic switch output goes to an OR gate network. This circuit can be a digital gate, or an analog mixing circuit of some type. Analog OR gates can be simple passive resistor networks, or sophisticated amplified multiplexer or mixer circuits. The specific circuitry used is not of concern here. Only be concerned with the functional operation of the circuitry—what it does, rather than how it does it.

An analog OR gate works in the same way as a digital OR gate. For the three OR gate inputs shown in Fig. 2-20, the output of the OR gate will go HIGH if, and only if, input A OR input B OR input C is HIGH. The output is LOW only if all inputs are LOW. The output of each electronic switch is LOW when the electronic switch is off (deactivated) and HIGH when it has been triggered on by an appropriate signal from its input sensor network. As long as all of the electronic switches are deactivated, the output of the central control box is LOW, or zero. No voltage is fed into the output alarm device, so it remains silent. As soon as one (or more than one) of the electronic switches is turned on, the central control-box output goes HIGH, feeding a voltage to the output alarm device, causing it to sound. Because the electronic switches are of the latching type, the alarm will continue to sound until the system is reset. (At this point, assume the reset function is accomplished only by a manual switch.)

A practical home alarm system should always have a timed shutoff feature, as emphasized elsewhere in this book. It is generally easy enough to add such a feature. The basic idea is shown in Fig. 2-21. Here is simply added a standard timer circuit. It derives its trigger input from the output of the central control OR gate, effectively in

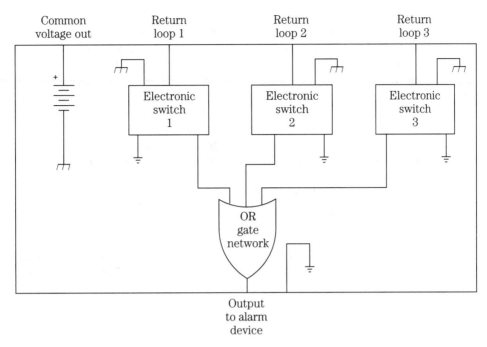

2-20 An alarm system of any degree of complexity will require multiple electronic switches in a central control box. This one has three.

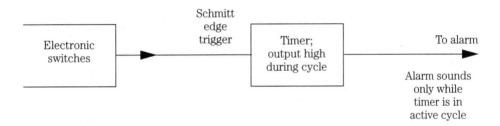

2-21 A practical home alarm system should always have a timed shutoff feature.

parallel with the output alarm device(s). In many practical circuits, greater reliability will be achieved by adding a Schmitt trigger stage as shown here. This stage will not always be required. With some timer circuits, additional circuitry to convert the continuous alarm output signal into a brief trigger pulse. Other timer circuits can use this signal directly, if they trigger on the LOW to HIGH transition, rather than the absolute HIGH state.

The output of this timer drives a nonlatching electronic switch that is in parallel with the manual reset switch. Opening either (or both) of these switches will reset the alarm system. Normally, when no sensor is triggering an alarm condition, the state of these switches is irrelevant. They are, in effect, ignored by the rest of the circuitry in the system. The electronic switch controlled by the shutoff timer is normally closed, but at this point this makes no difference. Now, assume a sensor is tripped, activating the associated electronic switch. The tripping action passes a signal through the OR gate to turn on the output alarm device, and initiate the timing period of the shutoff timer. The output of this timer immediately goes HIGH, opening its electronic switch. No reset signal passes through to the sensor's electronic switch. When the timer times out, its output goes LOW again. Because its electronic switch doesn't latch, it is immediately released to its normal position, which is closed. This action feeds a reset signal into the system, and the alarm is turned off.

With some circuits, it is difficult to come up with a normally closed electronic switch directly. In such a case, you simply have to add an inverter stage between the timer output and a normally open electronic switch, as shown in Fig. 2-22. Normally, when the timer is not activated, its output is LOW. This output is inverted to a HIGH signal that holds the electronic switch closed. When the timer is triggered, its output goes HIGH, which is inverted to a LOW control signal, releasing the electronic switch to its normal open state. After the timing cycle is completed, the timer output goes LOW again, which is inverted to HIGH, closing the electronic switch. In effect, the normally open electronic switch is forced to act as if it was a normally closed electronic switch.

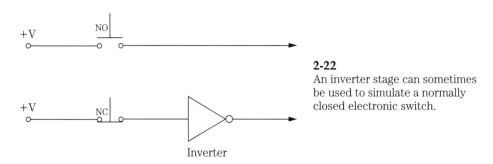

2-22
An inverter stage can sometimes be used to simulate a normally closed electronic switch.

If a door or window is left open, the alarm would be immediately retriggered, defeating the purpose of the shutoff timer. A solution to this problem is shown in Fig. 2-23. Here a second timer stage is added; it is triggered by the main shutoff timer. This timer has a very short timing cycle—just a second or two is enough. Some simple gating circuitry is added to the system so if the alarm is retriggered before this second timer times out, another latching electronic switch disables the output alarm device until it is manually reset.

Recall the discussion of the importance of an entrance delay timer to permit the legitimate occupants a chance to get in and out of the house without setting off the alarm. This delayed-response entryway sensor is fed to its own electronic switch with a timer at its input, as shown in Fig. 2-24. The alarm will not be set off unless this sensor is still in its triggered state when this timer completes its timing cycle. A timing period of 30 to 50 seconds is typical for this timer.

Many additional features can easily be added to the alarm system. The block diagram approach makes design of the central control box very easy. First determine what functional blocks are needed, then plug in the appropriate subcircuits, which are usually simple in themselves.

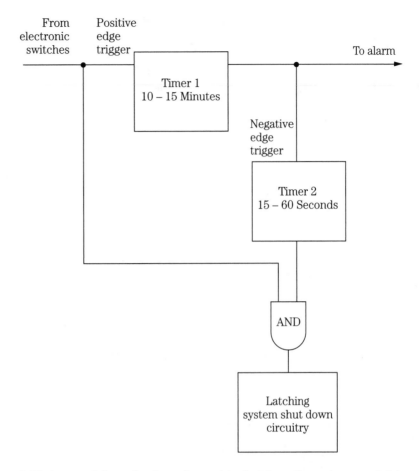

2-23 A second timer circuit can be used to shut down the system completely if it is immediately retriggered due to a stuck sensor from an open door or window.

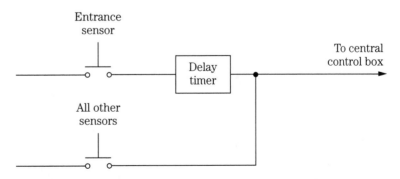

2-24 A delayed-response entryway sensor is fed to its own electronic switch with a timer at its input.

3

Structural considerations

An alarm system installer is primarily concerned with the electronics, of course, but there are many other aspects to a truly effective security system. Structural details of the house can play a crucial role. Even if you, as an alarm system installer, are not qualified to make structural changes, it is part of your job to note such items and advise your customer to have necessary work done.

The purpose of an alarm system is to frighten off any intruders, and/or to summon help to catch the intruder in the act. The ideal security would be to stop an intrusion before it happens. The goal is to keep intruders out.

If an intruder gets into the home, an alarm going off will probably help, but to some extent much of the damage has already been done. A cool-headed thief can probably grab something of value before fleeing. Even if the intruder doesn't actually take anything, the odds are good that some damage was done during the process of breaking in. Something almost certainly got broken or damaged, and the homeowner will have to pay for repairs. The aborted intrusion can still prove expensive to the homeowner, even if nothing was actually stolen. This risk shows why good solid structural details are a vital part of a home security system. If it's too easy to break into the home, an alarm system will only be of minimal value. It can limit but not prevent losses.

Doors

Outside doors are often the weakest security elements in many homes. You'd be surprised how easy it is to break through many home doors. Many doors are hollow, with just thin wood on either side of a frame, as shown in Fig. 3-1. There are some advantages to such doors for inside use—they are lightweight and inexpensive. They are relatively easy to hang. They are fine for bedroom or bathroom or closet doors, or the like. But they should never be used for an outside door. It doesn't take much physical strength to kick through each of the thin panels. Once there is a hole in the door, its no trouble for someone to reach in and open any inside lock. An intruder might make a hole big enough to crawl through without actually opening the door. In such

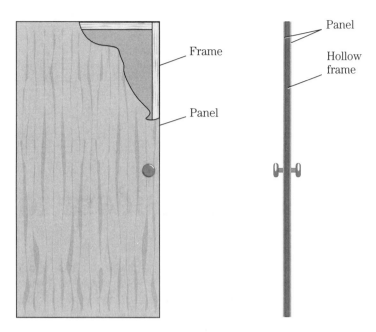

Frame

Panel

Panel

Hollow frame

3-1 Many doors are hollow with just thin wood on either side of a frame.

a case, a standard magnetic reed switch nominally protecting the door would remain undisturbed.

A light-weight door also can be forced completely off its hinges. A make-shift battering ram would do the job with only a minimal amount of physical effort for the intruder.

A hollow door keeps other people from seeing into your home, and keeps weather conditions (wind, rain, etc.) outside, but the security it offers is negligible.

With just a little experience, anyone can learn to recognize a hollow door just by knocking on it. The sound is decidedly different from that of a heftier solid door.

For reasonable security, exterior doors should always be either strong metal or solid wood. The thicker a wood door is, the harder it will be to break. Naturally, there are reasonable practical limits to door thickness. A fortress might use a foot-thick door, but that would be highly impractical for a home. It would be very difficult for the legitimate residents to get in and out. For reasonable security and practicality, the best choice for a solid wood door is about 1¾ to 2 inches thick. Anything thicker would probably be too heavy for convenience in day-to-day living, and anything thinner would be too fragile.

Of course the best, heftiest door in the world isn't going to offer much security unless it fits within its frame snugly and firmly without significant gaps. Gaps around the edges of an exterior door should be avoided in any case for reasonable energy use. Even a small gap can force a heating or cooling system to work much less efficiently than it really needs to do.

Exterior doors should be hung with the hinges on the inside. It should be impossible to remove the hinges or gain access to the hinge pins from the outside of the building. If a potential intruder can remove or damage the hinges, any lock on the door isn't going to accomplish very much.

Double locking is strongly advisable on all exterior doors to the home. Dead-bolt locks should always be used. Spring-loaded locks are simply too easy to pick. Often all an intruder needs to do is to wiggle a credit card between the door and the jam to pry the lock open. A dead bolt, on the other hand, goes securely through the door frame and cannot be forced back out of the way from the outside, except by using the key (see Fig. 3-2).

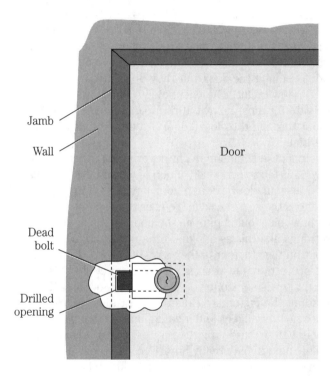

Jamb

Wall

Door

Dead bolt

Drilled opening

3-2
A dead bolt goes securely through the door frame and cannot be forced out of the way from the outside except by using the key.

A dead-bolt lock also has a long hard metal bolt that goes through the thin framing lumber used on the frame of most doors, passing directly into heavy structural studs. To be truly efficient and secure, the dead bolt should have at least a one-inch throw. A one-inch throw ensures that it goes at least 1 inch deep into the frame when the door is locked. With a 1 inch engagement, it is extremely difficult for anyone attempting to kick the door open. They're more likely to hurt their foot than force the dead bolted door open.

A steel *kick plate*, or *strike plate*, can help secure the door even further. Metal strike plates should be placed around the immediate area of the lock to prevent someone from drilling holes or bashing through enough to get past the lock mechanism. The best place to mount the strike plate is directly into the door frame on the side where the bolt goes through the stud framing. This placement spreads the force of any kick or blow over a larger area and makes it much less effective.

For maximum effectiveness, strike plates should be mounted onto the frame with screws that are least 3 inches long. This depth has a double advantage. It would take longer for an intruder to attempt to remove the screws. The intruder would still have to break through the lock. Exerting force or pressure on the plate will not pull the screws all the way out, which could occur with shorter screws.

Strike plates can be very effective security devices, and they are relatively inexpensive as well. They are highly advisable for homes located in high crime areas.

For security, a window in or near a door can be a mixed blessing. On the positive side, the person inside can visually identify a visitor before opening the door. On the other hand, an intruder might break a window and reach in to unlock the door.

If there is no window, it is worthwhile to install a wide-angle peephole viewer or an intercom. Such devices are almost the best of both worlds. They allow advance identification of callers without opening the door, but they don't give a prospective intruder any advantage, as a window might. The peephole viewer is not expensive, and it will be more than adequate for most homes. If occupants need to question a visitor's identity, they can shout through the closed door. An intercom is somewhat more elegant, but hardly essential.

People criticize peepholes because someone might cover it from the outside or stand outside its range of view. This tactic isn't really much of a problem. If you can't see the person who's knocked at your door or rung your doorbell, don't open the door. Call out and ask to see who is there. If the caller refuses to cooperate, the odds are excellent that this is someone you should not open the door for. Sure, sometimes friends will get cute and do things like this as a joke. Perhaps it wouldn't be a bad idea to leave them standing out on the stoop until they stop the childish pranks.

A peephole is not perfect protection, but what is? An intruder could hide in the bushes, or otherwise out of sight, while someone you know knocks or rings the bell. When you open the door to admit the legitimate caller, the intruder could rush in. Sure, this could happen, but it's not very likely, and it could happen that way with or without the peephole. The peephole is hardly increasing the risk. Under most circumstances, a peephole will help, and it can't really hurt. Because these devices are relatively inexpensive and can be installed without too much difficulty (it's usually just a matter of drilling a hole through the door), there's little reason not to include one in any windowless exterior door. Of course if there is a window in, or next to the door, there wouldn't be much point in installing a peephole viewer.

If there is a window, could an intruder break it and reach in to open the lock from the inside? Unless a door window is very small, this is a real possibility. The window should be protected by the alarm system. Here is a case where foil tape should probably be used, as aesthetics are not as much an issue and most other sensors would be less reliable for this job.

What about other windows near the door? If they are more than 40 inches or so away from the door lock, they only need to be protected like any other window in the home. It's unlikely that anyone could reach in and unlock the door from this distance or farther. If the window is less than 40 inches from the door lock, special precautions need to be considered. Any extra sensor protection to that one window is strongly advisable. You also might consider mechanical tricks. Is there some way to physically block off a potential intruder's reaching access to the lock?

Also consider any other potential access points through the door. Can the inside lock be reached from outside through a mail slot, a pet door, or anything similar? If so, it is necessary to add protection, either physically blocking access or adding a special sensor to trigger the alarm if an attempt to break in is made through this access opportunity. Protecting such access points with an alarm system can be tricky, because the system must allow for ordinary legitimate use. The mail carrier must be able to open a mail slot and drop in mail. The alarm should not go off every time your pet goes in or out through the pet door.

Every case is somewhat different, and it is difficult to come up with a universal solution to cover such cases. The most general approach might be a photoelectric sensor and a light beam above the opening, as shown in Fig. 3-3. In legitimate use, nothing should go high enough to break the light beam. For a mail slot, the letters come in and drop down. A pet is going to approach a pet door from below, not above.

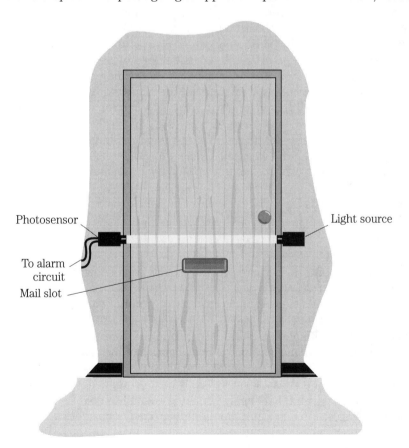

3-3 A mail slot or a pet door can be secured with a photoelectric sensor and a light beam above the opening.

But an intruder will stick an arm through and up to reach the lock. This action will break the light beam and set off the alarm. The biggest problem here would be the mounting of the light beam source and the photosensor in such a way that they will not interfere with ordinary use of the door. A little mechanical ingenuity is called for.

Screen or storm doors are often neglected in security system planning. Many homes have sturdy, well-protected front doors, but in warm weather, the heavy main door is left open, and the entrance to the home is "protected" only by a flimsy storm or screen door with only a simple spring-loaded latch to serve as a lock. The built-in latch in most screen or storm doors is good only for keeping the door from accidentally swinging open. They certainly aren't going to keep anyone of even moderate strength out if they are determined to get in.

The main door should always be closed and locked whenever no one is at home. But even when the family is home, don't tempt a possible intruder with an invitingly flimsy storm or screen door.

The screen or storm door should be at least reasonably sturdy and rigid. It should not be easily bent or broken. Make sure there is a decent lock on the screen or storm door. If the main door is to be left open often for extended periods, add sensors for the alarm system to the screen or storm door as well as for the main door. The system should guard against someone breaking through the glass in a storm door, or (even more likely) cutting through the screen of a screen door. Usually this wouldn't take anything more than a common pair of simple wire cutters. Test the screen for conductivity. In many cases, it will be insulated by paint, but often the metal screening will be exposed, and will serve as a fair conductor. It might not always be possible, but you might use the screen as a normally closed sensor switch. Connections to the alarm system are made to opposite ends of the screen. If the screening is broken or cut between the connection points, electrical contact will be broken, and the alarm will be sounding, as if any other NC sensor switch was opened.

Door guard chains

One of the most popular of all security devices is the door guard chain. Unfortunately, in most cases, these devices offer little more than a symbolic comfort. They give little or no practical security.

The principle of a door guard chain mechanism is shown in Fig. 3-4. There might be some minor variations in actual products of this type, but the basic principles remain the same. One end of short, relatively stout chain is fixed solidly and permanently to the door (on the inside). When the free end of this chain is attached to a hook mechanism mounted on the door jamb, the door (theoretically) can't be opened more than a few inches, limited by the length of the chain. The chain is usually sturdy enough. The weak element is usually the mounting of the hook mechanism on the door jamb. These devices usually come equipped with screws that are only ½ to ¾ inch long, and that simply isn't long enough to hold securely. It doesn't take much physical force to yank them out, especially considering the soft wood used on most door jambs. Unfortunately, the door jamb will be too shallow to accept longer screws without splitting. It's another good-sounding idea that isn't really practical.

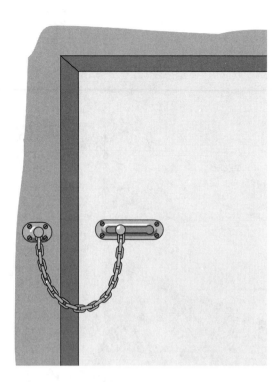

3-4
One of the most popular, but least
effective, of all security devices is
the door guard chain.

Door guard chains won't do any harm. They won't reduce the security of anyone's home, but they can't be counted on to add to it either.

Many customers will insist on door guard chains, and won't feel secure without them. Because they only cost a couple dollars and aren't much trouble to install, put them in if the customer wants them. It would be even more of a wasted effort to try to explain to many people why they aren't really worth much. They seem to be almost a superstitious icon for many. If it keeps your customers happy and doesn't add appreciably to the system cost or installation effort, it won't hurt to put them in. Be sure they aren't the primary basis of security in the home. As a designer or installer, don't suggest such items that do not add to real security. Use them only if the customer specifically requests them.

Basement doors

Be sure to consider all doors to the home. Front doors and back doors are obvious enough, but all too often, people tend to forget all about cellar doors, doors from the garage, and the like. These doors must be as secure and protected as well as the front door, or you might as well leave the front door wide open with a "Welcome" mat for any burglars in the area.

Many homes in certain areas still have old-fashioned outside cellar doors, as shown in Fig. 3-5. In more innocent days gone by, home security was not generally considered an issue. Often the cellar door was used for deliveries of coal, so it couldn't be left locked. On many such doors the only built-in "lock" is a simple hook and eye

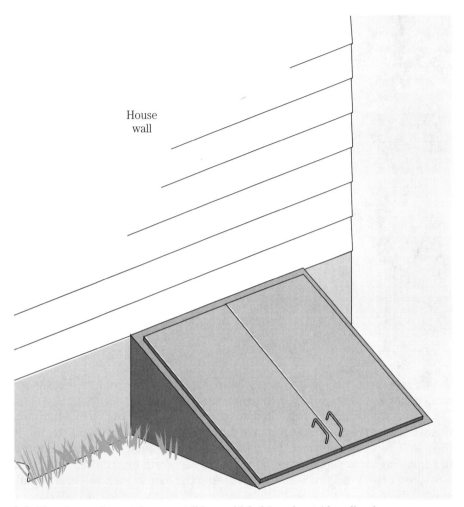

House
wall

3-5 Many homes in certain areas still have old-fashioned outside cellar doors.

latch like the one shown in the diagram. The latch keeps the door from blowing open in a light wind, but it obviously offers no security at all. There's nothing to keep any intruder from opening the latch and gaining access through the home through the cellar.

In any home with such a cellar door, special precautions must be taken, or the most elaborate alarm system in the world will be essentially useless. As an absolute minimum, the hook-and-eye latch should be replaced with a sturdy hasp and a good padlock. The choice of a combination lock or a key lock is pretty much one of personal preference and based on how many people should have legitimate entrance through the cellar door.

Don't forget that the hasp and all hinges should be mounted to make all mounting screws and hinge pins as inaccessible as possible from the outside. An intruder should not be able to get into the home by removing a hasp or disassembling a hinge.

In most homes, it is not advisable to use an automatically latching lock that engages whenever the cellar door is closed unless it can be easily opened from the inside. Many people have gotten locked in basements by such locks. Sometimes it might be a long wait until someone comes by to let you out. At best, it's an uncomfortable, irritating experience. In most cases it would be safer and wiser to use a manually controlled, rather than automatic lock. Of course, everyone must get into the habit of closing the lock every time. It would only take one careless exception to invite an intruder into the home.

In some cases, it is advisable to mount the lock on the inside of the door, instead of on the outside as is the normal tradition. This arrangement is good if the cellar door is not being used by the current occupants of the home. But if the cellar door is likely to be used, consider if it will be a problem or a major inconvenience to limit outside access to the cellar door to legitimate users. If the cellar is used for storage, bringing things in from outside will make an external rather than internal lock almost mandatory.

Of course, the home alarm system should include appropriate sensors to monitor the cellar door. In most cases magnetic reed switches can be used in a manner similar to any standard type door. A single panel door, as shown in Fig. 3-6, offers no special installation problems in most cases. If there are two door panels that open in the center and move out in opposite directions (as shown in Fig. 3-7), a little ingenuity and extra care is required to install an effective magnetic reed switch sensor. The most obvious approach is shown in Fig. 3-8. The wired section is mounted on one of the two moving door panels. This means the connecting wires must be slack enough to prevent undue excess stress when the door is opened, yet not enough loose slack to permit the wires to get tangled. Fortunately, a cellar door is one area in a typical home where aesthetics aren't likely to be a significant issue. It's okay for the installation to look a little unattractive. But try not to make it too ugly or untidy. Keep it neat, not just for appearance sake, but to avoid potential mechanical problems in the future.

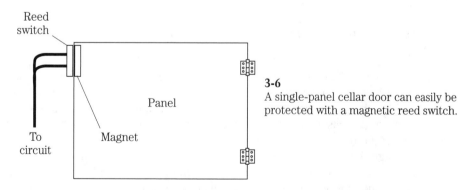

3-6
A single-panel cellar door can easily be protected with a magnetic reed switch.

It also is very important to check the condition of the door. These cellar doors were almost always made of wood and are probably quite old. They have been exposed to the elements for years. There is a good chance that the wood might be at least partially rotted or significantly weakened in spots. How easy would it be for a po-

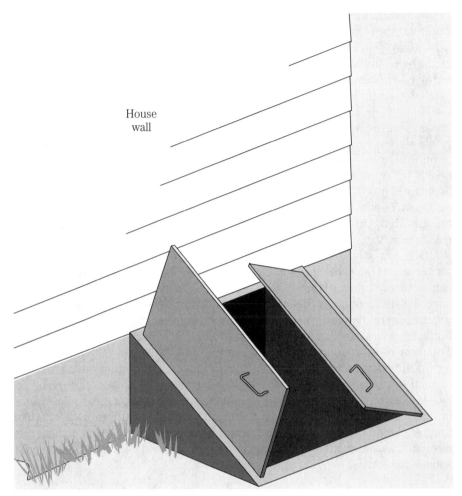

House
wall

3-7 A cellar door with two panels that open in the center and move out in opposite directions is a little trickier to protect in an alarm system.

tential intruder to kick through the door? If there is any doubt at all, replace the door. Use a good solid wood or, even better, sheet metal. Make the door as strong and secure as possible, without making it too heavy to be easily opened by legitimate users.

At the top of the basement stairs, there almost certainly will be a door to the main portion of the house. This door also should be protected against potential intruders who might have somehow gotten into the basement. This door, even though it is actually completely inside, should be treated as if it were an exterior door. That is, it should be solid, not hollow, and it should have a good quality lock. It also should be protected with sensors for the alarm system.

Once again, an automatically locking door is risky. It can be surprisingly easy to lock oneself in the basement when no one else is home. Being locked in the basement can be more than an annoying inconvenience under some circumstances. But

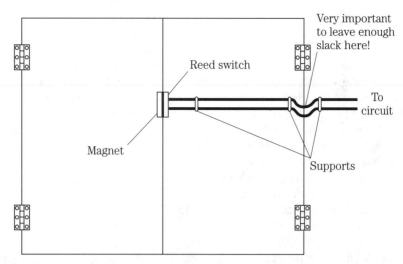

3-8 This is one possible solution to the problem of Fig. 3-7. The wired section of the magnetic reed switch is mounted on one of the two moving door panels.

with a manually operated lock, everyone in the household must get into the regular habit of always keeping the basement door locked when no one is legitimately downstairs. If the cellar door and any basement windows large enough for someone to crawl through are kept locked, locking the basement door will be somewhat less critical than a true exterior door, especially if the door is monitored by an adequate alarm system. If the basement is properly protected, any intruder attempting entry that way will probably have set off the alarm before reaching the basement door. The basement door acts as one last protective barrier.

Of course even a locked basement door will be of very limited protection if the door's hinges are on the basement side where the intruder would have access to them.

Garages

If the home has an attached garage, there must be protection against unauthorized entry through the garage. Typically there are three access points to be considered in laying out the home security system. There is the actual garage door, where vehicles are driven in and out, of course. This door should always be kept shut except when it is actually being used. An automatic garage door opener is somewhat more secure than a comparable manual garage door, but most automatic garage doors have a (very sensible) fail-safe system permitting manual operation of the door in case something goes wrong with the remote, or the automated system. Unfortunately, if the homeowner can manually open the garage door in an emergency, so can an intruder. For adequate security, a lock is a must. Regrettably, this might eliminate the convenience of an automatic garage door. You'll have to get out of the car to unlock the garage door. But compared to a break-in and burglary or violence from an intruder, it might be the lesser of two evils in high-risk neighborhoods.

Several sensors for the alarm system should monitor the garage door. This arrangement often introduces some tricky, but not insurmountable, mounting problems. It is difficult to protect many garage doors adequately, so this is often a weak link in a security system. This makes it vitally important to consider the garage in the early stages of planning out the security system to strengthen the weak link as much as possible.

One fairly simple trick can serve both as a security and a safety measure. A reasonably bright light should be turned on over the entire driveway area whenever the garage door is opened. A timer should keep the light on for five or ten minutes after the garage door is shut. If it is dark outside, this will aid in visibility for anyone legitimately coming or going. As stated several times throughout this book, burglars like to work in the dark and shun well lighted areas as much as possible. If it is dark, they are less likely to be seen, and if they are seen, the odds are good the witness won't be able to positively identify them later. Security lighting increases the chances of a potential intruder being caught in the act, or, even better, being discouraged from even attempting entry in the first place.

If you want, you can add photosensors so the driveway lights will only be turned on when it is dark outside. The lights won't normally be on very long, so even if heavy-duty flood lamps are used, the electrical drain will be minimal. There's also a possibility that a neighbor would notice if the lights come on for no apparent reason during the day. For example, assume the Smiths next door know about this part of the Green family's security system. If they see the light go on in middle of the day when everyone in the Green family is at work or school, the Smiths might report this suspicious incident to the police. That possibility could make a couple extra pennies (if that much) on each month's electrical bill a very worthwhile investment.

Most home garages also have a standard access door, usually in the rear of the garage. This door is often forgotten and neglected in many home security systems, and professional burglars know this. It should be protected like any other exterior door to the home. Because it is just a regular door, making it secure introduces no special problems, as long as the garage access door is remembered. Of course it must be a good, sturdy door suitable for exterior use.

The third door in a garage is the most important one, and it too is often neglected in many home security systems. This door is the one that goes from the garage to the interior of the home. (If there is no such door, of course, the garage would not be a point of access to the home and would not have to be included in the security system, except to protect items in the garage.) Although this is in a sense an interior door, for security purposes it must be considered an exterior door, and protected accordingly. This door should be solid, not hollow, and it should have a good-quality lock. It also should be protected with sensors for the alarm system. The hinges should be inside the house, and not on the garage side where an intruder might tamper with them to gain entrance to the house.

Sliding doors

Standard doors usually don't present many problems to the alarm-system installer. Sliding glass doors, popular as patio doors, are at the opposite extreme. From the standpoint of security, sliding doors offer nothing but problems.

For one thing, the built-in locks on sliding doors are typically lousy. In fact, they often aren't really locks at all, just a simple, inexpensive latch like those used on many windows. Such a latch usually can be forced or pried open without much difficulty.

Some sliding doors do have key locks, but even here, only a small inexpensive lock is typically used. Such locks are pretty easy to pick. Some aren't really built into the door, but have an extended lock body, as shown in Fig. 3-9. Being a cheap lock, it is built of fairly soft metal. The entire lock mechanism can easily be crushed to bits with a moderately large pair of pliers or some similar tool.

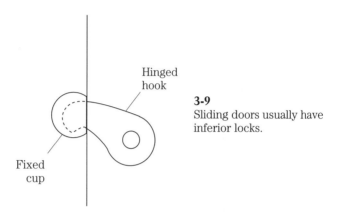

Hinged
hook

Fixed
cup

3-9
Sliding doors usually have inferior locks.

Unfortunately, the very design of most sliding doors makes installation of a truly effective lock very difficult, if not completely impossible.

Rather than rely on a lock that can be opened from the outside, it's usually more secure to block the sliding door from opening from inside the house. Use some other (standard type) door to leave or return to the house.

The following method is simple and effective, if somewhat inelegant. The only piece of equipment required is a piece of 1 × 2 lumber or a large dowel cut to a length slightly less than the distance between the door jamb and the sliding portion of the door when it is fully closed. To secure the sliding door, simply lay the wood into the track where the door slides back and forth. With the wood in place, it blocks the door's path in the track, and the sliding door can't be opened until the wood is removed.

Some hardware stores stock a bar for sliding doors, which is designed to be attached to the middle of the jamb on the stationary side. A small clip is screwed above this bar on the same jamb. When the bar is not in use, this clip holds it in an upright position. To secure the sliding door, simply close it and lower the bar from its upright position, snapping it into a second clip that is mounted on the frame of sliding door (the movable portion). With this metal bar across the opening, the door cannot be opened. It would be difficult to force your way past it.

The basic design of most sliding doors make them somewhat an inherent security risk. During the original installation of the sliding door, the frame is put into place first, then the actual doors (both the movable and the stationary sections) are dropped into place. The door sections fit into grooves or ruts in the top and bottom fittings, which provide a track for the sliding door to move across. To make the in-

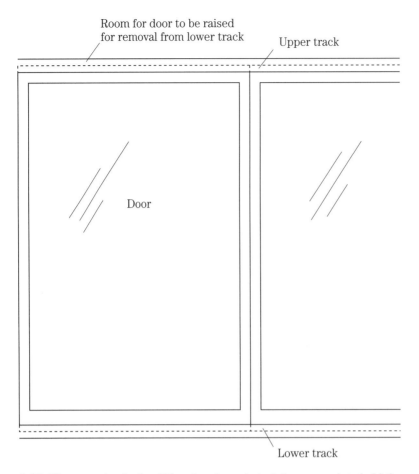

Room for door to be raised
for removal from lower track

Upper track

Door

Lower track

3-10 The upper track of a sliding door is made just deep enough to hold the door, but shallow enough to permit the door to be lifted up enough to clear the retrainers in the lower track.

stallation or any future repairs possible, the upper track is made just deep enough to hold the sliding door, but shallow enough to permit the door to be lifted up enough to clear the retrainers in the lower track as shown in Fig. 3-10.

Unfortunately, the same design that permits the sliding door to be installed in the first place, makes it pretty easy for that same sliding door to be removed by anyone who knows how it works. It is simply a matter of prying it up from the bottom and pulling the bottom of the door section outwards. This is usually easier to do from the inside, but it is far from impossible from the outside. A standard sliding door lock certainly isn't going to be strong enough to prevent this. Even a locking bar will probably permit enough play to make it possible for someone with a steady hand. The bar wouldn't have to be broken, just tilted a little.

Fortunately, there is a fairly simple solution to this security problem. Drill three or four evenly spaced holes into the upper track of the sliding door assembly, between the track guides, on the inside of the sliding door. Sheet-metal screws should then be inserted firmly into these holes. The screws should be long enough to extend down toward the top of the sliding glass door when they are screwed into place. The heads of the screws will not get in the way of removing the sliding door, as shown in Fig. 3-11. This modification will be a bit of a nuisance if there is ever a legitimate reason for removing the sliding door, perhaps for repairing a broken pane of glass or a bent track. But this is unlikely, and the nuisance is only a minor one. The holding screws can be removed from inside the house. It would just be a little more work. But these screws are inaccessible from outside the house, so they will do the job of thwarting a potential burglar trying to get in by removing the sliding door.

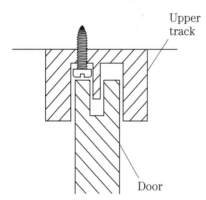

Upper track

3-11
Three or four evenly spaced protruding screws in the upper track of the sliding door assembly (between the track guides) prevent the door from being removed.

Door

Windows

Ordinarily, people enter or leave a house through a door, but burglars often find it easier to come in through a window. All too often people forget just how easy it is for someone to crawl in through an open window. Therefore, it is absolutely vital for an alarm system to guard against windows being opened, as well as doors.

In some installations, it might be desirable for the system also to protect against the glass in the window being broken. Unfortunately, the two most common ways to do this aren't very good. Foil tape is very unattractive, and only of limited effectiveness, and acoustic glass break detectors often suffer from reliability and sensitivity problems. Both these methods of protecting windows (and their inherent limitations) are discussed in more detail in chapter 1.

Actually, statistics show that burglars rarely get into a house by breaking a window and climbing in through the broken glass. There are undoubtedly many reasons for this. One obvious explanation is that a lot of glass would have to be broken to make a large enough hole, and it would be difficult if not impossible to do that quietly. A burglar obviously doesn't want to make a lot of noise that could draw attention. Another discouraging factor for the burglar is that climbing through broken glass can be dangerous or at least exceedingly uncomfortable. The remaining shards of glass are likely to be very sharp. Broken bits of glass would almost surely be on the floor in front of the window after the burglar has broken it. If the intruder crawls through, stepping on these shards could make noise and could cause loss of footing. A loss of footing or fall could result in more noise and possible injury from landing on the broken glass.

When intruders do break windows, they usually just make a big enough break to reach in and unlock the window or a nearby door so they can open it and get inside. The main concern around windows is detecting if the window is opened while the alarm system is armed. The most common method is to use a set of magnetic reed switches, as discussed in chapter 1.

Our interest here is the physical security of the window. The glass is not as much of a security issue as it might seem at first glance. Most home windows do not have actual locks, but simple latches, which are usually easy to defeat. The typical window latch is just a metal pin or hook on the movable window that is held in place by a latch clasp on the stationary portion of the window. A typical window latch is shown in Fig. 3-12. This latch is commonly used on sliding windows. The same type of latch is used for windows that slide up and down as shown in Fig. 3-13 or sideways as shown in Fig. 3-14.

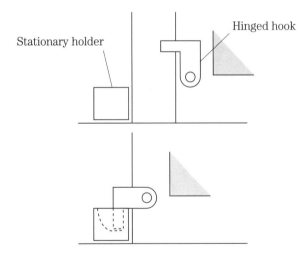

3-12
The typical window latch is just a metal pin or hook on the movable window that is held in place by a latch clasp on the stationary portion of the window.

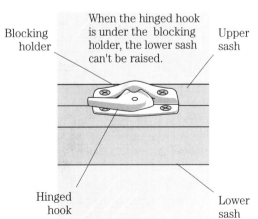

3-13
This is a typical window latch for a window that slides up and down.

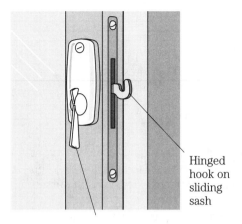

3-14
This is a typical window latch
for a window that slides
sideways.

Hinged
hook on
sliding
sash

Less commonly, you might encounter windows that swing open (either inwards or outwards), as shown in Fig. 3-15. This window is usually only found in very old homes, but they couldn't really be called rare. They are actually pretty common in some parts of the country. The standard latch for this window is a simple hook and eye, as shown in Fig. 3-16.

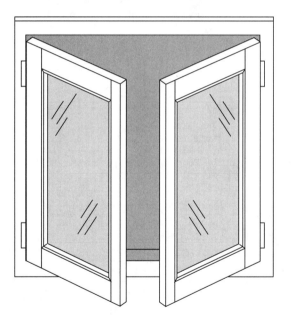

3-15
A few home windows are designed
to swing open, either in or out.

In either window (sliding or swinging), the latch provides only minimal security. Because it is small and weak, it can be forced from outside without too much effort. Certainly a crowbar would do the trick. Under even moderately concentrated pressure, the small clasp will bend, break, or be yanked out of its hold-down fastenings (usually very short, small-diameter screws). Also, both types of latch would be very easy to open by feel if the burglar breaks the glass and reaches inside.

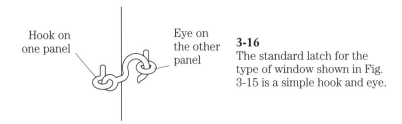

Hook on one panel

Eye on the other panel

3-16
The standard latch for the type of window shown in Fig. 3-15 is a simple hook and eye.

Some better-quality window locks are available, including dead bolt types for maximum security. Unfortunately these devices can be hard to find, and they tend to be expensive. In many cases it might be more practical to use a do-it-yourself approach to window security.

Swinging windows can easily be secured with a crossbar, as shown in Fig. 3-17. The heavier the crossbar, the greater the level of security it will offer. For a window that swings inwards when opened, the holding mounts for the crossbar only need to be mounted onto the wall on either side of the window. The sections of the window cannot push past the crossbar when it is in place. If the window swings outwards, however, additional holding clamps for the crossbar must be mounted on the window sections themselves, as shown in Fig. 3-18. The mountings will necessarily be shallower here, limited by the thickness of the window frame, but you can still get very strong crossbar protection this way.

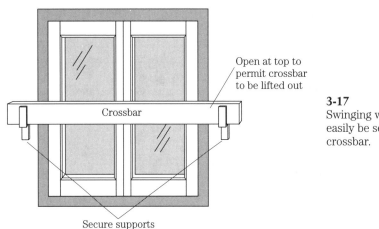

Open at top to permit crossbar to be lifted out

Crossbar

Secure supports

3-17
Swinging windows can easily be secured with a crossbar.

For sliding windows of the type that are often called *double hung*, the process of securing them is just a bit more complicated but still not really difficult. Close the windows and drill a small hole through the window frame from inside the house towards the outside where the two frames meet. On most windows, there isn't much margin for error. The hole must be precisely located, and kept as much as possible in the thickest part of the wood frame. It would be very risky to come too close to the

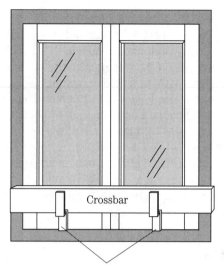

3-18
For windows that swing out, the crossbar must be mounted on the window sections.

Crossbar

Supports fixed on sashes

glass, which might crack or shatter from the vibrations of the drill. Also, if the hole is drilled too close to the edge, it will not be very effective as a security device. Don't drill all the way through the window frame. Just go completely through the inside window sash and about halfway through the outside window sash.

The hole should be just large enough to comfortably hold a 8 penny common nail. The hole should be just slightly wider than the diameter of the nail. The idea is to make it easy to insert or remove the nail, but for it to fit snugly enough to hold securely when in place. Sliding the nail into the hole while the window is closed, prevents it from being opened. To open the window, just remove the nail, which can only be done from the inside. This simple but effective security modification to a window is shown in Fig. 3-19.

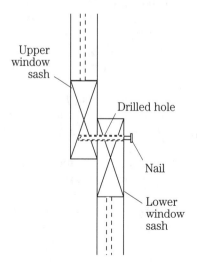

Upper window sash

Drilled hole

Nail

Lower window sash

3-19
A simple removable nail in a drilled hole can prevent a window from being opened from the outside.

The nail should be long enough to stick out of the hole far enough to be easily grasped for removal, but not so long that it will tend to fall out due to its own unsupported weight. For most standard home windows, a good length is 2 to 2½ inches.

A nice extra is a simple holder mounted on the wall next to the window to store the nail conveniently when it is not in use. Without a holder, it would be easy to misplace the nail while the window is opened. The holder does not have to be anything fancy, just a simple piece of wood with a hole in it large enough to hold the body of the nail but not big enough to let the head pass through it. A stiff wire loop also could be used for this purpose. Whatever holder is used, its appearance should not be neglected. It should be as unobtrusive as possible, and if it can be made decorative, at least try not to make it actively ugly. In some cases, the holder could be mounted so it is hidden behind the edge of the curtain. In such cases, the appearance would be much less of a concern.

Vents and fireplaces

In some houses, there might be alternate ways to get inside other than the obvious doors and windows. In some architectural designs, vents and fireplaces can be vulnerable to intrusion. The alarm system designer must consider and examine all such possibilities carefully. If intrusion is possible, even if it seems unlikely, the security system should take it into account and provide at least some minimal protection.

These potential entry points should already be marked on your basic security map introduced in the previous chapter, but it would probably be a good idea to take an extra walk around the entire house, both outside and inside, and look for any openings in any of the walls large enough for a human being to pass through. (Don't forget that some burglars might be crafty enough to use a child as an accomplice to get in spaces too small for an adult, and then unlock a door or window from the inside.) Don't ignore openings covered up with gratings or plates, assuming they are already secure. Any covering can conceivably be removed or broken. Would a potential intruder have access to the inside of the home if the obstructing cover was out of the way? If you can do so conveniently and nondestructively, try removing the covering yourself and looking inside. Is there a large enough passageway for an intruder. Consider the opening safe only if it is structurally too small for anyone (including a child) to crawl through, or if it doesn't lead anywhere that would provide a security risk.

In modern houses with fireplaces, the chimney is usually (though not always) designed with security in mind, and portions of the flue are made too narrow for reasonable passage. In other designs, gates or gratings are mounted as obstacles, but gates and gratings can be removed.

Although specialized sensors are not generally available for such unusual intrusion access points, in most cases, by their very nature, they are relatively easy to secure adequately with an alarm system.

The first step is to include sensors to detect if any cover plate or grating is opened, removed, or broken. Often magnetic reed switches will do the job as well as for standard doors or windows. A metallic grating can be used as its own sensor in some cases. The idea is similar to foil tape, which is discussed in chapter 1. Contacts are placed at either end. If the grating in between is cut or broken, the circuit between the two contacts will be broken, and will act like a normally closed sensor being opened, setting off the alarm. Do not, however, consider booby trapping such a metallic grating by electrifying it to give an intruder a shock. The booby trap could be a fire hazard, a booby trap could backfire and harm someone who is innocent (perhaps someone you were trying to protect), and it could open you up to a law suit, or even criminal charges, even if the person injured or killed was breaking into your home. The law does permit the use of force in self-defense or to protect other persons or property, under certain conditions, but this is severely limited for some very good reasons. Citizens are not permitted to take the law into their own hands and act as judge, jury, and executioner. The defensive force must be reasonable in response to the original threat. Deadly force is never legally permitted in the protection of property. Dangerous booby traps are almost always illegal, and they have a nasty tendency of harming the innocent.

If an intruder gets into the house via a vent pipe or a chimney, he or she will have to pass through a fairly narrow passageway, and upon reaching the end of the pipe or chimney, will be restricted in the choices of how to get out. The location of his first step is liable to be more or less forced to a specific spot. This makes the use of pressure mats a good security choice. Some could be placed inside a large vent pipe, for example, on the floor immediately in front of the vent inside the house. A typical example is shown in Fig. 3-20. Of course, as always, the pressure mats should be covered or disguised. They should not be visible to the intruder. This precaution includes any pressure mats inside the vent pipe. Don't count on it being too dark in there for the intruder to see. A burglar of any intelligence at all is going to carry at least a small flashlight, especially if she or he often crawls through dark vent pipes.

Most modern fireplaces have safety screens to protect against possible flying embers. The safety screen is usually in the form of a folding or swinging gate assembly. Such safety screens also can be used as part of the home security system. Add a sensor to set off the alarm if the safety screen is opened or removed.

Fences and landscaping

The security system is not just inside the house. The landscaping around the house also can be of considerable significance.

In most cases, the professional alarm system installer will have to work with the landscaping that's there. People have often put considerable time and expense into the decorative aspects of their lawns, and they'll probably be reluctant to make major changes to make your job easier, even though your job is ultimately to make their own home safer. You might make a few gentle suggestions but be prepared to work around them.

The usual problem is shrubbery or decorations that block the view in critical areas and could provide an excellent hiding place for an intruder attempting to get into the home. Check the visibility of all potential entrance points to the house (doors, windows, and whatever) from the street and neighbors' houses. The places you can't

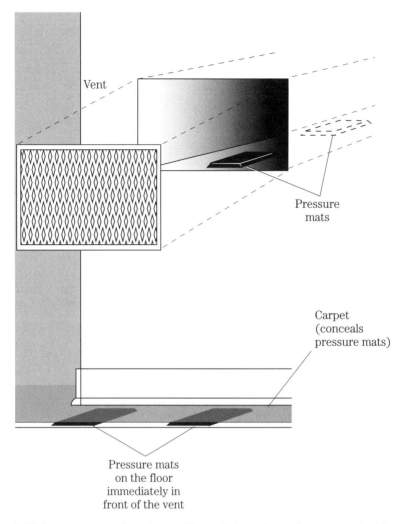

Vent

Pressure
mats

Carpet
(conceals
pressure mats)

Pressure mats
on the floor
immediately in
front of the vent

3-20 Large vents an intruder could crawl through can be protected with
well-placed pressure mats.

see well are where a potential intruder will see a "Welcome" sign. Your job is to find
a way to make them a little less welcome.

Often installing some lights over the most critical areas will increase visibility,
and help discourage intruders. Even if the intruder is not directly visible, cleverly
arranged outdoor lighting could cast very visible telltale shadows.

If visibility is a problem at a particularly critical entrance point, such as the front
or back door, it would be a good idea to add some appropriate outdoor sensors to the
alarm system. These exterior sensors must be designed for outdoors use, or enclosed in suitably weather-proof housings. They also should be extra durable and
tamper proof. It is absolutely vital for them to be very well hidden and not obvious to
any potential intruders.

Generally, modified pressure mats are one of the more obvious choices. Placement is a major problem, however. You can't count on an intruder cooperatively stepping right where you've placed a pressure mat. You have to figure out those places where an intruder is likely to be more or less forced to step.

Sound sensors are often used to protect such outside areas, but sensitivity can be a problem. The sound sensor must be sensitive enough to low volume sounds from an intruder who is presumedly trying to be as quiet as possible. The sensor must avoid setting off false alarms to other, perfectly innocent sounds in the area, which might be loud (such as kids playing, dogs barking, or passing cars backfiring). The problem is complicated further by the fact that naturally occurring sounds in the environment could occur at any frequency so tuning a sound sensor to respond only to specific frequencies (assuming you can determine what frequencies need to be specifically monitored) is unlikely to eliminate false alarms, though it might reduce their occurrence somewhat.

A more effective approach is to use well-positioned photosensors. These devices are most effective with a directed beam source directly aimed at them, as shown in Fig. 3-21. When an intruder passes between the beam source and the photosensor, even momentarily, this is sensed by the system, and sets off the alarm. Infrared beams and photosensors are the best choice, because the light beam will not be visible to the intruder at night, and the photosensor is less likely to be confused by ambient light, whether daylight, or the artificial light protectively illuminating the area.

For homes in wealthier areas, where more tempting valuables are likely to draw burglars, one or more video cameras could be used to help guard less directly visible

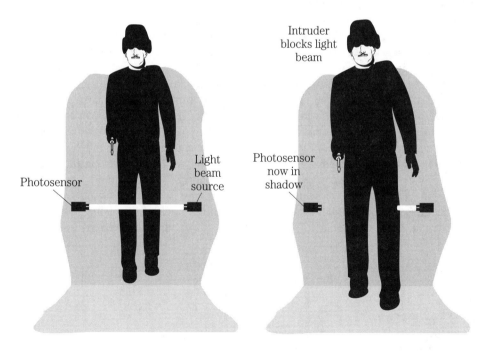

3-21 A directed light beam aimed at a photosensor can help an alarm system determine when an intruder has entered the area.

areas around the house. In some installations it might be desirable to hide the camera, but in most cases, a visible camera might act as a deterrent to potential intruders, discouraging them from even making the attempt to gain entry. You might even get away with just installing some nonfunctional dummy cameras to act as high-tech scarecrows. These dummy cameras must look identical to the real thing, but even so they are sure to be far less expensive than true video cameras. Relying too heavily on such dummies is always a risky business though. Sharp burglars are familiar with such tricks and can be very tough to fool.

Whether real or dummy video cameras are used, they must be securely protected themselves. They should be mounted high up or otherwise in an inaccessible position. It certainly shouldn't be possible for an intruder to come up behind the video camera. If possible, it would be a good idea to enclose the video camera in a locked cage assembly. Don't give an intruder an opportunity to break or blind the video camera (or find out if it is a dummy), or worse, to steal it. Security cameras are stolen, especially when they use a taped system rather than a nearby live guard viewing a monitor continuously. There's a healthy market for video cameras these days, and a burglar could easily sell hot ones.

Some customers might say there is little need to protect the back yard, for example, because the yard is fenced in, and the fence is kept locked. Even a high fence will do little to slow down a professional burglar. Someone who makes a living by breaking into houses is hardly going to be deterred by a simple backyard fence. In the real world, fences offer only very limited (if any) protection to a home, other than perhaps against children, vandals, and trespassers taking a short cut through your yard. A tall fence might protect the family's privacy against nosy neighbors, but a good burglar will willingly climb it or find some other way to get past it. It's almost always very easy to do. Fences are almost always completely irrelevant to a home security system.

In some cases, it might be worthwhile to include a sensor to set off the alarm if the gate is opened while the system is activated, but usually even this will be a waste of effort and expense. If a potential intruder suspects that the gate might be protected by the alarm system, he or she will simply go over the fence or cut an opening in it away from the gate. In practice, a gate sensor is unlikely to do much noticeable good. The alarm system designer and installer usually will find it best simply to ignore the presence or absence of any fences on the property to be protected. They are just another decoration as far as security purposes go. The greatest significance of a fence to a security system installer is that it could be an obstacle to disability, giving potential intruders a better chance of hiding while they gain illicit entry to the home.

4
Installation procedures

Installing a home alarm system is not really a difficult process, although it often requires some delicate precision work. It's picky work rather than truly hard work. Do not rush the job. It requires patience and careful attention to detail. A careless installer can do considerable harm to the building fixtures and decor. Remember, this is somebody's home. Neatness in your work is essential.

Realistically, it takes at least two people to install a decent alarm system properly unless it is a very, very simple one (which wouldn't require a professional installer anyway). If nothing else, you'll need an assistant on those many occasions when someone is needed at both ends of a long wire running through the house at once.

There is considerable variation in prices, of course, depending on the general economy and the specific requirements and special features of a given alarm system. Normally, the material costs of a typical full-featured home security system will be $500 or so. In most areas, the consumer cost a professionally installed alarm system is about $1500 to $2500. Even with the labor costs for you and your partner or assistant, there is a decent if unexceptional profit margin available if you work efficiently. Naturally you want to avoid wasting time and (especially) the need for call backs. On a call back, you pay for the labor, not the customer, because you are correcting problems that are your responsibility. Careful planning is never wasted time in this field.

Remember from the first chapter that an alarm system can be divided into three sections as shown again in Fig. 4-1—the sensors, the control center, and the alarm. Installing the control center and the alarm output device(s) is pretty straightforward. A few special notes on these sections are offered in this chapter. The bulk of the actual installation work is in the sensor section—mounting the sensors themselves and running all the wires from the various sensors in the system to the control center.

Wiring the sensors

Compared to most electronics systems, a typical home security system covers a very large area. In a sense, you are dealing with a circuit that is virtually the size of the house. You will deal with very long runs of wires. It is vital to install this wiring in a

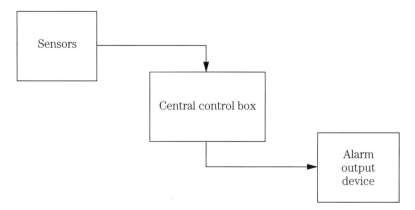

4-1 Any alarm system can be divided into three basic sections.

way that minimizes (if not eliminates) the possibility of getting entangled or anyone tripping over it. Because you are making installations in homes, take the effort to make the room-to-room wiring as inconspicuous and attractive as possible. Whenever a length of wire can be hidden, it should be.

The least unattractive and most out of the way method for running groups of wires from room to room is to go through the walls, just like the normal electrical wiring. Unfortunately, this is not always a practical option. It can be very difficult running wires inside the walls after a house has been completely constructed. Normal house wiring is all done before the inner walls are actually put up. In a rented home, getting behind the walls to add alarm system wiring will probably be forbidden, or at least strongly discouraged by the lease. There are good reasons for this. If the installer isn't skilled, considerable damage to the building can result. In some areas an electrician's license is required to do such work legally. A careless or uninformed worker could easily come into contact with the existing electrical wiring, causing a major shock and fire hazard.

It is beyond the scope of this book to adequately cover through-the-wall wiring, so unless you have professional training in such techniques from other sources, it's best not to take chances.

In most cases, the safest and least expensive method of running wires from room to room is to use conduit. The wire is positioned in a shallow tray affixed to the baseboards, then a fitted cover is placed over the top as shown in Fig. 4-2. The wires are securely protected, making stress-related short circuits highly unlikely. If the conduit is properly fastened to the baseboard, it should be impossible for anyone to trip over it. The conduit is designed to lie as flat as possible to accommodate the thickness of the wires it contains, so it is relatively unobtrusive. Sometimes conduit is available in decorator colors, or it can be painted to suit the decor, becoming almost invisible to anyone not actually looking for it. In some cases, it could even be made a contrasting color and serve as a decorative touch. (Check with the people who live there first, of course. Any decorative details should always be their decision.)

When conduit is not available or practical for any reason, the best alternative is to use *U-nails*. A U-nail is a special curved nail (or tack) with a point at either end,

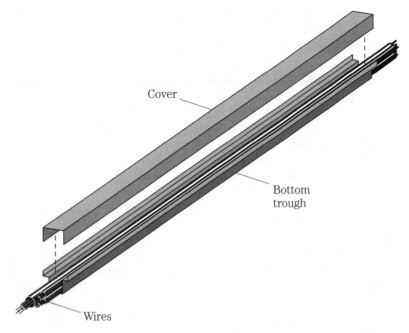

4-2 In most cases, the safest and least expensive method of running long wires is to use conduit.

as shown in Fig. 4-3. These devices are sometimes called staples, because of their appearance. In fact if just a few relatively thin wires are to be mounted, a staple gun can be used, but you must be very careful not to let the staple points pierce the insulation of any of the wires at any point.

To use, place the wire or cable under the center curve of the U-nail and then hammer it in place while holding the wire securely. A number of U-nails should be

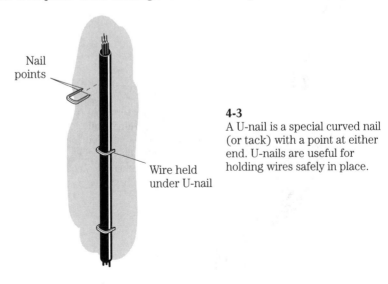

4-3
A U-nail is a special curved nail (or tack) with a point at either end. U-nails are useful for holding wires safely in place.

used to hold the wires as tight as possible. Don't permit wires to sag between support points. The sagging is unattractive, and it also invites stress to the wires that could eventually cause problems. Loosely mounted wires also can be tripped over, or something could get caught in them. Proper mounting will hold the wires tight enough that someone would have to deliberately work at it to get anything caught between them.

Another way to keep things as tidy as possible, which can be combined with any of the earlier techniques, is to use multiconductor cable for places where several wires must be run together over some distance. This cable is just two or more individually insulated wires bundled together in a single insulated jacket. A typical cable of this type is shown in Fig. 4-4. There is no need to use shielded or coaxial cables for most alarm system applications, because the wires aren't carrying any data other than simple on/off switching states. Either the switching voltage is present (switch closed), or it isn't (switch open). Electrical or *RF* (radio frequency) interference is highly unlikely to be a problem. Certainly coaxial or other shielded cables will do the job, but they will tend to be thicker and bulkier for a given number of internal conductors, and they will surely be significantly more expensive per foot than simple unshielded multiconductor cable. Because a typical home security system installation will require at least a couple hundred feet of room-to-room cable, using unnecessarily shielded cable can result in a noticeably higher overall materials cost for the installation, without offering any practical advantage.

A typical home alarm system includes dozens of separate sensors. A moderately large house could need more than a hundred sensors. Each individual sensor in the system needs at least two wires leading back to the control center. A few specialized sensors might require more than two wires, but usually each system will be some form of SPST switch, opening or closing an electrical circuit, as shown in Fig. 4-5.

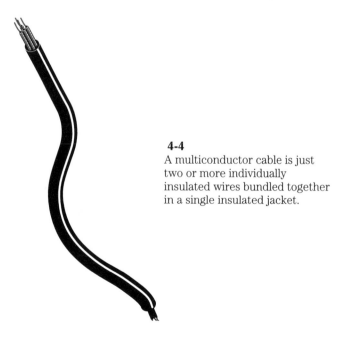

4-4
A multiconductor cable is just two or more individually insulated wires bundled together in a single insulated jacket.

Normally open   Normally closed

4-5 Most sensors used in practical alarm systems are specialized SPST switches.

Obviously even a fairly simple home alarm system is going to call for a lot of wires running from room to room. The installation will be made a lot easier and less expensive if you can find ways to reduce the number of wires in the lengthy room-to-room runs. Fortunately, there are a number of fairly simple tricks that can reduce the wire count considerably in most home alarm systems.

One of the most obvious of these tricks is to wire multiple sensors in series or parallel, depending on the type of sensor used. Multiple normally open sensors can be wired in parallel as shown in Fig. 4-6. Closing any one (or more) of these sensor switches will trigger the alarm. You can add as many NO sensors in parallel as you want, and it will only take one of them to complete the circuit that activates the alarm.

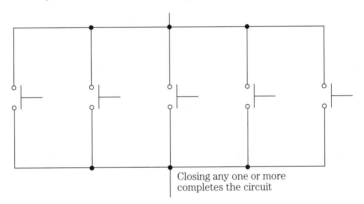

Closing any one or more
completes the circuit

4-6 Multiple normally open sensors can be wired in parallel.

Multiple normally closed sensors, on the other hand, must be wired in series, as shown in Fig. 4-7. In its normal state, an NC sensor acts as part of a complete circuit. Tripping the sensor opens the circuit, activating the alarm. Opening any one (or more than one) NC sensor in a series string will be sufficient to set off the alarm, regardless of how many individual sensors there are in the circuit.

Normally open sensors and normally closed sensors trigger the alarm in exactly opposite ways. Different control circuitry will be required for each type for the alarm system to operate properly. Most practical alarm systems use both sensors, so ap-

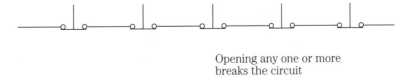

Opening any one or more
breaks the circuit

4-7 Multiple normally closed sensors must be wired in series.

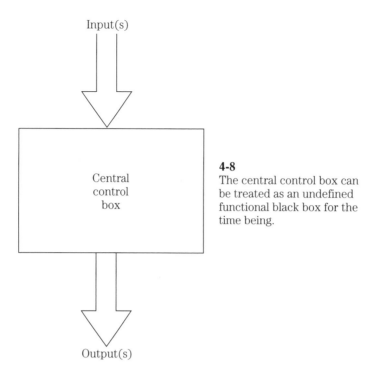

Input(s)

Central
control
box

Output(s)

4-8
The central control box can
be treated as an undefined
functional black box for the
time being.

propriate provisions must be made in the control center circuitry. You can learn the
details of the control circuitry in this chapter. For now, just treat it as a black box, as
in the simple system diagram of Fig. 4-8.

Normally open and normally closed switching devices cannot be used directly in
the same circuit, either in series or in parallel. The circuits shown in Fig. 4-9 will not
work. Try tracing the circuit path as each sensor is moved from its normal (inacti-
vated) state and see why such a circuit is nonfunctional.

But in many practical alarm systems it would be very desirable to combine NO
and NC sensors on a single pair of wires leading back to the control center. Actually
it's not too difficult to do, although the required circuitry is necessarily a bit more
complex than the nonfunctional circuits of Fig. 4-9. Figure 4-10 shows how to add a
normally open device to a normally closed circuit. A simple relay is shown, but almost any form of electronic switching can be used. For example, the relay could be
replaced with a suitable SCR or transistor switch or, in some digitally based systems,
a digital gate. The switching device is really irrelevant for this discussion. The same
general principles apply in any case.

Whatever electronic switching is used, the switch function must be normally
closed. When no control voltage is applied to the electronic switch, the circuit is
closed. Applying a control voltage activates the electronic switch, and opens the circuit. The electronic switch is connected in series with all the other NC sensors in the
circuit, because it is to function in the same way. Usually, the normally open sensor
on the control side of the electronic switch is open, of course, so no control voltage
reaches the electronic switch to activate it. Its switch contacts remain closed. But if

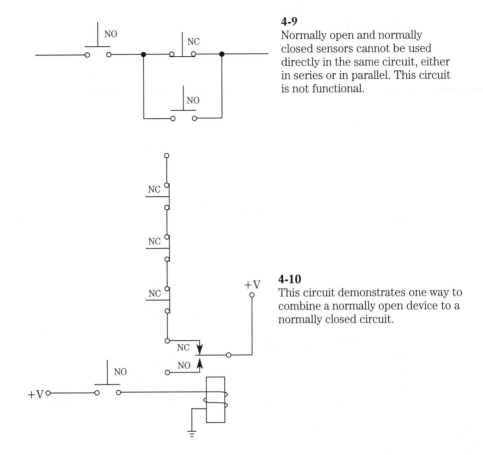

4-9
Normally open and normally
closed sensors cannot be used
directly in the same circuit, either
in series or in parallel. This circuit
is not functional.

4-10
This circuit demonstrates one way to
combine a normally open device to a
normally closed circuit.

the NO sensor is tripped, closing its switch contacts, this completes the circuit to the
relay coil (or other input to the electronic switch), activating the relay (electronic
switch), causing its contacts to open. Just like opening a normally closed sensor, this
triggers the alarm.

Additional normally open sensors can be placed in parallel with the one shown.
Closing any one or more of several NO switching devices in parallel is sufficient to
complete the circuit.

A normally closed sensor can be added to a normally open circuit in a very similar way, as shown in Fig. 4-11. Again the relay (or other electronic switch) has normally closed contacts, even though you might have expected to use a normally open
electronic switch in this application. The NC electronic switch is wired in parallel
with the other NO sensors, as if it were one of them. The control voltage operating
this electronic switch must pass through the normally closed sensor. Usually, this device will be closed, of course, completing the control voltage circuit, so the electronic
switch is held in its activated state—the switch contacts are open. If the NC sensor
is tripped, it opens its internal contacts, breaking the circuit, so the control voltage
is removed from the relay's coil (or input of the electronic switch). The relay or electronic switch is released from its active to its normal state, closing its contacts. In ef-

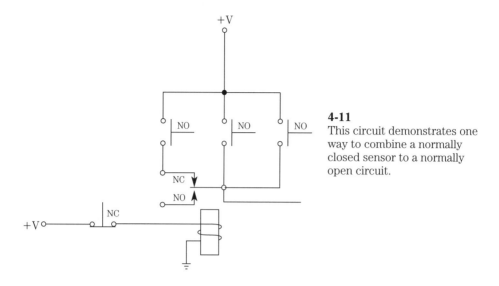

4-11
This circuit demonstrates one way to combine a normally closed sensor to a normally open circuit.

fect, the NC sensor and the NC electronic switch work together to simulate the functioning of a NO sensor.

Of course, multiple normally closed sensors can be added in series to the one shown in the diagram. Opening any one of several NC switches in series is sufficient to break the circuit.

In principle, just two wires are needed between the sensor location(s) and the control center. Additional sensor locations can be hooked up either in series (if NC) or in parallel (if NO), using the same pair of lead-in wires. For simple alarm systems, this is well and good. However, it eliminates the possibility of many special features.

The security offered by an alarm system can be greatly increased by designing it to inform the user what area has been breached when the alarm is set off. This information is very important in a moderate to large house. Was there an intrusion detected in the kitchen, in the living room, or in one of the bedrooms? Generally the only way the control circuit can tell the difference is to have different independent sensor circuits. A simplified block diagram is shown in Fig. 4-12. For convenience, only one sensor is shown in each area, but additional sensors can be wired in series or parallel, as discussed in this chapter. At the expense of a few additional wires from the protected rooms to the control center, the alarm system can give more information. LEDs (or other indicator devices) can be mounted on the main control panel indicating which circuit (or circuits) has triggered the alarm. These indicators can even be arranged into a simplified map of the house, as shown in Fig. 4-13, for maximum ease of use. The homeowner can tell at a glance where the problem is. Separate circuits also can be used for intrusion and fire alarms. In fact, it can be helpful for the alarm system to produce a different sound for a fire than an intrusion, so everyone in the household can know immediately what action to take. Tell children to stay put or go to the parents room if there is a late night break-in. But tell them to go outside immediately if there is a fire.

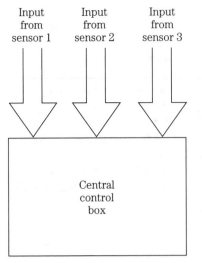

Input from sensor 1 · Input from sensor 2 · Input from sensor 3

Central control box

4-12
Generally the only way the control circuit can tell which sensor, or group of sensors, has been activated is to have different independent sensor circuits.

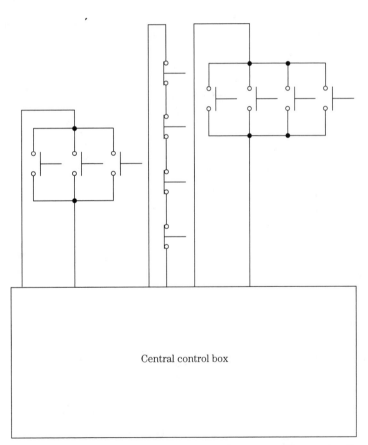

Central control box

4-13 The sensor area indicators can even be arranged into a simplified map of the house.

There is some duplication of circuitry required for such refinements to a home alarm system, and additional wires must be run, but the long-term advantages make this well worthwhile in most cases. Of course there would be little point in such modifications in a security system for a small apartment.

Depending on the specific design of the alarm system's control circuitry, it might be possible to reduce the number of long wires needed by almost half. Each sensor or set of sensors requires two wires, which you can call *signal*, and *common*. In most systems, a single common wire can be used for the entire system. There is no need to run a separate common wire from each room all the way to the control center. Instead, each set of sensors can tap into a single main common wire as it passes the area. Only the signal wire must be added to the cable or wire bundle for each new section. This arrangement is shown in Fig. 4-14, which is a modification of Fig. 4-12.

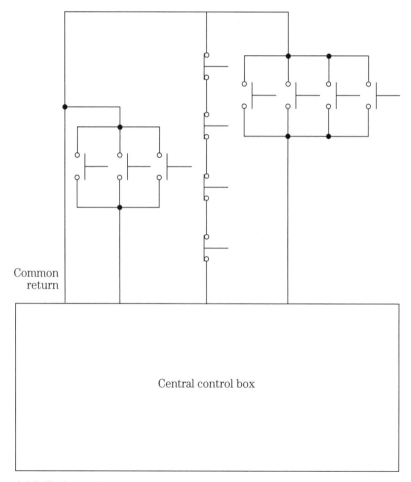

4-14 Each set of sensors can tap into a single main common wire as it passes the area.

The control center

Certainly the portion of a home alarm system that can be expected to vary the most from design to design is the control center. In fact many manufacturers take great efforts to protect their individual designs in this area. If you are installing alarm equipment supplied by a specific company, you will be using their approach to system control centers, of course. If not, you will quickly find your own favorite control center.

There are so many different types of alarm system control center circuits available, that it would be impossible to cover them all here, or to give much general information that would apply in all or even most cases. Because this is not a book of do-it-yourself circuits, it seems inappropriate to go into specific detail in this area. For this discussion, treat the control center more or less as a black box. The switching data from the sensors is fed into it, and the appropriate control signals for the actual alarm and any other indicator devices come out. Don't concern yourself how the various signals are treated within the control center between the input and the output. Instead, take a quick look at some general principles of placement and installation that are likely to be applicable in many home installations.

A home alarm system's central control box should be centrally located, of course. It should be readily and conveniently accessible to the legitimate residents of the home, but preferably not to an intruder. There is little point in going overboard on protecting the central control box, even though an intruder is likely to attempt to interfere with or destroy it. Assuming the system was well thought out and properly installed, the alarm should have been set off long before an intruder could reach the central control box location. Still if it's too easy for an intruder to sabotage the system once he or she reaches this point, a genuine alarm could be mistaken for a false alarm that was legitimately turned off. In some cases, this could make the difference between whether help is summoned or not, especially if no one is at home, and the system depends on the reaction of neighbors or passers-by.

Similarly, don't worry about cleverly hiding the central control box. A smart intruder is almost certain to find it anyway—there are usually just so many possible hiding places, and most people will tend to make similar choices. On the other hand, there's no sense in tempting fate by leaving it right out in the open and in plain sight. The central control box should be readily available to legitimate members of the household, who will presumedly be under some stress if they need to get to it in a hurry, but not overly obvious. The best approach is to keep things simple.

The central control box, and the wires leading to it, should be reasonably well secured. Don't tempt an intruder to attempt to defeat the alarm system by yanking out the central control box and destroying it. Sensor wires and especially the wires leading from the control box to the actual alarm sounding device should be covered and not directly accessible. An intruder is likely to try yanking out any wires connected to a central control box. That might silence the alarm. Removing wires from normally closed sensors won't do the intruder any good. That will simply trigger the alarm (if it isn't already sounding), just like tripping a NC sensor. But a yanked-out wire will electrically "look" like an untripped normally open sensor. On the output end, pulling out the wires will prevent the necessary signal from reaching the alarm sounding device.

In most cases, the best practical protection for the system wiring is to enclose it in well-designed, sturdy conduit, which cannot be opened easily or quickly. The conduit should be securely fastened to the walls or other structural items as much as possible. Do not give an intruder direct access to any wires if it can possibly be avoided.

Mount the central control box securely with sturdy mounting screws. Use more screws than are really necessary to support the weight of the box. Yes, that means a bit more work during installation and if any future repairs are needed, but that is precisely the point. You don't want someone (like an intruder) to open or remove the control box quickly or easily. Perhaps you might even want to add a bit of melted wax over the screw heads. The screws can't be removed without scraping the wax away. The wax can be a nuisance if you ever have to service inside the control panel, but not a monumental one. It will be a much bigger nuisance for an intruder who is trying to disable the system under considerable time pressure. One or two "secret" hidden screws also can be a good idea. Placement of a few critical holding screws in locations that are not obvious will not be too big a hassle during possible future repairs, if you know where they are. But they can frustrate and slow down a desperate intruder. These tricks are scarcely guaranteed to keep someone else out. If the intruder is determined enough and has enough time, she or he will get past these obstacles. But they will surely slow an intruder down, perhaps enough for him or her to get caught in the act, or to give up and flee.

Even if an intruder doesn't actually damage or destroy the central control box, what is to stop the intruder from simply turning off the alarm system? Yes, the alarm has presumedly already sounded before anyone ever reaches the central control box, but if the intruder can turn it off promptly, neighbors or passers-by are likely to assume it was just a false alarm. Obviously, an effective home security system must include provisions to minimize such an occurrence. Rather than relying on physical security measures, such as hiding the central control box, it is generally more effective to use electronic security. A security switch of some sort can go a long way toward discouraging unauthorized operation of system functions.

There are three possible approaches to such a security switch. The first is simply a secret hidden switch that must be operated before any of the other system controls will function. This approach is inexpensive and simple, but probably not very effective as a security measure. There are just so many practical locations for such a hidden switch. Once an intruder has figured out that such a switch exists, which shouldn't take long at all, she or he probably won't have much trouble finding it, especially if the intruder happens to have any knowledge of electronics systems.

A little more security can be had with a locking key switch. This device is discussed in the section on arming and disarming the alarm system. In this application, a lock switch has two major disadvantages. It is likely to be something of an inconvenience to the legitimate system operator(s), especially under emergency conditions (a false alarm or a genuine intrusion), when nerves are likely to be jangled. The key must first be found before it can be used. Yet the key can't be kept anywhere too handy, or an intruder is likely to be able to find it. If the intruder gets hold of the key, it will obviously serve no purpose as a security device. In addition to being a potential convenience to the legitimate occupants of the house, it could be a major convenience for an intruder.

Probably the best approach to securing the central control box is to use an access code to enable any or all critical controls. Two or more switches must be depressed in a specific sequence. An error will lock out use of the control panel for some predetermined amount of time. Similar access codes were discussed earlier in the section on arming and disarming the alarm system. Actually, things can be kept somewhat simpler here than for the system arming switch at the main entrance. An intruder might try to quickly turn off the alarm if he comes across the system's central control box, but because the intruder is already in the house, he or she is not likely to want to spend a lot of time trying.

The access code can be entered via a calculator-type keypad, but the results can be as good if a half dozen or so push-button switches are used. A very simple, but surprisingly effective security circuit is shown in block diagram form in Fig. 4-15. There are three timer circuit sections and a handful of push-button switches, and

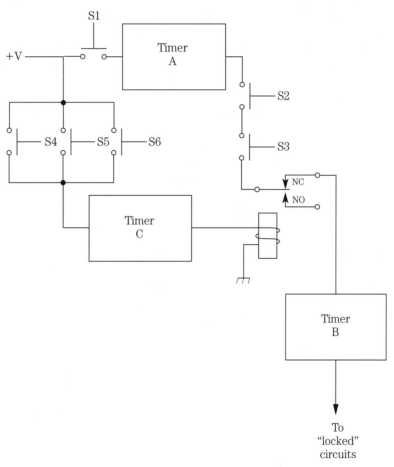

4-15 This circuit, using just three timer circuit sections and a handful of push-button switches, is a very simple but surprisingly effective security circuit.

that's about it. Any standard timer circuit can be used in this application. High precision wouldn't be of any advantage here. The simple and popular 555 timer *IC* (integrated circuit), for example, will do the job just fine.

In operation, to release the electronic lock, switch S1 must be pressed first, triggering timer A. This timer is set for a relatively short timing period of just a second or two. Before timer A times out, switches S2 and S3 must be simultaneously pressed to activate timer B, which activates the "locked" controls until it times out. A timing period of two or three minutes is appropriate for timer B.

At any point in the sequence, pressing any of the other switches (S3 through S6) will activate timer C, locking out the correct switches until it times out. A good choice for the timing period of timer C is 20 to 30 seconds. More of these "booby-trap" dummy systems can easily be added in parallel, to make guessing the correct combination even more difficult. Because two switches have to be depressed at once, an intruder is even less likely to guess correctly—an intruder is more likely to try one switch at a time. Every time there is an incorrect guess, there is a waiting period of about half a minute before another attempt can be made. But the intruder doesn't even know how long to wait or when the code switches are locked out or when they are functional. If the intruder just keeps pushing buttons, hoping to get lucky, she or he will never get access to the system controls, because the lock-out timer will be repeatedly retriggered. Simple, but very effective.

To complicate matters (for the intruder, but not for you), you might even include a few dead switches that aren't connected to anything at all inside the central control box. This ploy makes it even more difficult for an intruder to guess what is going on. Some wrong guesses activate a lock-out timer, and others don't.

More important, the correct sequence is very easy for the legitimate members of the household to remember and use. They just have to remember three buttons in a simple sequence. First S1, then S2 and S3. Of course, these switches will not be mounted in simple numerical order. Mix them up. The legitimate system users only need to remember the correct positions. One possible arrangement is shown in Fig. 4-16. The buttons don't even have to be labelled. Notice how easy it would be to remember the correct sequence of buttons to press, if you know the secret of the system.

You could even intermingle the electronic lock's switches among the actual system controls on the front control panel to confuse an intruder even more.

The numbered buttons of a calculator-type keypad can certainly be used in place of the individual push buttons shown here.

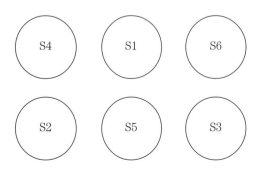

4-16
The control code switches are not mounted in simple numerical order. The legitimate system users only need to remember the correct positions.

In most home alarm systems, the central control box is, by far the most complex section on the level of electronic circuitry. Even so, it still is relatively simple, at least on the conceptual level. It is just a signal switching multiplexer/demultiplexer. It accepts input signals and routes them to the appropriate output or outputs. In any electronic system, the electromechanical parts are far more likely to develop problems than the purely electronic circuitry. The central control panel will rarely develop problems. In almost all cases repair calls after installation has been completed (and all bugs and errors corrected) are with an external sensor or the interconnecting wires. Such problems are almost always mechanical. Common alarm system repairs are discussed in another chapter. For the purpose of this discussion, be concerned with preventing repairs before any problems arise and making them easy and convenient to deal with.

It is a very good idea to tag each wire into the control box. Make it easy to determine just what sensor or area it comes from. A color code would certainly be a good idea. The code eliminates the need for bulky tags that can be pulled off or smudged or otherwise made illegible. Because every system is unique, a standard all-purpose code might not be appropriate. Mount a card with an explanation of the color code inside the system's main control panel. Don't rely on memory. Someone else might someday have to service the system. Why make the job more difficult for them? Also, if you are in the business of alarm system installation, you are going to face many different situations, calling for individualized modifications in any generalized color code. There are just so many different colors available to choose from. A particular color will probably have to mean different things in different systems. Are you really going to remember all the specific details of such a variable color code if you are called back to work on an installation you did a year or more ago? If you don't have an on-site color code chart, you might as well not bother with a color code at all. The odds are against it being really helpful when it is needed. Certainly it is worthwhile to devise as generalized and standardized a color code as you can, but be prepared for very frequent exceptions. Include even the "standard" elements of the color code in the reference chart to permit someone else to understand the system, if necessary, and to allow future in the standard code. A brown wire might have meant one thing five years ago, but now its old meaning is obsolete and has been superseded by a different new meaning. Why risk the possibility of confusing yourself? Especially because it is so unnecessary. (There is more discussion of general color codes in this chapter.)

A standardized approach to hidden mounting screws (for security purposes) is usually appropriate. If you are in the habit of putting these disguised screws in the upper left corner and at the center slightly up from the bottom of the control box, you won't frustrate yourself if you have to do repairs later.

Make a detail sheet of hidden mounting screws, color codes, or any other features for a specific installation. Make two copies of this detail sheet. Keep one in your office files, and give the other copy to your customer, advising the customer to keep it in a secure place. A safety deposit box would be ideal, but might be overkill. A locked box in a closet should be sufficient to prevent an intruder from reading the "juicy details" of the alarm system. If you ever need to make repairs on the system, you can easily consult your office copy. The customer's copy is in case someone else must do future repairs for any reason. This act is not foolishly giving business to someone else. It is part of giving the customer a well thought-out, complete system. You might not be available for some reason when repairs are needed. Your installation company might go out of business (many companies do). On the other hand, your business might become too busy to handle the repair call when it comes in. You might move from the area. If your company is very small, an emergency repair situation might occur while you're on vacation. The customer might, for whatever reason, prefer to go to someone else. These are all fully legitimate reasons why someone else might need the detail sheet to do the repairs efficiently. Not giving the customer a copy of the detail sheet is, in a very real sense, cheating your customer.

It would be foolish and risky to give the customer the only copy. Some people are careless, and accidents and mistakes do happen. You don't want to be placed in the embarrassing position of having to repair your own installation blindly because the customer no longer has a copy of the detail sheet, and you didn't keep a copy in your files. Such an awkward situation is so easy to prevent.

Installing the output alarm device

On one level, it isn't appropriate to say any one portion of a home security system is more critical or important than the rest. After all, everything must work together as a system. The system, as a whole, will only be as good as its weakest element. However, given all that, it is still true that installing the output alarm device calls for extra care and planning. If the alarm can't sound, the rest of the system certainly isn't going to accomplish much. Even if the alarm does sound, it must be heard, or it isn't going to accomplish anything useful.

The important issues are the proper location and protection of the alarm output device. For the most part, assume the device is an audible alarm of some sort—a bell, a siren, or other sound-making circuit. Such an audible device will be the primary (if not only) output device for the vast majority of home alarm systems. Supplemental silent alarms also can be included in such a system, but they are more or less incidental. Alarm output devices that do not rely on sound include such things as indicator lights and autodialers to summon help from some other location.

An audible alarm should normally be used in any home alarm system, unless there are strong, special reasons to make an exception. An audible alarm serves so many purposes so easily. It can immediately alert any legitimate occupants of the house to an intrusion or other emergency condition. It can alert neighbors or passers-by that something is wrong, and the authorities should be notified or other help summoned. It also can let an intruder know that the odds of escaping with the goods are sharply reduced and fleeing is not the best plan. Audible alarms are usually effective in frightening off potential burglars, often before they get a chance to take anything (or at least before they can get much).

The choice of the sound of the alarm is for the most part a matter of personal preference. Usually one of four basic types of alarm sounds are used:

- Bell
- Buzzer

- Continuous-tone siren
- Multitone alarm or "whooper"

Bells and *buzzers* are electromechanical devices. When the appropriate electrical system is applied, a clapper strikes a bell, or a piece of metal is set into vibration and amplified to produce a harsh, well-carrying buzzing sound. Some sirens also are electromechanical in nature, but most modern siren devices are electronic oscillator circuits.

A *continuous-tone* siren is a straightforward oscillator circuit of one type or another. As long as it is fed a suitable supply voltage, it emits a tone through a speaker (or similar device). This tone is a constant tone with a single, specific frequency. For discussion, the wave shape doesn't really matter, although a harmonically rich wave shape such as a square wave (as shown in Fig. 4-17) or a sawtooth wave (Fig. 4-18) will carry farther and sound louder for a given amount of power consumption, than a pure sine wave (Fig. 4-19), which nominally has no harmonic content at all. The sound of an amplified sine wave becomes very piercing and irritating very quickly, so it is likely to bring complaints from the neighbors if the alarm ever sounds for more than a minute or so.

The siren tone can be emitted continuously, but it is usually more effective to pulse it on and off, as shown in Fig. 4-20. The pulsing makes the sound more distinctive and harder to ignore.

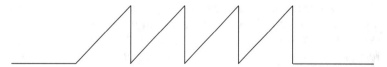

4-17 A square wave is a harmonically rich waveform.

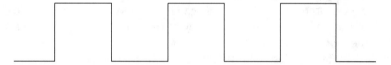

4-18 Another common harmonically rich waveform is the sawtooth wave.

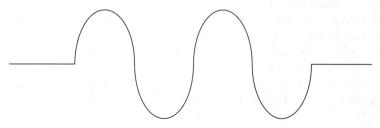

4-19 A sine wave is very pure harmonically and is therefore a weaker signal for alarm purposes.

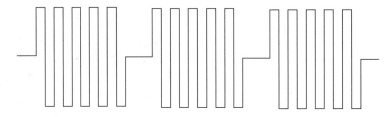

4-20 It is usually most effective to pulse an alarm tone on and off.

A *multitone* alarm, or *whooper* siren can be even more effective. By producing two or more frequencies in a rapid sequence, the alarm sound is more demanding of attention, and harder to ignore. There are several ways the multiple frequencies can be combined. Usually the main circuit will be some type of *VCO* (voltage-controlled oscillator). Changing the input voltage changes the output frequency. To get the multitone alarm effect, an ac waveform is the control voltage input. A square wave will switch back and forth between two discrete frequencies. The effect is similar to a British police car siren. Using a sawtooth wave as the control voltage input will cause the sound to smoothly glide from one extreme frequency to another, passing through all intermediate frequencies; then the signal will jump back to its original frequency and start over. The effect is a distinctive *whoop-whoop* effect, so this siren is often called a *whooper*. Other wave shapes also can be used for the control voltage signal. Regardless of the wave shape, the frequency of the control voltage signal should be well below the audible limit. Control frequencies of 0.5 to 5 *Hz* will usually be best. Lower switching frequencies will lose the ear-catching effectiveness, and higher frequencies will tend to blur the sound into a single, apparently continuous complex tone with a lot of harsh sidebands. In the later case, you might as well use a continuous tone siren that will involve less expensive and simpler circuitry.

Any of these alarm sounding devices, electromechanical or purely electronic, can be made more effective by pulsing them on and off every few seconds, rather than sounding continuously. A continuous sound fatigues the ear very quickly, and the brain starts to mask it out. A pulsing alarm is considerably more difficult to ignore.

In complex alarm systems, it can be very helpful and perhaps even life-saving to use different alarm sounds for different purposes. For example, a fire might produce a different sound than an intrusion. The residents of the house will immediately know what the problem is and what protective actions to take as soon as the alarm sounds. Of course, the sounds must be as distinctive and obviously different as possible. In a large house, you might consider dividing the house into two or three sections, each with its own unique alarm sound, so when the alarm goes off, the residents not only know what the problem is, but approximately where it is.

The most obvious way to produce different alarm sounds is to use separate and differing alarm sounding devices. For example, a bell could be used for a fire, and a whooper siren is used for an intrusion. This approach might be obvious and logical, but it is a bit wasteful and unnecessarily complex. It will usually be easier and less expensive simply to design the control circuitry to produce different pulsing patterns. For example, if an intrusion is detected, the alarm might be turned on and off

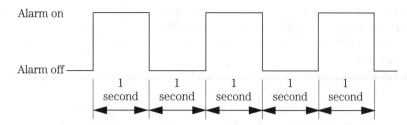

Alarm on

Alarm off

| 1
second | 1
second | 1
second | 1
second | 1
second |

4-21 In a typical coded alarm system, a detected intrusion can be indicated by the alarm being turned on and off at even one second intervals.

Alarm on

Alarm off

4-22 In a typical coded alarm system, a detected intrusion can be indicated by groups of three short bursts of tone, separated by about a second and a half of silence.

at even, one-second intervals, as shown in Fig. 4-21. If there is a fire, the alarm will be sounded in groups of three short bursts separated by about a second and a half of silence, as shown in Fig. 4-22.

Another important question to consider is just how loud should the alarm be. Most people would probably immediately go for the obvious answer—as loud as possible. After all, the louder an alarm is, the less likely it will be to be ignored or unnoticed. True enough, but only within certain limits. An alarm can be too loud. Excessively loud sounds can be annoying or even potentially harmful. Many areas have local ordinances limiting the volume of such things as alarms to avoid unnecessarily disturbing the peace. The alarm can certainly be loud enough to do its job without becoming a public nuisance. Bear in mind the possibility of false alarms, as well as the fact that if no one is at home when the alarm is set off, it will continue to sound for some time. Even with a shutoff timer (as discussed in this book), an excessively loud alarm can be a significant hardship on your neighbors. A deafeningly loud alarm sounding for 15 to 20 minutes can seem like hours, if not years. By all means check out all local ordinances thoroughly to determine at what point legal complications might set in if (when) the alarm is set off. Don't subject your customers to unnecessary fines for a too-loud alarm.

Will the alarm sounding device be mounted indoors or outdoors? An indoor alarm must usually be at a much lower volume than an outdoor mounted unit. Inside, the sound will reflect from the walls, and the reverberation will make the sound seem considerably louder than outside in the open air. If anyone is at home when the alarm is triggered, excessive volume can be painful and possibly disorienting. This sound level might be fine if the effects could be limited to the intruder, but legitimate members of the household will be equally affected by the noise level. For use inside the house, it's usually better to mount several small, low-volume alarm devices throughout the building, so their covered areas overlap and at least one can be heard at every point in the house. This arrangement has the added advantage of extra reliability. If one of the alarm output devices is defective (or damaged by the intruder), the others will continue to sound.

For an outdoor alarm, consider how far away the alarm needs to be audible if no one is at home when the emergency arises. In a heavily populated area, the sound doesn't have to reach very far, because there are several neighbors and other people close by. In a sparsely populated rural area, with considerable distance between neighboring homes, a much louder alarm will naturally be needed. Also consider the normal noise levels of the area. In an inner city district with considerable traffic or noisy factories or train tracks nearby, an alarm might have to be somewhat louder than normal to be obvious over the normal noise level.

It is easy enough to control the volume of an amplified electronic siren. Just add a volume control to the amplifier circuitry. Some electromechanical bells and buzzers are designed with a crude volume control that adjusts the force of the striker or the strength of the vibrations, which controls the volume of the sound produced. In many of the devices, the sound level can be controlled somewhat by adjusting the voltage applied to the input/control terminals. Usually a higher voltage will produce a louder sound. In most cases the useful range will be limited, but at least you have some degree of control over the alarm volume. On some electromechanical devices, however, changing the input voltage will have little or no effect on the sound level. These units are essentially fixed volume devices. Once a size is selected, you're stuck with whatever volume it produces.

For electromechanical devices, the sound level is more or less directly related to the size of the unit. For example, a 12-inch alarm bell will be considerably louder than a similar 8-inch alarm bell. Buzzers are usually small and low in volume. They are best suited for indoor use. The sound might not be loud enough to carry outdoors. Of course, you can combine both indoor and outdoor sounding devices in any alarm system to maximize the protection.

Any outdoor alarm must be adequately protected from the weather. Reputable manufacturers will indicate if an electrical device is rated for outdoor use or not. An additional weatherproof housing never hurts, even if the device is designed for outdoor use. This idea is a good one in areas frequently subject to heavy rains or other rough weather. Of course, the weatherproof housing must be as acoustically transparent as possible. Make sure it does not significantly deaden the sound produced by the alarm. A grill with downward-facing slits, as shown in Fig. 4-23, will usually do a reasonably good job of keeping most rain, dust and other troublesome particles out of the mechanism, but permit the sound to pass through with no noticeable reduction in volume.

Some electronic sirens are built into a single unit, with an attached speaker or similar transducer. Others are separate circuits where the output is fed to an external speaker or horn. It is a good idea to mount the actual circuitry inside the building, if possible, with only the speaker, horn, or whatever mounted outside (with suitable weather protection).

In addition to weather protection, protect an external alarm against tampering. You don't want your alarm system to be disabled by vandals, or worse, by an intruder

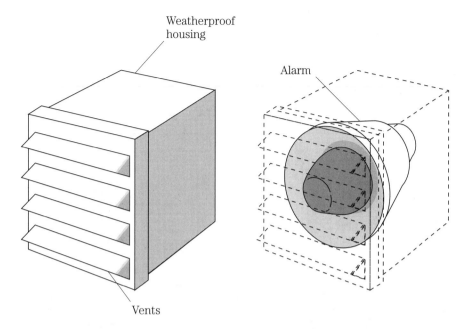

Weatherproof
housing

Alarm

Vents

4-23 To protect an outdoor speaker or siren, a grill with downward facing slits will usually keep out most rain, dust, and other troublesome particles.

before he or she gets in and sets off the alarm. (Indoor alarm sounding devices also
should be reasonably protected against tampering, but it is less critical here, and less
solid protection is required.) All wires and especially connections must be enclosed
in a sturdy housing. It should not be possible for anyone to cut the wires. The alarm-
sounding device should be very securely mounted, and ideally enclosed in a locked
cage or similar protective structure.

Mount outdoor alarm sounding devices physically as far off the ground as possible. Make them as inaccessible as possible. Obviously they won't be completely inaccessible, or how would you mount them? Do your best to discourage a potential
intruder from trying to get at them. You might not be able to make it impossible, but
you can make the task require a lot of time, and make the intruder risk attracting
attention.

The area around the exterior alarm sounding devices should be well lit and as
visible as possible from as many directions as possible.

For maximum protection, use multiple alarm sounding devices at different locations. An example is shown in Fig. 4-24. If they are all relatively inaccessible, it would
take a very determined intruder to attempt to disable them all. It wouldn't hurt to
mount one or more extra alarm sounding devices in less-obvious, less-visible places.
Even if an intruder does tamper with the main alarm sounding devices, she or he
might miss the hidden units. There is no guarantee, of course, but this little trick can
help improve the odds.

There's no reason why you can't use a few intrusion sensors in the immediate
area of each alarm sounding device. For example, opening the housing could set off

4-24 For maximum protection, use multiple alarm sounding devices at different locations.

the alarm. Even if the intruder immediately destroys that alarm sounding device, others in the system will still alert the neighbors.

For most home installations, there's no need to go overboard protecting the outdoor mounted alarm sounding devices. Just take reasonable precautions. The greatest risk to unprotected units is probably from vandals.

Planning for serviceability

Another chapter of this book explores troubleshooting problems that might come up in a home alarm system. Part of a good installation involves limiting the possibility of such problems before they happen and making them as easy as possible to repair if they do crop up later. A good alarm system designer always designs the system with serviceability well in mind.

The failure rate for modern electronic alarm systems is generally low. With occasional exceptions, it is usually reasonable to say that most problems are due to installation error, especially in the first year or two after installation. Clearly, these are problems and defects that should have been avoided in the first place. Fortunately, in the majority of cases, if system failure is going to happen due to faulty installation, it will probably happen within the first few days of use. However, some installation problems might not show up for some time. Such problems can involve some element of the system that is infrequently used or tested, such as a specialized sensor. There might be no reason for the occupants of the home to assume there is anything wrong until the sensor or other element doesn't work when it is needed. Other problems are cumulative in nature. The system might work okay for a while, but gradually "invisible" problems might become critical and could cause erratic operation, or even complete system failure.

The installer can and should be held responsible for any problems due to installation errors. Part of an alarm system installers job is to make sure everything is correctly installed and working properly. This responsibility extends even to unreasonable promises and substandard materials. If you promise your customers that no intruder can get past the alarm system, you could be held liable for any future burglary that does somehow take place. No security system is ever going to be 100% effective. Make sure your customers know the practical limitations of the alarm system, or you could face legal problems later. At the very least, you will end up with dissatisfied customers and poor word-of-mouth publicity. Similarly, make sure all materials used in your system installations is of suitable quality to do the job well and reliably. It is never good business to cut corners on materials or labor. Such short-sighted economy will certainly catch up with you sooner or later. If the system fails because of faulty materials or poor workmanship, you could be held legally responsible for repairs, reinstallation, or even damages due to the fault, even if the system is out of warranty or if there is no explicit warranty. In most areas, the law recognizes implicit warranties. That is, commercial products and services are required to meet certain minimum standards. A customer has the right to expect paid-for products and services to meet reasonable expectations. Even if you win a case in court, a lawsuit along such lines certainly isn't going to do your business any good. Not only can the time and court costs involved in fighting a lawsuit drain profits, a small business can be badly hurt by negative publicity. If you are sued by a dissatisfied customer, you are sure to lose some other potential customers who hear about the suit, even if you legally win the case. Many potential customers will consider your company tainted and somewhat less trustworthy anyway.

The only practical defense against such difficulties is to do everything you can to prevent such problems from ever arising. There is no way to guarantee you won't be hit with a nuisance suit without a reasonable or preventable basis. Some people will sue with little or no real provocation or justification. By planning and using proper care and materials, you can minimize your chances for facing such difficulties.

No matter how much advance planning and careful effort you put into an installation, a certain number of repair calls are pretty much inevitable. Problems do sometimes occur with any system. They're nobody's fault really; they just happen. So design and install the system with the assumption that you will have to get back into at a later date for servicing. There is much you can do during installation to minimize the effort and nuisance value of making future repairs. A number of tips in this direction are covered in this section.

Of course, if you want to stay in business long, you must respond to any service calls as soon as possible when they do come up. Where security systems are concerned, any service call qualifies as an emergency. This alone could make all the difference between staying in business or not. Service calls to past customers are not a nuisance preventing you from making money. Responding to such service calls promptly and efficiently is the very best possible advertising for winning your new business from additional customers—the relatives, friends, and neighbors of your satisfied past customer.

Keep a complete file of any manufacturer's warranties for all relevant materials used in the system. Items such as specialized sensors, commercially manufactured circuit boards, and alarm output devices generally carry warranties. Often such manufacturer's warranties are only good if the materials in question were installed by a professional installer. Make sure you qualify for coverage under the manufacturer's warranty. The exact qualifications might vary considerably. Read the fine print on the warranty card supplied with the product. If you don't keep track of what items are covered by the warranty and how to get credit for defective items, no one will. If you don't have or don't take proper advantage of manufacturer's warranties on your alarm system supplies, you will be the one to get stuck for the cost of any replacement or repair due to manufacturing faults. No, you didn't cause the problem, but by commercially installing the item, you accept legal responsibility for it. The manufacturer's warranty is between you and the manufacturer. As far as your customer is concerned, you, the system installer, provide and cover all applicable warranties and related responsibilities. You are responsible for defective materials used during your installation.

Before you can prevent potential breakdowns, first have some idea of what type of repairs are most likely to be needed. Modern electronic components are very reliable. Electromechanical parts, especially those that physically move in any way, are more likely to develop mechanical faults than electrical faults. Lengthy connected wires also can develop tiny breaks or short circuits to other adjacent wires due primarily to mechanical stress from being bent or moved back and forth. A wire that is stretched too tight also will be subject to considerable mechanical stress. All of this means that critical problems occur in the control panel itself fairly rarely. On most repair calls, it makes sense to suspect problems with one or more external sensors or the interconnecting wiring first. Naturally, during installation of the alarm system, take special care with such elements to minimize such mechanical stress problems before they ever get a chance to occur.

The most obvious preventive measure is to use high-grade components wherever possible, especially for the sensor switches. Cheap switches (of any type) often tend to jam, short, or stop making contact. These switches are usually momentary-action switches. A durable return-spring mechanism is an absolute must. If the return-spring mechanism breaks or losses its springiness, the sensor switch will be useless. Either it will cause intermittent or continuous false alarms, or it will do nothing at all when tripped, making a vulnerable point in the security system. A defective sensor will not detect an intruder (or whatever else it is supposed to detect).

Often the small business alarm system installer has only limited choices of sensor quality. After all, you can only buy and use what is available. For most sensors, especially highly specialized devices, there are only a few manufacturers and models to choose from. Although a bargain is always attractive, use some common sense. If manufacturers A, B, and C all charge $5 to $6 for widgets, but manufacturer D charges just 79 cents, be very suspicious of the quality of manufacturer D's products. The considerably lower price is probably due to poorer-grade raw materials or less-careful manufacturing procedures. On the other hand, if griblets made by manufacturers E, F, and G all sell for $1.00 to $1.50, but manufacturer H retails griblets for $7.00 apiece, don't automatically assume they are inherently significantly better. Some manufacturers overprice heavily for the quick profits they can get from suckers jumping to conclusions. Try just one or two of H brand griblets and compare them to a few samples from the lower priced competitors to determine if the extra cost is worthwhile. If there is a noticeable improvement in quality, using the higher priced devices will give you better profits overall, even though your purchasing expenses will be higher. The savings will appear in the form of fewer service calls and improved customer satisfaction and word of mouth.

Mount all electromechanical sensors carefully, keeping the mechanical stresses in mind at all times. For example, a sensor with a plunger type switch will probably last longer if the plunger is usually (if not always) hit head on, as shown in Fig. 4- 25(A) than if it is frequently hit on an angle as in Fig. 4-25(B). The extra mechanical stress could eventually break or bend the plunger, or it could cause the switching mechanism to jam or short itself out.

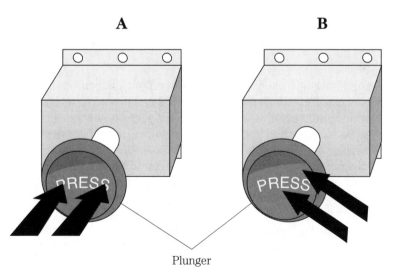

4-25 A sensor with a plunger type switch. It will probably last longer if the plunger is generally hit head on (A). Frequently hitting it at an angle will place it under greater mechanical stress (B).

Aside from manufacturing quality, the greatest cause for alarm system sensor problems is dirt. If dirt and grime can get into the mechanical mechanism of a switch (and usually it can, very easily), it can clog and block movement of some small moving part, or it can cause sticking. Either way, switch operation is very likely to become increasingly erratic, and it might eventually stop working altogether. In some cases, the damage might be permanent. The only repair possible is to replace the entire sensor.

Mount sensors to minimize their exposure to dirt and other foreign elements as much as possible. This precaution is obviously most critical for sensors mounted outdoors or in areas that are likely to be very dusty or frequently filled with smoke. (Although most people don't stop to think about it, cigarette smoke is a health hazard for electronic and electromechanical systems, almost as much as human beings. Take extra care when installing systems in homes with one or more heavy smokers.)

Use inset mounting whenever possible, as shown in Fig. 4-26. Insetting takes more time and effort, but it will leave less of the sensor mechanism exposed to airborne dirt. The sensor also will be less susceptible to tampering or other damage.

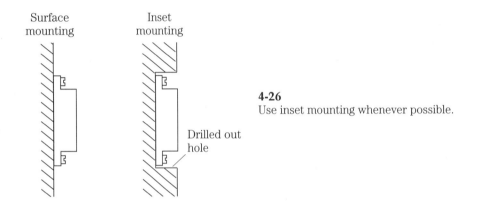

Surface mounting   Inset mounting

Drilled out hole

4-26
Use inset mounting whenever possible.

Some specialized devices might require a free flow of air through some or all of the mechanism, usually to avoid overheating or related problems. In such cases, providing proper and sufficient air flow is much more important than shielding against dirt. Try to do both as much as you can, but remember that the air flow takes precedence. Few such devices are likely to be used in home alarm systems, but you should be aware of the possibility. If clear air flow is required, the manufacturer of the device will usually clearly indicate this on the packaging or installation instructions. Usually you can use simple common sense. If something inside the device is likely to run very hot, a cooling air flow will be necessary. Or, if a device is designed with air vents built into its body, they must be there for a reason. Don't defeat their purpose by blocking them off. But if the mechanism is open just because the manufacturer didn't enclose it in its own housing, (generally to maximize the installation options available), it should be protectively housed in some way to protect it from dirt and other environmental conditions.

The interconnecting wires throughout the alarm system should be mounted to minimize potential mechanical stress as much as possible. Runs of wire should be tight enough that a person passing by can't trip over them or get anything caught in them. As mentioned, a protective conduit is very strongly advised for any otherwise exposed wires in a security system. In addition to limiting the possibility of intentional tampering from an intruder, enclosing the interconnecting, room-to-room wires in conduit will minimize the possibility of accidents and externally applied stresses.

The wires, even in a conduit, should not be left too loose, or they could become snagged or tangled, creating stress points. On the other hand, they should not be pulled so tautly that they are permanently under a stretching strain. Ideally a wire should be tight enough that it remains in position but can easily be plucked and moved slightly with a fingertip.

Any external wire or group of wires that runs more than a couple feet should have intermediate supports along its length. Use common sense and reason in determining how many support points to use. For example, assume you are running a cable along a 12-foot long straight hallway. One support at either end would be hopelessly insufficient, as shown in Fig. 4-27. The cable will sag in the middle, and could get caught in something. Even if the cable is enclosed in a conduit, this is far from enough support. The conduit will tend to sag if unsupported, unless mounted directly at floor level. It will eventually crack, or break at one or more stress points, defeating its purpose. On the other hand, 12 supports along the hypothetical hallway at one foot spacings would unquestionably be overkill. It wouldn't do any harm to use too many supports, unless the wires have to be removed or redirected later. Basically, it just makes unnecessary work and looks ridiculous. In the example of a 12-foot straight run down a hallway, four or five more-or-less equally spaced supports should be sufficient, unless the cable being run is exceptionally heavy. (See Fig. 4-28.)

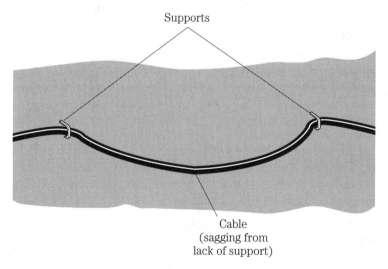

Supports

Cable
(sagging from
lack of support)

4-27 One support at either end of a long run of cable is hopelessly insufficient.

Any time the cable is routed around a corner or otherwise changes direction, a support is required at this point. In many cases, use two closely spaced supports immediately before and after the turn to minimize mechanical stress on the wires at the

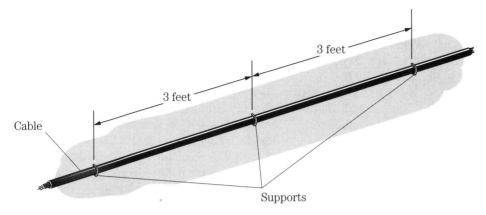

4-28 For a 12-foot straight run of cable, four or five more-or-less equally spaced supports should be sufficient, unless the cable being run is exceptionally heavy.

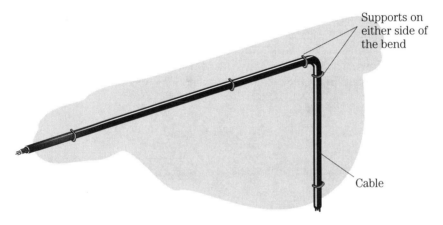

4-29 If a cable is routed around a corner, put a support at the turning point. In many cases, two closely spaced supports immediately before and after the turn should be used to minimize mechanical stress on the wires at the bend.

bend (Fig. 4-29). The mechanical stress of the turn is spread out over the distance between the two supports. Leave a reasonable amount of slack between the supports but not enough to permit tangling or catching.

When you use conduit, prefer curved conduit to a sharp right-angle turn, for the same reasons. Unfortunately, this is not always a reasonable choice. In a home system, the conduit will typically be laid along the baseboard, and should follow the walls without significant gaps. Because few homes have curving walls, the conduit must follow the straight turns. Make sure the wires are laid in the conduit loosely enough at the turn points to be curved within the sharply bent conduit. It can help considerably to secure the wires within the conduit in a fashion similar to that described for openly mounted wires described previously. An example of this mounting is shown in Fig. 4-30.

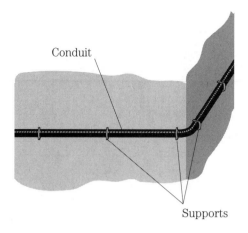

Conduit

4-30
Often conduit can be mounted in a fashion similar to that described for openly mounted wires shown in Fig. 4-28 and Fig. 4-29.

Supports

Most modern alarm systems are really simple, at least on the conceptual level. The central control panel, being primarily electronic, with few or no mechanical parts will rarely develop problems, although it can happen. In most cases repair calls after installation has been completed (and all bugs and errors corrected) are problems with one or more external sensors or with the interconnecting wires. Such problems are overwhelming mechanical in nature. Common alarm system repairs are discussed in another chapter of this book. For now, be concerned with preventing the need for repairs and making them easy and convenient to deal with.

As mentioned in another chapter, it is always a good idea to use a color code. As an alternative, tag each wire, especially where they lead into the central control unit. Make it as easy as possible to identify each individual wire and what is at the other end of it. Where does this wire go? What sensor does it come from?

If you work with many similar installations, a semistandard color code of some sort would certainly be a good idea. There will almost certainly be a number of special exceptions and unusual cases, but most of the basic connections can probably be standardized to a reasonable degree. You will have to devise your own color code. Because every system is unique, a standard all-purpose code might not be appropriate for many cases, and it would be impractical to try to include any universal color code scheme in a book like this.

Because the color coding in home alarm systems cannot be fully standardized, you must allow for the possibility of forgetting some or all of it if you have to service the system a few years after installation. And there is always the possibility that you won't be available to make needed repairs later, so be kind to your fellow technicians. Don't expect them to read your mind about your color coding. Mount a card with an explanation of the color code inside the system's main control panel. That way you don't have to rely on (potentially faulty) memory. It would be strongly advisable to keep a copy of the color coding for each individual system you've installed in the permanent file for that customer, in case something unforeseen happened to the on-site original.

In many systems, a color code for the incoming wires will be insufficient. In such cases, you can attach small tags to each wire (on the inside of the control box) as

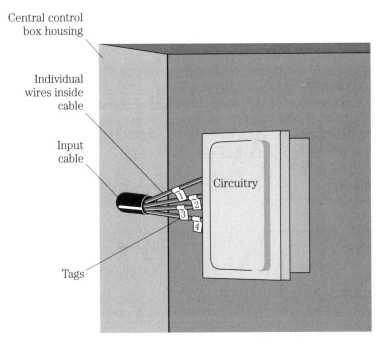

Central control
box housing

Individual
wires inside
cable

Input
cable

Circuitry

Tags

4-31 In some cases, you can attach small tags to each wire (on the inside of the control box) to indicate the wire's individual function

shown in Fig. 4-31. In some cases you might be able to write the full function of the wire on the tag, but it's usually a better idea to use a number or letter code. Again, mount a key to reading the code inside the control box (with a copy in your office files). Make this key listing as concise, yet informative as possible.

One possible system would be to use colors to indicate the type of sensor, and a letter/number code to indicate the location. For example, a blue wire marked *FD* might be a magnetic reed switch on the front door. Another blue wire might be labelled *MBW1*, which would identify a magnetic reed switch on window #1 in the master bedroom. A yellow wire marked *FH-LR* could indicate a pressure mat in the front hallway near the entrance to the living room. A red wire marked *UH-B* could be a temperature sensor in the upstairs hall closest to the bathroom. This general idea must be adapted to suit the needs of the system you are working on. It might seem like a lot of fuss and bother, but it can be a major time (and frustration) saver. It could be the difference between making troubleshooting of an unexpected problem a nightmare or a breeze.

In constructing the alarm system central control box, give yourself enough room to work with the circuit reasonably, without making the box too bulky, unwieldy, and unattractive. There is a strong tendency in electronics today to make everything physically as small and compact as possible, for no good reason except the capability of doing so. The prevailing attitude, even among major commercial manufacturers is "You can't make it too small." This is utter nonsense. Anything, including electronic equipment must be large enough to do its job and to permit someone to work with it adequately. A design of electronic circuitry that is too compact can very often lead to overheating and unnecessarily higher failure rates. Maximum possible compactness is essential only in a few specialized cases, not as a general principle. It's good design practice to make a circuit as small and compact as is reasonable, without reducing things to the level of impracticality.

The following is an example of needless problems that can result from getting carried away with the "small is better" attitude. This example isn't directly related to alarm systems, but the same basic principles apply.

Some years ago, I bought a function generator made by a well-known, major manufacturer of electronic equipment. It was a very compact unit. The case was as small as it could be to fit the front panel controls. Even these were smaller and more closely placed than was really comfortable, but it was usable. In inches, the case measured about 4 (wide) × 3 (deep) × 1.5 (height).

After about a year or so, this function generator developed a minor problem. Because it was out of warranty, I decided to repair it myself. On opening the case, I discovered it was an incredibly poor design. The case contained a lot of empty space. All of the circuitry was crammed onto a printed circuit board measuring ¾ × 1½ inches. This board was so tightly packed, taking measurements and desoldering the defective component were tedious nightmares. There was scarcely enough room to remove the bad part and insert a replacement using the narrowest pair of tweezers I could find. Because of the tight spacing of components, most of them quickly became too hot to touch after just a couple minutes of light-duty operation. There was plenty of room inside that case (whose dimensions were dictated by the necessary front panel controls) for a much larger printed circuit board with adequate and reasonable spacing of the components. Yes, interconnecting wires, leads, or PC (printed circuit) traces in any circuit should be kept as short as possible, but this consideration is far from the only one. For a function generator designed primarily for use at audio frequencies, there would be no detectable difference in operation if all leads and traces were increased by a factor of three to four, or even more. The larger circuit would have been much easier to service, less costly to manufacture, and most important, more reliable. The defect I serviced was almost certainly due to overheating.

The ridiculously undersized printed circuit board was not the only serious design flaw in this function generator. All the connecting wires between the PC board and the front-panel controls and rear-panel connectors were 30 gauge. These tiny wires also were stretched as tightly as possible to install them. There was virtually no slack in them. Inevitably, about half these wires broke as soon as the case was opened, making the total repair job much longer and more tedious.

Thirty-gauge wires should never, under any conditions, be used for any off-board connections. They are far too thin and fragile. Such misuse virtually guarantees breakage under the slightest mechanical stress. Thirty-gauge wire simply isn't made for such purposes. Wire that thin should only be used for on-board wire wrapping, or possibly short, on-board jumpers.

Even with a reasonably heavy wire for off-board connections, it is essential to leave a reasonable amount of slack, especially to any wire connected from the chassis to the removable part of the housing. Obviously you don't want to leave so much slack that the various wires will become hopelessly entangled. But it is absolutely vital to make it possible to open the case and make repairs without breaking on or more wires.

Despite the highly respected brand name, the fact is, this function generator was unquestionably incompetently designed in terms of the mechanics involved. Do not make the same foolish and inexcusable mistakes in your own work. When you encounter such design flaws in commercial equipment you are servicing, it would probably be worthwhile to correct the errors as much as possible. Replace too-thin off-board wires with wire heavy enough to do the job adequately. Unfortunately, you usually can't do much about a too tightly packed circuit board short of total redesign of the board, which is usually not practical. But you can add extra heat sinking if it seems needed (and if you can physically fit it in.)

In most cases, the case size of the central control box in a home alarm system will be dictated by the necessary (or desired) front-panel controls and indicators. Usually, this will give you more than enough room to keep the circuitry comfortably spaced—neat, but not cramped and impractical. All electronic components work best with a little breathing room to permit cooling air to pass between them. Risk problems of overheating only when it is absolutely essential to do so.

Design the front control panel with convenient use in mind. Remember your customers might have to operate the controls under some emotional stress. Don't make it harder on them to get the desired results from their security system. Use controls that are large enough and spaced out well enough that they can easily be grasped by adult fingers. Make indicators large enough to be seen clearly and easily.

In summary, the central control box should not be too large or too small. Simply put, it should be as big as it needs to be to do its job properly.

Finishing touches on the job

Once you have all the elements and components of the alarm system mounted and hooked up, the installation job is still not quite finished. A few important finishing touches remain.

By all means, clean up after yourself. To ensure customer satisfaction, make it look as much as possible like no one has been at work in the home. Don't just pack up your tools and any spare parts and leave. Clean up and remove debris, including component wrappers and packaging, cut-off leads, bits of stripped off wire insulation, and dust and particles from drilling and other work. Look for and clean off any footprints, hand prints, fingerprints, or other marks of any sort left by you or any of your assistants. Make sure any pencil marks you made for measurement and alignment purposes are fully erased and cleaned off.

The installation is not really complete when you've mounted the last screw or connected the last wire. You must check out the entire system before leaving the premises. If you don't, you're almost sure to be called back to fix something that should have been taken care of in the first place. The extra trip and labor will end up coming out of your profits, and 9 times out of 10, there is no real need for it. A thorough check-out of the entire system at the time of the installation will save you a bit of time and money in the long run. Don't be in a hurry to pack up your tools and go home (or to the next job). Even under the best of circumstances, it will waste more time to come back to an installation location than to go ahead and take care of everything you can while you are already on the premises.

Before you leave, test everything. Make certain that everything in the system is hooked up correctly, and working as it should. Taking a little extra time here can significantly reduce the nuisance and customer dissatisfaction of immediate call-back service calls to correct problems that should have been taken care of as part of the original installation.

Check all of the connections throughout the system with an ohmmeter. Don't assume that a connection is good just because it looks good. Open and close each sensor switch as you watch the ohmmeter pointer. Precision measurements are not necessary or even relevant. You just need to check to make sure there is circuit continuity wherever it's supposed to be, and not where it shouldn't be. The small mechanical parts in many such switches can get bent and not make proper contact, or short circuit themselves. It is especially important to make quick continuity checks of all switching type sensors, whether of the NC and NO type. Be sure to keep them straight as you make these tests, or you will become confused by the results.

Before hooking up the main alarm device, hook up a small, temporary alarm. This device is strictly for testing purposes. It should be just loud enough for you to know when it's working, without disturbing any of the neighbors, or even anyone else in the house where you're working. A low-volume test alarm also will help preserve your own ears and sanity. You could go even further, and use a totally silent "alarm." Simply hook up a test lamp across the system output, in place of the usual alarm.

Also disconnect the secured arm/disarm or reset switch, whether it is a lock-key type or a coded keypad. Temporarily replace it with a simple push-button switch for convenience during testing. You will be repeatedly arming and resetting the system many times over during the testing procedure. Turning a key or punching in a code repeatedly can quickly become a real nuisance and a bit of a distraction. A temporary simple reset switch will make the system testing procedure go a lot faster and more smoothly. Temporarily replacing the reset switch is not absolutely essential, but it is definitely worthwhile. Using a smaller, quieter test alarm device, however, is not optional. No one would appreciate the numerous deliberate false alarms you'll be setting off during testing if they are at full volume. Keep the disturbance level down to an absolute minimum.

Now you can test the entire system thoroughly, without disturbing the peace. This job requires two people. A pair of walkie-talkies helps considerably. One person remains by the central control box and the temporary test alarm device. The other person goes through the entire house or protected area and deliberately trips each sensor throughout the system, one by one. The first person makes sure each individual sensor activates the alarm properly when it is tripped, and resets the system to prepare for testing the next sensor. One person could do this job, but it would involve an awful lot of running back and forth.

Don't get lazy and just spot check the sensors. Test each individual one. In a typical home installation there won't be all that many sensors, and it just takes one bad one to make the entire system vulnerable. According to Murphy's Law, the one sensor you don't bother checking out will be the one that doesn't work properly.

In addition to testing all the sensors, this procedure also gives a near total checking of the central control box, especially its arming, disarming, and resetting functions.

Also test each panic button throughout the system. Perform these tests twice—once with the system armed and once with it disarmed. Remember, a panic button should set off the alarm when pressed whether the system has been activated or not.

While you're at it, check out any special features and functions of the central control box. Make sure everything is working as it should. Remember, you are dealing with a security system. Any security system will only be as good as its weakest element. One defect can effectively neutralize the security of the entire system under the right circumstances.

Now, disconnect the temporary reset switch and reconnect the permanent lock switch or code keypad. Trip a few more sensors and make sure this device arms or disarms and resets the system properly. Make sure the system cannot be reset without the key or the correct code. Also test the entrance arm/disarm switch device carefully. Trigger the alarm by tripping several different sensors in various areas throughout the house. This time it is not necessary to test every single sensor in the system. The sensors themselves have already been checked out and found good. At this point you are just testing the arming/disarming functions.

Don't forget to check the entry timer function. It is easy to check. Just arm the system, leave the front door (or whatever entrance is connected to the timer function) open and wait. The test alarm should soon go off.

As long as the timing period is approximately correct, consider it acceptable. Don't worry about great precision. In practice it isn't going to make much noticeable difference if the timing period is 37 seconds or 51 seconds, instead of the 45 seconds you intended to set it for. In either case. It is close enough. On the other hand, if the timing period is supposed to be 45 seconds, but the alarm goes off after 10 seconds, or not until after a minute and a half, something is wrong. Check out the timer circuit, and make the necessary adjustments.

Set off the alarm once more with the test alarm device. Take a coffee break or use the time to begin packing up your tools and supplies. Wait long enough to make sure the system's shut down timer is working properly. As discussed earlier in this book, the system shut down timer is a vitally important feature, and should not be considered an optional or negligible element.

Finally, disconnect the temporary alarm output device, and hook up the real system unit(s). Conduct one brief test to make sure all alarm output devices are working properly. It is very important to keep this test as brief as possible to minimize disturbing the neighbors more than you have to. It would be a nice courtesy to warn the closest neighbors just before this test.

As soon as you've determined the alarm output device is working, reset the system. The alarm should cut off immediately when the system is reset, but be prepared to quickly cut off power to the system or unplug the lead(s) to the alarm output device(s). It's not unheard of for a short circuit to make it impossible to shut off the alarm by ordinary means once it has been set off. If this should happen, check the wiring from the output of the central control box to the affected alarm output device. In extremely problematic cases, it might be easier simply to rerun new wires. The fault can be assumed not to be in the central control box circuitry, because it presumedly did not occur with the temporary test alarm device. (If any such problem did show up during the earlier testing, you should have taken care of it then, of course.)

There is some vague possibility that the short might be in the alarm output device, and it must be repaired or replaced. But this is very rare. If this problem does crop up, the odds are there is a short in the external wiring.

At this point, you know all the elements in the installed alarm system are correctly connected and operating properly, with one important exception. An extremely important, though often ignored, element of any security system is the human element. You can't just physically install the system and leave without talking with the customer(s). Make sure all members of the household understand what the system does and doesn't do, and how to use it for maximum security benefits. Specific issues to discuss with your customers are covered in the next section of this chapter.

Advice for your customers

Your customers themselves are vital parts of their own security systems. Your work, no matter how good a job you've done, could be functionally worthless if the customer makes one or more of the errors described in the next few paragraphs.

Take the time to sit down and talk to each customer before leaving any installation. If possible, include all members of the household, or at least all adult members. Don't rush this discussion. Make sure the environment is reasonably quiet and conductive to the customer understanding what you have to say. It also might be a good idea to print up a list of instructions, but too many people foolishly never read instructions. So consider spelling out these warnings orally as part of the installation. Nothing else matters if this information is not properly "installed" in the customer's mind.

Many people assume that a professionally installed alarm system is somehow magic and will free them of all responsibility. The system should be designed to be as automatic and to require as little active attention as possible, but there are certain things the residents of the protected home must do for the system to be able to do its job. There also are several things they could unthinkingly do that could defeat their own security system.

The following are some important warnings you should give to each and every customer. Some of them might seem too obvious and common sense to be worth mentioning. But common sense often seems incredibly uncommon. Many, many people have committed every one of these obvious errors. They are worth mentioning.

Don't rely too much on secret hiding places for anything. A lot of people try hiding their valuables, or worse they hide a spare key to disarm the alarm system somewhere near the front door. It doesn't hurt to conceal valuables, of course, but such hiding won't offer much practical security. Hiding a key outside is very risky. There are usually only a limited number of possible hiding places available, and (for various psychological reasons) most people will tend to make similar choices. A smart burglar can usually find any secret hiding place quickly.

If a secret hiding place is used (hopefully in addition to other security measures), by all means keep its location as secret as possible. Never reveal it to anyone who doesn't absolutely need to know. Similarly, don't reveal any critical details of your alarm system to anyone, except on a need-to-know basis only. For instance, if you go on vacation, you would obviously need to tell the house sitter what he or she needs to know to use system effectively. But there might be details that are irrelevant to the house sitter's legitimate duties, and there's no need to mention them. Avoid the temptation to play "Can you top this?" about your alarm system, especially with people you don't know well. Don't even do this with good friends. This hush-hush attitude is not a matter of not trusting your friends, it's just a matter of reasonable security. Someone else might overhear the key details you reveal to your trusted friend. Even a good friend might innocently and inadvertently reveal some important information to someone who might be somewhat less trustworthy.

Remind your customers to always lock the doors, even if the alarm system is on. Yes, the alarm will offer its protection by going off when the door is opened, whether it was locked or not. But this could cause unanticipated and unnecessary problems. For example, suppose you run to the neighbor's house for just a moment, but you end up being there somewhat longer than anticipated. Meanwhile, a relative shows up at your house, perhaps earlier than expected. Because your car is in the driveway, the natural assumption is that you're home. The relative knocks on the door, and getting no answer, tries the door and sets off the alarm. Under some circumstances, both you and your relative could face some trouble explaining what happened to the police.

Aside from such difficulties, it's important to remember that no security system is perfect or absolute. A determined professional burglar could find a way to defeat any home alarm system. Locking the door gives one more obstacle to slow any such burglars down a little.

Yet another problem with leaving the doors unlocked even with the alarm system armed is that casual burglars often get in simply by trying doors. Such an opportunistic burglar could get in and grab something valuable before the time delay sounds the alarm. Such a run and grab action takes less time than you might expect. If the burglar is a cool-nerved type and doesn't get rattled, she or he could go ahead and take items while running out. The burglar wouldn't have time to clean you out, but you might lose your most prized possession. Even if it is an item of only moderate value, its unnecessary loss is bound to hurt.

There's certainly nothing wrong with supplementing an electronic alarm system with other security techniques, but they should be carefully considered. Often they sound good but are really a waste of time and money, adding little to practical security, and might even increase the risk.

A fence around the yard might be decorative or add privacy from nosy neighbors, or it can keep the family dog from wandering off. These are all good reasons for putting up a fence, but security isn't one of them. Fences offer only very limited protection to a home, other than perhaps against trespassers taking a short cut through your yard, and kids who might casually vandalize your property, litter, or trod through your freshly planted seed. If someone is going to go to the trouble of burglarizing your home, their not going to stop short at the prospect of climbing a fence. In a residential area, you can't use the type of security fences used in industrial settings. Barbed wire and electrified fences simply aren't reasonable choices for home security, and are almost guaranteed to get you into trouble with local ordinances.

5
CHAPTER

Fire and smoke alarms

Most of this book focuses on intruder alarms, as this is what most people automatically think of when the subject of security systems comes up. But there are many other dangers that a home alarm system can protect against, in addition to keeping the bad guys out. One of the most important and deadly is mentioned several times already in previous chapters—fire. Every year, hundreds of people die or are badly injured, and millions of dollars worth of property is damaged or destroyed by fire. For most homes, the risk of a fire is statistically somewhat more likely than the risk of an intruder breaking in. In most cases, a fire can do a lot more harm. A fire is much more likely to kill. Sure, there have been cases of people being killed in their own homes by intruders, but such incidents usually make the news, because they are relatively unusual. Most intruders in homes are burglars, interested in stealing property, and the good ones plan ahead so no one will be home when they break in. If no one is at home, no one will get hurt. It's considerably safer for the burglar that way. Most home intrusions result only in loss or damage of property. Certainly that is bad enough, and protection against it is appropriate, and the risk of being one of the rarer cases involving personal injury or death is real, but it is a minimal risk compared to the potentially catastrophic consequences of a major fire in the home.

Unfortunately, many homeowners install extensive intrusion alarm systems and neglect the risk of fire altogether, except perhaps for a simple (often legally required) smoke alarm or two. This approach is not reasonable for home security. A real home security system will guard against intruders, fire, and possibly other less common risks such as gas leaks or flooding (discussed in the next two chapters).

Some of the material in this chapter is repeated from comments about fire alarms in other chapters, but it makes good sense to consolidate the relevant information here. The repetitions are minor.

Methods of fire detection

There are two basic approaches used in most fire alarms. Each has its advantages and disadvantages. Neither can provide true security by itself, but either is better than nothing. The greatest security will always come from a system that simultaneously uses both of these methods of fire detection. These two methods are based on the two most obvious attributes of fire—it is hot and it produces smoke.

The first fire detection approach (and the one most commonly used today) is smoke detection. Where there's smoke, there's fire (presumedly) and vice versa. Smoke can be electronically detected by using either optical or chemical means.

The second, less popular approach to fire detection is to monitor the temperature in the protected area. If the monitored temperature exceeds some preset limit, there is a very strong likelihood that a fire is in progress. Some sort of thermal sensor triggers the alarm when the area grows too hot. There are a number of different types of thermal sensors (or temperature-sensitive devices) available. The range of sensors leads to a much wider range of different designs of thermal fire detector circuits, compared to the narrower range for smoke detectors.

Smoke detectors are by far the popular choice among most homeowners, largely because of their very low expense and simple maintenance. Today an off-the-shelf smoke detector alarm can be bought for ten to thirty dollars and sometimes even less. If properly placed, a single smoke detector can provide as much protection as a single thermal sensor, although it is usually a simple enough matter to add multiple thermal sensors to a single control circuit. The first smoke detector will cost less than the first thermal sensor (which must be supported by appropriate circuitry), but additional smoke detectors will almost certainly cost more than additional thermal sensors. Detectors will be a higher cost because they are entirely self-contained, and all of the control circuitry must be duplicated for each desired location. A single control circuit, however, can support numerous thermal sensors at various locations, at just the cost of the sensor device and some wire.

The currently accepted wisdom is that a smoke detector is the better choice for home protection if only one type of fire alarm is used. Few responsible people would argue that a thermal alarm working together with a smoke detector wouldn't offer a significant increase in actual security.

The popular notion that a smoke detector is automatically the best choice in a home is very debatable, however. Maybe it is, and maybe it isn't. Before selecting, weigh the inherent strengths and weaknesses of both types.

Many fires smolder for a long time, before much heat or active flames build up. It will be hot at the actual starting point of the fire, but this heat might be very localized. A few feet or even a few inches away, there might be no significant increase in ambient temperature until the smoldering fire finally bursts into flames, often with explosive force. The fire suddenly goes from a small, localized smoldering fire to a large-scale blaze in a matter of seconds. In such fires, a thermal detector fire alarm would not do much good. Unless it just happened to have its sensor mounted right at the actual fire source, the alarm system would ignore the fire as long as it continued to smolder. By the time it sensed the fire, there's a good chance it would be too late for the alarm warning to help much. Moreover, the materials that are smoldering could be releasing toxic fumes into the house. The fumes could be especially dangerous at night. Residents of the house could inhale very dangerous or even deadly amounts of poisonous gasses without waking up.

But such a smoldering fire does tend to produce fairly large quantities of smoke, making it readily apparent to a smoke detector, even at the early stages of the fire. The alarm will be set off and household residents can safely escape, or even extinguish the fire before it builds enough to do significant property damage.

Such smoldering fires are fairly common among house fires. All it takes is for a spark (that can come from almost anywhere, even a discharge of static electricity) to hit a flammable material just right. Usually carelessness of some sort is the ultimate cause of such fires.

Such smoldering fires are particularly common in households with one or more smokers, for the simple reason that a lit cigarette is a very good source of stray sparks. Smoking in bed has caused many fires. The smoker could doze off and drop the lit cigarette into the bed clothes. Blankets and mattresses will tend to smolder a very long time before bursting into flames. The fumes from some mattresses can be toxic. Even out of bed, a careless smoker might accidentally drop a hot ash into a crevice in a sofa or easy chair without noticing it. If he or she leaves the room before the smoke from the smoldering furniture becomes noticeable, the fire might not be discovered in time to prevent damage or tragedy.

Other common causes of smoldering household fires also are due to carelessness. Improper storage of flammable materials can be a big problem. Often this hazard can occur in unexpected ways, where someone does really stop to think that they are, in fact, storing flammable materials. For example, assume someone has been working on a car and has gasoline or oil smeared on his or her clothes. The person might toss the soiled clothes into the laundry hamper until wash day. A stray spark landing in a pile of clothes or clothing is always a possible cause of a smoldering fire. But if any of the clothes in the pile is soaked with gasoline or oil, a fire is virtually guaranteed if a spark or a localized heat source gets too close to it. Oily rags stored in a garage or basement are a smoldering fire just waiting to happen.

Another possibility would be someone neglecting to turn the stove all the way off. Then someone carelessly tosses a towel or hot pad over the low-heat burner. Eventually, its got to burn.

Smoldering fires can occur in many ways, and in situations that are not unusual in the average home. Yes, most such fires could have been prevented if carelessness on some level was not involved, but you must make reasonable allowance for human nature. People don't always think about all the possibilities of every little action. Occasional carelessness is an inescapable part of being human. However, there's no excuse not to try to limit and reduce it as much as possible.

Not all home fires in the home are of the smoldering type so well suited to smoke detection. Another very common type of household fire is an electrical fire. Electrical fires can be started by careless misuse of electrical equipment, of course, or by improperly selected or installed materials in the building's electrical system. But usually, no one is really at fault for an electrical fire. A small chip of critical insulation might have been nicked or otherwise minimally damaged in some way, but the damaged area was so small it could only be found by someone actively looking for it. Having the electrician check every inch of wire before installing it simply is not a reasonable expectation when you consider that the average home wiring system contains hundreds, if not thousands of feet of wire. Further, insulation can become brittle and small pieces might chip away with age. Mechanical stresses (from hanging pictures, termites, mice, severe weather or any of dozens of other causes) also can create weakened points in the electrical wiring behind the walls of the house. If conditions are just right, a fire can start.

Because the electrical fire is behind the walls it is hidden from view, and any smoke produced is likely to be contained for some time. Eventually the fire will burn through the walls, but by that time it will almost surely be well advanced into a large blaze. A smoke detector will not catch this fire in its early stages. However, if there is a fire behind a wall, it is inevitable and obvious that the wall will get hot. A thermal sensor mounted on or near the wall could detect the abnormal increase in heat while the electrical fire is still at a fairly early stage. Because of the nature of this type of fire, it would be difficult for the residents of the house to extinguish it themselves—in most cases, holes would have to be broken through the wall. But a thermally based fire alarm could give the household residents ample warning to escape safely and summon help. With luck, the fire department might arrive in time before the electrical fire breaks through the wall and starts to do damage to anything inside the house, as well as the structure of the house.

Neither type of fire detection can be relied upon to detect and give warning of all common household fires. By using both methods of fire detection, the home is much better protected against the various possibilities.

The functional simplicity of a smoke alarm also can work against its effectiveness. A home smoke alarm is almost always a self-contained unit, and not actually part of a larger security system (although it can be a valuable added support to such a system). Most people tend to install a smoke alarm, then forget about it. All standard smoke alarms today are battery powered, and no battery lasts forever. Many people forget or don't bother to check and periodically replace the batteries in their smoke alarms. A smoke detector with a dead battery offers no protection at all. Some models do give a visual or audible indication when the battery gets low, but even this might not always be noticed before the battery fails completely.

Even worse, people often take the battery out of a smoke alarm, and forget to put it back. Why would anyone do this? There are two common reasons—one pretty stupid and inexcusable, but the other is almost a necessity. First, someone might decide to borrow the smoke detector battery for use in some other piece of equipment, like a radio or a camera. There might be some rare incidents where an unusual emergency situation requires the use of a smoke alarm's battery elsewhere, but 99% of the time, this should be considered an absolute no-no. The smoke detector does you no good whatsoever while its battery is missing, and it's all too easy to forget to return it.

On the other hand, people far more frequently and excusably take the battery out of a smoke detector because on most designs that's the only way to shut it off once it has been triggered. Smoke detectors are notoriously prone to false alarms, especially if they are installed in or near the kitchen, which all too many people, who really should know better, think is the ideal location. Their argument is that the kitchen is a likely source of fire, because the stove and oven produce heat, along with the toaster, the microwave, and other common kitchen appliances. Yes, but their normal use is inevitably a common source of smoke, especially if food is accidentally over cooked. Some foods produce smoke when cooking normally. If you can smell it, there's a chance the smoke detector might react to it if it contains the right chemicals. I lived in one apartment that had a smoke detector that functioned as a super-sensitive lamb chop detector. Every time I cooked lamb, the smoke alarm would go off almost immediately. If an oven is due for a cleaning, opening the oven door while cooking could be enough to set off a too close smoke detector. Naturally no one wants to listen to the loud alarm until dinner is through cooking or all harmless smoke has been cleared from the area. Even if there is a simple reset button on the smoke detector, the alarm will just immediately go off again until all the smoke is cleared. The only way to silence most smoke alarms is to remove the battery. This design flaw is very serious, because it's very easy to forget to put the battery back later when you've finished cooking.

The best way to correct this problem is for smoke detector manufacturers to build in a time-delay reset switch. If the alarm sounds, pressing the reset button will disable the smoke detector for five or ten minutes, then the device will automatically rearm. No one has to remember to turn it back on. The reset switch would add to the cost of smoke detectors, of course, but it also would add a great deal to their practical reliability and efficiency.

The only other solution is to mount the smoke detector away from likely sources of frequent false alarms—such as the kitchen. Yes, a grease fire or something of that nature is most likely to start in the kitchen, but someone is likely to be nearby to check on the cooking food. At worst, the type of smoke produced by a kitchen fire is unlikely to be highly localized. It will drift throughout the house, and will soon reach the nearest smoke detector. A smoke alarm mounted a little farther from the kitchen will certainly detect any fire a lot better than a unit mounted right in the kitchen, but with its battery removed to stop a false alarm. The kitchen is unquestionably the worst possible place to mount a smoke detector.

Smoke detectors

Smoke detectors are wonderful devices, that have saved hundreds of lives. They have the additional advantages of being inexpensive and easy to install and use. However, be cautious of relying on smoke detectors exclusively for protection against fire. Although many home fires do smolder (and produce smoke) for some time before bursting into active flames, many other fires that might occur in a home might not produce much or any detectable smoke until the fire has already reached an advanced stage.

As stated, smoke can be electronically detected by using either optical or chemical means. Other more obscure methods might be theoretically possible, but, all smoke detector circuits seem to use one of these two methods, particularly the chemical method.

Anyone who has ever seen smoke knows it is less transparent than ordinary air. It partially, though not completely, blocks light. If a small light source and a photo-

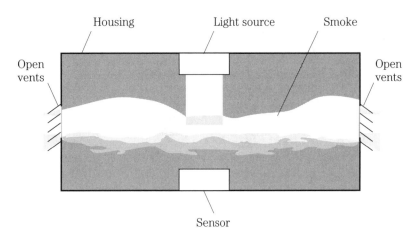

5-1 In an optical smoke detector, the smoke blocks the light from a source before the light reaches a photosensor.

sensor are placed in a semi-enclosed housing, as shown in Fig. 5-1, no object can get
in to block the light from the source before the light reaches the photosensor. But air
can get in easily, and that includes smoky air. The smoke will come between the light
source and the photosensor, blocking off some of the light. The photosensor will respond to this reduction in the amount of light striking its sensing surface. The circuitry connected to the photosensor is calibrated to trigger the alarm when the
detected light is slightly reduced, indicating the presence of smoke. Unfortunately,
dust or other airborne particles also might set off an optically based smoke alarm.

Alternately, special electronic sensors can detect the change in the chemical
composition of smoke-filled air. This approach is considerably more reliable, though
more complex than the optical method, and it is used in one form or another in virtually all commercial smoke detectors now on the market. This method of smoke detection is rather complex and requires too much space to describe it adequately.
Fortunately, there is little or no need for the practical alarm system technician to
know the details of the inner workings of smoke detectors. These units are widely
available commercially at low cost, and are self-contained. They are almost never
cost effective to repair. It's almost always cheaper simply to replace a defective
smoke detector with an entirely new unit. Therefore, the alarm system technician
can reasonably treat a smoke detector as a black box. Either it works or it doesn't
work, and how it's supposed to work doesn't really matter.

Although it is foolish and risky to consider one or two smoke detectors to be adequate protection against fire in any home, it would be equally foolish to leave these
devices completely out of a home security system. In many areas, local ordinances
require the installation of smoke detectors in homes, and even where they aren't
legally required, they are very much a good idea. A smoke detector is so inexpensive
compared to the home alarm system as a whole, that there is little or no reason for
not using it. A smoke detector does provide excellent, if limited, protection. For certain types of fires (slow smoldering fires), there is no better way to detect them in
their early, less destructive stages.

In a large house, use several smoke detectors. Remember, they are cheap. There's no need to scrimp. It's better to install too many smoke detectors than too few. The down side of installing too many smoke detectors in a home is a little added expense, typically ten to twenty dollars per smoke detector. An alarm system installer should be able to buy smoke detectors in quantity, lower the unit price even more. The down side of installing too few smoke detectors is the possibility of hundreds or thousands of dollars of property damage or serious injury, or even death of one or more members of the household in the event of a smoky fire. Which alternative seems like the more reasonable trade off?

In most homes, the most critical location(s) for smoke detector(s) is near any sleeping areas. Noxious fumes from smoke are most likely to have tragic results when everyone is asleep. A person who is awake is more likely to smell or hear something suspicious and investigate. Many people have died in their beds from extensive smoke inhalation, without ever waking up. A hall outside several bedrooms is a logical place to install a smoke detector. A more cautious approach is to install a smoke detector in each bedroom.

A garage or a basement also would be a good place to install an extra smoke detector. A slow smoldering fire could continue in such locations for some time, even during waking hours, without anyone noticing, because most people don't spend much time in these areas. A garage or basement also is the most likely place for possibly flammable materials to be stored, making a fire somewhat more likely to start there.

As stated, the very worst place to install a smoke detector is in or near the kitchen. A detector in the kitchen will accomplish little but numerous false alarms. At best, this would be extremely annoying, and possibly tragic if the smoke detector is disabled by having its battery removed to stop a false alarm and not replaced.

Whatever the location in the house, it is usually best to mount a smoke detector high up on a wall or on the ceiling. The high location will help prevent accidental damage from anyone bumping into it, or from too curious children. More importantly, a smoke detector will tend to function more reliably at a higher physical level. In the event of a fire, even the slowest burning smoldering fire, the smoke is going to be hot, at least hotter than the normal air in the area. Hot air, including smoke, tends to rise. The rising of hot air is why experts recommend crawling on your hands and knees if you ever have to escape from a major fire with the room filled with smoke. The safest, most breathable air will be down close to the floor.

Installing a smoke detector is not even remotely difficult. It's just a matter of mounting it in place. Most commercial smoke detectors are designed to be held by one or two standard screws. Other than that, the installer just has to make sure a fresh battery is correctly installed in the unit, and the installation of the smoke detector is complete.

Thermal sensors

Too many homes are currently protected against fire only by a smoke detector. Many well-meaning but short-sighted officials have irresponsibly led the public to believe this is adequate protection. It most definitely is not. Certainly a smoke detector by itself is better than nothing, but it can only protect against some types of fires. How can anyone guarantee they'll only have the "right" type of fire?

No, an adequate home security system must offer double-barrelled fire protection, incorporating both smoke detectors **and** thermal sensors. There is no rational excuse for making this an either/or choice. Use both to do the job right.

Commercially manufactured thermal-sensing fire alarms are not widely available now, unfortunately. But a wide variety of thermal sensors are commonly available, and they can easily be incorporated into an existing alarm system, pretty much like the sensors used for detecting intruders. Some thermal sensors will require some specialized support circuitry, usually in the form of a comparator circuit for a continuous-range type sensor, and others can be wired directly into the alarm system, just like any other switching sensor. The support circuitry, if required, rarely needs to be very complex or expensive.

A *thermal sensor* is generally any electronic device that produces some electrical response to a detected change in temperature. Of course, if you get too loose with this definition, almost any electronic component could qualify, if the temperature changes sufficiently. Most capacitors will vary their value in response to the ambient temperature. If a resistor is heated sufficiently, it also will change its value, perhaps permanently. Any semiconductor device is always heat sensitive to some degree, which is why heat sinks are frequently used to protect such components. A semiconductor component will change its performance characteristics in response to changes in temperature, and the delicate crystalline structure of the semiconductor can be easily damaged or destroyed by over heating. Of course, a sensor that is destroyed by the condition it is supposed to detect would hardly be practical or reliable.

A practical thermal sensor offers a predictable and repeatable (that is, nondestructive) response to changes in the detected temperature. Of course, any electronic component or device will be damaged or destroyed by sufficient extremes of temperature, but a practical thermal sensor can stand up to much higher temperatures than most standard electronic components. The thermal sensor is unlikely to be damaged unless it is actually engulfed by the fire, in which case, the damage to the sensor is probably the least of your worries.

Thermal sensors are available as either continuous-range or switching devices. *Continuous-range* thermal sensors usually (but not always) work by varying their resistance in response to the sensed temperature. A device that changes its resistance proportionately with temperature is known as a *thermistor*. The word *thermistor* is a blending of *thermal* and *resistor*. There are many different devices that fit into the relatively broad heading of thermistor.

The standardized schematic symbol for a thermistor is shown in Fig. 5-2. Notice that this is basically just a slight variation on the standard schematic symbol for an ordinary resistor. The important element here is the letter t° for *temperature*, or *thermal*. The t° is the only part of the symbol that identifies the indicated component as a thermistor rather than some other type of resistor. Some technicians omit the circle, as it adds no information to the symbol. The circle is more eye catching than the small t, so it more clearly indicates that this component is something other than an ordinary resistor. A few schematics will add an arrow through the thermistor symbol as shown in Fig. 5-3 to indicate the variable resistance of the component, but

5-2
This is the standard schematic symbol for a thermistor.

5-3
A few schematics add an arrow through the thermistor symbol to indicate the variable resistance of the component.

this really isn't necessary, because the t° already implies the resistance varies with temperature.

Especially in hand-drawn schematics, neatness is vital. A sloppy t° could be mistaken for a +, indicating a positive value of some sort. The sloppy t° could cause unnecessary confusion very easily.

Thermistors can be divided into two broad subcategories, based on the way they function. Any thermistor must be either an *NTC* or a *PTC* type. *NTC* stands for *negative temperature coefficient*, which means the device resistance is inversely or negatively correlated to the sensed temperature. That is, increasing the temperature results in a corresponding decrease in the thermistor resistance, and vice versa.

Not surprisingly, a PTC thermistor operates in just the opposite way. You've probably already guessed that *PTC* stands for *positive temperature coefficient*, which means the device resistance is directly or positively correlated to the sensed temperature. Therefore, increasing the temperature results in a corresponding increase in the thermistor resistance, and vice versa.

For a variety of reasons that needn't really be of concern, NTC thermistors are much more common in practical use than are PTC thermistors. For that reason, focus just on NTC devices. Everything said about NTC thermistors here also will apply to PTC thermistors if the resistance response is simply reversed.

Thermistors come in a very wide range of shapes and sizes. A few typical body types for thermistors are shown in Fig. 5-4.

Most standard thermistors are formed from special ceramic materials, which function as semiconductors. Powdered metal oxides (particularly nickel oxides and manganese oxides) are often used to fabricate these components. In some cases, other oxides might be mixed in as well. The powdered oxides are mixed together with water and various electrically neutral binders, and the resulting material can be shaped as desired and fired into a solid ceramic. A coating of silver, or occasionally some other conductive metal, is placed over the ceramic center. Leads are added; then the assembly is enclosed in an insulating housing, usually made of epoxy, glass, or plastic.

An ideal thermistor would be perfectly linear over its entire range, as graphed in Fig. 5-5. Real-world components aren't nearly so perfect, of course. A typical resistance/temperature graph for a practical thermistor is shown in Fig. 5-6. The exact curve, and the placement and size of the linear portion depends on the design of the

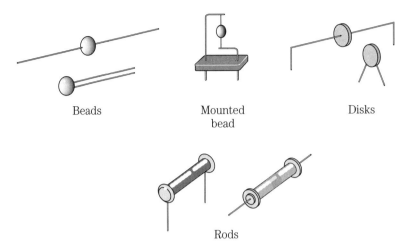

5-4 Thermistors come in a very wide range of shapes and sizes.

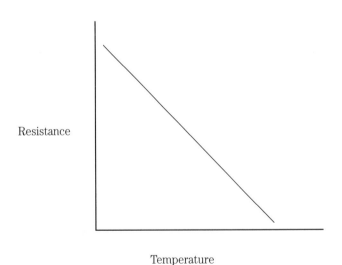

5-5 An ideal thermistor would be perfectly linear over its entire range.

thermistor used. In precision-measurement applications, a thermistor must be very carefully selected to be as linear as possible over the desired measurement range. For use in fire alarms, however, a thermistor is combined with a comparator circuit of some sort, and all that you are interested in is whether or not the sensed temperature is greater than or less than the preset trip point. Linearity is not generally a significant issue in this application.

In selecting a thermistor for use in a fire alarm system, the only really important specification is that the desired trip-point temperature is well within the rated oper-

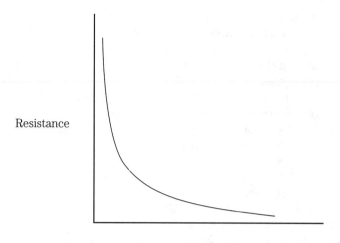

5-6 This is a typical resistance/temperature graph for a practical thermistor.

ational range of the device. This requirement will rarely be a problem in home environments, when a temperature above about 150 to 200°F would almost certainly indicate trouble, and should trigger the alarm. This is still a fairly low temperature as far as most thermistors are concerned.

Most commercial thermistors are rated by their nominal resistance at 25° Celsius (about 77°F). This nominal resistance is just an approximation except for specialized (and expensive) high-precision devices. The higher this reference resistance is, the higher the effective temperature range of the thermistor will be (see the comparison chart of Table 5-1).

**Table 5-1. Comparision of the temperature/
resistance trip points for some typical thermistors**

Temperature		Reference resistance at 25°C			
°C	°F	100	1 kΩ	10 kΩ	1 MΩ
–50	–58	2.32 kΩ	35.4 kΩ	441 kΩ	—
–30	–22	846	11.4 kΩ	135 kΩ	—
–10	14	354	4.23 kΩ	47.5 kΩ	—
10	50	166	1.79 kΩ	18.8 kΩ	2238 kΩ
30	86	85.4	834	8.19 kΩ	775 kΩ
50	122	47.5	425	3.89 kΩ	296 kΩ
70	158	28.3	233	1.99 kΩ	123 kΩ
90	194	17.8	136	1.08 kΩ	55.5 kΩ
110	230	—	—	624	26.8 kΩ
130	266	—	—	376	13.7 kΩ
150	302	—	—	237	7.48 kΩ

Closely related to this type of thermistor is the RTD, or resistance temperature device. An RTD is usually a wirewound coil or metalized film that exhibits a positive temperature coefficient response. Nickel and platinum are popular materials for use in RTDs. In fact, some technical literature refers specifically to PRTs, which are platinum resistance temperature devices.

Another continuous-range temperature sensor is the thermocouple. A thermocouple is not truly a resistive type, but if you're not too particular about precise definitions, it could be loosely considered a sort of thermistor. In many ways, the effect is the same. If thermocouples and thermistors are not in the same immediate family, they are at least cousins.

The intricacies of the theory behind a thermocouple's operation are a bit on the complicated side, but the physical construction of this device is simple—it's just a junction of two different types of metal. This mismatched junction will produce a voltage that increases with the ambient temperature at the junction. A practical thermocouple can be as simple as just two wires of different metals wound around each other, as shown in Fig. 5-7. In most practical thermocouples intended for long-term use, the junction will be welded together for maximum reliability.

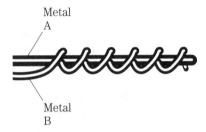

Metal
A

Metal
B

5-7
A practical thermocouple can be as simple as just two wires of different metals wound around each other.

A working thermocouple can be made from almost any pair of dissimilar metals, but, not surprisingly, some combinations work considerably better than others, particularly in the areas of stability, linearity, and overall temperature range. Some examples, as recognized by NIST (National Institute of Standards and Technology—formerly the National Bureau of Standards) include:

- Chromel and alumel
- Chromel and constantan
- Copper and constantan
- Iron and constantan
- Nicrosil and nisil

Other effective thermocouples use various platinum alloys.

Thermocouples are more suitable to industrial and laboratory applications than home alarm systems, but they can certainly be used for home systems.

Thermal switches also are available, and they are more directly suited to alarm system applications. As the name suggests, a thermal switch is a switch that is activated when the temperature exceeds some specific preset level. For most common thermal switches, the temperature trip point is permanently set by the manufacturer of the device, and is not user adjustable. Some thermal switches are adjustable over a limited range, however. A few can be adjusted for any of a moderately wide range of trip-point temperatures, but wide ranges are the exception rather than the rule.

For most fire alarm applications, the exact trip-point temperature isn't too critical. The trip-point temperature needs to be high enough above the normal expected ambient temperature to avoid false alarms, but low enough that the heat from a fire will set off the alarm before it gets too far out of control. Generally speaking, a reasonable trip-point temperature in a home would be in the 120 to 180°F range. It wouldn't take much of a fire to produce such temperatures, but it is highly unlikely that it will ever get that hot inside a home, unless something is very seriously wrong.

There are some special case exceptions, however. Even in air-conditioned homes, the attic is usually not cooled, and during summer months it can get extremely hot inside an attic. In some climates, a temperature of 130 to 160°F might not be unusual inside an uninsulated attic. Because attics are normally used for storage, and aren't generally occupied most of the time, they are a likely starting point for a fire. But such high normal attic temperatures could create some serious false alarm problems if a fire alarm thermal switch mounted in the attic has a trip-point temperature of about 140 or 150°F. It is supposed to be a fire alarm, not a hot sunny day alarm. The solution is obvious enough. Use a thermal switch with a higher trip-point temperature. Something between about 200 to 250°F should do nicely. Certainly you should avoid using a thermal switch with a trip point temperature much higher than 300°F. This is not a reasonable temperature that should be expected in a home under normal conditions. In certain heavy industrial settings, temperatures over 300°F might be only moderately warm, but you are concerned with home systems here, and people generally just don't live under such conditions.

Near a water heater is another place in the average home that reasonably calls for a thermal switch because of the likelihood of a fire starting there. A switch near a water heater requires a higher than normal trip-point temperature to avoid false alarms.

You also might consider mounting a moderately high temperature tripping thermal switch over the stove. Don't mount it too close, or ordinary cooking might set it off.

One of the simplest and most common types of thermal switch is similar in some ways to the thermocouple. This switch also is used in most electromechanical (as opposed to purely electronic) thermostats for household heating and cooling systems.

Once again, there are two dissimilar metals, but here they are normally close, but not quite touching. Usually the metal will be in the form of strips, rather than actual wires. In an adjustable thermostat, one (or sometimes both) of the metal strips will be coiled as shown in Fig. 5-8. Tightening or loosening the tension of the coiled strip will control the actual trip-point temperature.

This thermal switch is based on the principle that most materials, including metals, tend to expand as they are heated. Ordinarily, this expansion is so slight it goes unnoticed, but it is sufficient for electromechanical switching.

This expansion effect is most clearly demonstrated by the mercury inside an ordinary thermometer. Mercury is a metal with an extremely low melting point—so low, in fact, that mercury will only solidify at what to humans would be an abnormal and unbearably cold temperature. Generally, a liquid expands more readily for a given increase of temperature than a solid. At cold temperatures, the mercury con-

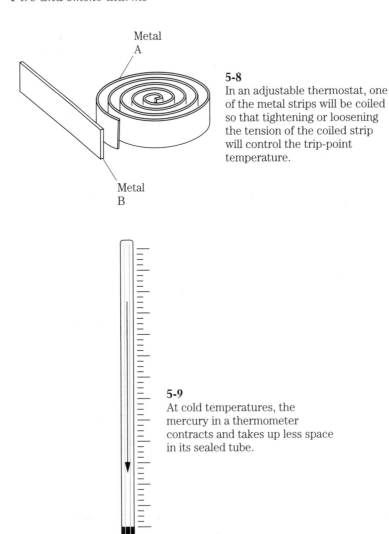

Metal
A

Metal
B

5-8
In an adjustable thermostat, one of the metal strips will be coiled so that tightening or loosening the tension of the coiled strip will control the trip-point temperature.

5-9
At cold temperatures, the mercury in a thermometer contracts and takes up less space in its sealed tube.

tracts, and takes up less space in its sealed tube. It only reaches up to a fairly low level on the scale, as shown in Fig. 5-9. When the temperature increases, the mercury expands. Because it is in a sealed tube, the only way it can expand is by moving upwards in the tube, filling more of it, up to a higher point on the scale, as shown in Fig. 5-10. A similar effect occurs with solid metals, but the differences are less obvious to the naked eye under most normal circumstances.

The two metal strips inside a thermostat or thermal switch are made of different types of metal because different materials naturally expand at somewhat different rates. If you have two strips of different metals expanding at differing rates, correct

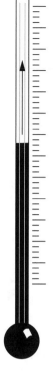

5-10
At high temperatures, the mercury in
a thermometer expands and takes up
more space in its sealed tube.

physical placement will cause the two metal strips to normally be separate, but to
touch each other if the temperature exceeds a specific trip-point value, as shown in
Fig. 5-11. If electrical terminals are connected to each of the metal strips, you have
a simple, but effective temperature-activated normally open switch. If the temperature is below the trip point, the switch contacts (the dissimilar metal strips) will be
open, but if the temperature exceeds this critical value, the switch contacts will be
closed (the two metal strips touching).

Other types of thermal switches also are available, but are less common. Most
still operate on some variation of the expansion with temperature principle, although
in somewhat different ways.

Installing thermal sensors

A thermal switch or other temperature sensor can be installed in much the same
way as the more standard sensors used for intrusion detection in a home alarm system. There are a couple of special points to keep in mind.

First, as with a smoke detector, it is usually best to mount a thermal sensor high
on a wall or on a ceiling. This location will help prevent accidental damage from anyone bumping into it and from curious children. The most important reason for
mounting a thermal sensor closer to the ceiling than the floor is that hot air rises and
cold air falls. The thermal sensor's job is to watch out for abnormally increased tem-

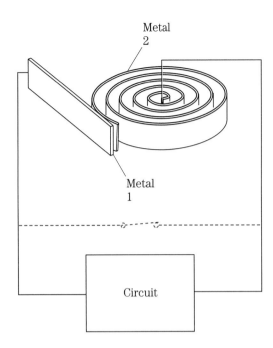

Metal
2

Metal
1

Circuit

5-11
When the trip-point temperature of a
thermal switch is reached, the two
strips of dissimilar metals touch each
other, making electrical contact.

peratures, and this will be most detectable and obvious at higher positions. If there
is a fire anywhere in the area, the temperature near the ceiling will soon get abnormally warm, but it might be some time before the increased heat is detectable near
the floor level, especially if there are any cool drafts in the area.

Try to anticipate areas where fires are most likely to occur when choosing where
to mount thermal sensors. Typically, a thermal sensor can cover a somewhat smaller
area than a smoke detector, so you will probably need more of them. Certainly a
thermal sensor should be placed near any potential fire or heat source, such as a water heater, a furnace vent, or a fireplace. But don't mount it too close, or the residents will be plagued with false alarms. Remember, it is the intended function of a
water heater to get hot, and a furnace vent or a fireplace is supposed to send out
some heat into the room. The thermal sensor must be selected and mounted to detect only **abnormal** amounts of heat, not the normal functioning of such common
household features.

6
CHAPTER

Gas detectors

Dangerous gas leaks aren't too common in the average home, but they can occur and the results can be deadly. Some poisonous gases betray their presence with a distinctive smell, but some of the most poisonous gases are odorless, colorless, and tasteless. They can be silent, invisible killers. Even if the gas does have an odor, it might not be noticed until too late, unless someone is paying attention to the possibility of a gas leak. Under most circumstances, a strange odor is likely to go unnoticed unless it is strong, especially if there are other smells in the area that could mask that of the gas.

Gas leaks are relatively rare occurrences. When gas leaks happen, they are much more likely to have disastrous results than most other comparable accidents because many gases can do considerable damage, or even cause death, before their presence is detected. Often the presence of the poisonous gas is only detected after the fact, from its effects. Obviously it is more than desirable to detect a gas leak before an accident happens.

In addition to directly poisonous effects, many gases that might leak are highly flammable or even potentially explosive. Again, the leaking gas is all too often only discovered after the fact. The rubble in the aftermath of an explosion might reveal that gas must have been the culprit, but by then it's clearly too late for the information to help avert disaster.

In any house that uses a gas stove or gas heat, a potentially dangerous gas leak must be considered a real possibility. Even if there is no direct use of natural gas in the house, there might still be a risk. If any of the neighboring houses use natural gas, the odds are good that pipes carrying gas are buried in or near the property. If a gas main ruptures or leaks, anyone in the vicinity is at risk.

Many dangerous gases have nothing to do with ordinary home gas use (heating or cooking) but come from other sources. One of the deadliest common gases—carbon monoxide—can be found in any garage. Fumes from stored gasoline or alcohol also can be dangerous in high concentrations or where ventilation is poor. People who like to camp might keep a portable propane tank in the garage or basement, and this too can leak dangerously. There are numerous other possibilities, of course. It is foolish to assume any given home is safe from gas leaks without very carefully considering all the factors and variables.

Deoxidizing gases

Most of the potentially dangerous gases that are likely to show up in the home are the type known as *deoxidizing* gases. As the name suggests, a deoxidizing gas is one that tends to reduce the amount of available oxygen in the area. Of course, oxygen is vitally needed by your body. Oxygen deprivation that lasts more than a few seconds can cause permanent damage, if not death.

A deoxidizing gas is one that is relatively unstable and tends to bond chemically with any oxygen atoms it might encounter, even "stealing" them from other molecules with weaker bonds. The stolen oxygen atoms help stabilize the gas by changing its chemical composition.

An example of a deoxidizing gas, how it works, and why it so dangerous, is carbon monoxide. As you know, you breathe in oxygen from the surrounding atmosphere. When your body is through with the inhaled oxygen, the oxygen is combined with carbon atoms to form carbon dioxide, which you exhale. The prefix *di-* means *two*, so a carbon dioxide molecule consists of one carbon atom bonded to two oxygen atoms.

If there is just one oxygen atom to each carbon atom, the result is carbon monoxide, instead of carbon dioxide. (*Mono-* means *one*.) A carbon monoxide molecule has room for one more oxygen atom, and would be more stable with it. It will try to complete itself by latching on to the first oxygen atom it can.

Carbon dioxide is a fairly stable compound, and it acts as if it is functionally complete. It would be very difficult to force a carbon dioxide molecule to bond with a third oxygen atom, and even if such a bond could be made, it would be inherently very weak and unstable. The excess oxygen atom would drop off from the molecule at the earliest opportunity.

If you inhale carbon dioxide, it won't do you any good. You can't extract and reuse the oxygen atoms that have bonded to carbon atoms. But in itself, breathing in carbon dioxide is not harmful. That's a good thing, because you can't avoid breathing in quite a bit of carbon dioxide, no matter how hard you might try not to. Every time you exhale, you are adding more carbon dioxide to the nearby environment. Some of it will inevitably be drawn back into your lungs the next time you inhale. Ordinarily, this is no problem, and your body is well designed to cope with it. The only time you might have trouble with carbon dioxide is if you spend some time in a small enclosed area with poor or no airflow from the outside. As you exhale more and more carbon dioxide, the available oxygen in the area will be used up, and eventually you could run out of breathable oxygen. The problem here is not with the carbon dioxide, but with the local scarcity of usable oxygen.

There also might be problems breathing in areas with very high concentrations of carbon dioxide, even if the oxygen isn't really in short supply, but even in this case, the carbon dioxide isn't really acting as a poison or a problem in itself. Your lungs can draw in just so much air at a time. If there are large amounts of carbon dioxide in the inhaled air, it's going to take up more room than normal, leaving less room for good oxygen. If the concentration of carbon dioxide is high enough, you might not be able to take in enough oxygen. Lack of oxygen is biologically dangerous, of course, but the carbon dioxide is really just acting as a neutral space filler, and isn't doing any active harm on its own.

With carbon monoxide, you have a very different situation, however. Carbon monoxide is functionally incomplete. You could say that a carbon monoxide molecule wants to become a carbon dioxide molecule, and will do anything it can to achieve this ambition.

What happens if you inhale some carbon monoxide molecules? They will grab any free oxygen molecules in the lungs, making them unavailable for biological purposes. If any carbon monoxide gets into your bloodstream, it will steal the oxygen atoms being carried by the red blood cells to various parts of the body, which will therefore not receive the oxygen they require for proper functioning. Even at relatively low concentrations, carbon monoxide can quickly take hold of most of the oxygen in the body, leaving it too little oxygen to carry on the essential biological functions. Particularly sensitive body parts, such as brain cells, will quickly start to die off due to oxygen deprivation. Within a matter of minutes, the entire body will die.

Because of its inherent deoxidizing characteristic, carbon monoxide, unlike carbon dioxide, acts as an actively poisonous gas. Because it is odorless, colorless, and tasteless, a person cannot detect it directly, until the harmful oxygen deprivation effects set in, and the presence of carbon monoxide (or some similar deoxidizing gas) can be deduced. By then it might already be too late.

Other common deoxidizing gases include methane, propane, and hydrogen, as well as fumes from gasoline or alcohol. Not all deoxidizing gases are equally powerful in their poisonous effects. It would take a significantly higher concentration of hydrogen (which occurs naturally in the atmosphere) or alcohol vapors to cause death than carbon monoxide. However, the effects can be just as deadly. It just takes more of certain deoxidizing gases than others to do the job.

The Taguchi gas sensor

Because potentially deadly deoxidizing gases are very difficult, if not impossible, to detect directly with your senses, an electronic alarm of some sort surely makes sense in areas at risk. A commonly used sensor device for detecting the presence of deoxidizing gases is the Taguchi gas sensor, often abbreviated as *TGS*. In much technical literature, references to unspecified gas detectors usually imply some form of the Taguchi gas sensor.

The Taguchi gas sensor is a semiconductor device made up of a combination of N-type metal oxides, such as tin, zinc, and ferric oxide. These materials respond electrically in the presence of a deoxidizing gas. As the concentration of the deoxidizing gas increases, the resistance of the sensing material decreases. This decreasing resistance can easily be electronically monitored to drive a meter or other continuous level indication device or circuit. Alternately, and more appropriately for discussion purposes, the varying resistance of a TGS can be used to control the input voltage to a comparator circuit of some sort. When the monitored resistance becomes lower than some preset calibration level (that is, when the detected concentration of the deoxidizing gas exceeds safe limits), the comparator circuit can trigger an alarm, alerting any occupants in the area to the dangerous condition.

The internal resistance of the Taguchi gas sensor is normally very high. In the presence of a deoxidizing gas, the resistance of the Taguchi gas sensor is proportionately reduced. The higher the gas concentration, the lower the resistance. The response of the Taguchi gas sensor is not instantaneous, because a chemical reaction is involved. It takes a few minutes for the sensor to stabilize to its normal high resistance state after power is first applied, or after a detected concentration of deoxidizing gas is removed. Typically a wait of about 5 to 10 minutes is required for the Taguchi gas sensor to clear and stabilize, before any further readings can be accurately made.

A wide variety of gas-sensing applications can be accommodated by the Taguchi gas sensor, thanks to its wide operational range and high sensitivity. This device can sense tiny concentrations of a deoxidizing gas, on the order of just a few *ppm* (parts per million), but it also can function reliably under very high concentration conditions, such as inside an automobile exhaust pipe for a pollution-emission control system.

The power requirements for a Taguchi gas sensor also are conveniently low. A typical Taguchi gas sensor can be operated with about 1 V (volts), and will consume a little less than half an ampere or 500 mA (milliamperes). (Some units are specified for 1.2 V.) The current consumption is a bit high compared to many other semiconductor devices in use today, but it is still far from excessive. Undoubtedly improved Taguchi gas sensors designed to consume less current will eventually appear on the market.

Battery life for a Taguchi gas sensor will be only moderately good, but if ac power is used, the power consumption would be virtually negligible. The circuit would have to run about 2000 hours (almost three months) to use up one kilowatt hour—the smallest unit that can be indicated on a standard home power meter. In most areas it might add literally just a penny or two to the monthly electric bill. You could use rechargeable battery back-up power for a gas-detection alarm, but this would probably be unnecessary overkill in most home situations. A gas leak is highly unlikely to coincide with a power failure, so the temporary lack of gas protection if ac power in the home is cut off for some reason is unlikely to be a serious risk, unlike the case for an intruder alarm or fire alarm. The darkness and other effects of a loss of ac power would be a decided advantage to an intruder, and many burglars deliberately disrupt the power to homes they intend to rob before going in. The risk of intrusion can be considered somewhat higher than normal during a loss of ac power, so the intrusion detection alarm circuits are needed more than ever. An electrical fire can often interrupt ac power before it is detected by the fire alarm system. If the power outage is caused by a short circuit somewhere in the house, a failure in the fuse box, or a lightning strike, there is a fairly good chance a fire might be started from the same cause. Battery back-up is essential for fire and intrusion alarms, but this need doesn't really apply to extra alarm functions such as gas leak alarms or flooding alarms.

There have been several different designs for Taguchi gas sensors, but most commercially available devices of this type follow a common pattern. The standard Taguchi gas sensor has two electrically isolated sections—an input section and an output section. Although the input section cannot be interchanged with the output section, either section is bidirectional, and nonpolarized. Electrical current can flow through each section in either direction.

Most Taguchi gas sensors have 4 or 6 pins, and are designed to fit into a standard 7-pin miniature tube socket, making installation convenient. (One or three of the socket pins are left unused.)

Because the Taguchi gas sensor is not a commonly used electronic component, it has not yet been assigned a fully standardized schematic symbol. Most technical literature dealing with the Taguchi gas sensor uses similar symbols for this device, indicating its input and output sections and their resistive nature. Some typical schematic symbols that have been used to represent the Taguchi gas sensor are shown in Fig. 6-1.

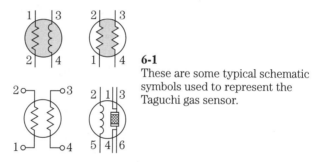

6-1
These are some typical schematic symbols used to represent the Taguchi gas sensor.

Response of the Taguchi gas sensor is reasonably linear, even over its wide operational range. This characteristic makes this device well suited for metering and measurement applications. Most gas meter circuits built around the Taguchi gas sensor use this device as part of a Wheatstone bridge network.

In an alarm system, you only need a simple yes/no type response, so the alarm can be activated when the detected concentration of deoxidizing gas exceeds a specific, preset level. Because the Taguchi gas sensor is primarily resistive in its response, the voltage drop across its output section can be used as the variable input of a comparator circuit. A fixed reference voltage that is equivalent to the desired critical trip point can be selected or adjusted to calibrate the sensor for almost any desired concentration level of deoxidizing gases in the monitored area.

The Taguchi gas sensor is singularly reliable, with an expected lifespan of at least several years.

Gas sensor circuits

A typical gas meter circuit is shown in Fig. 6-2. This device is a simple and direct circuit, with nothing complex or fancy. Despite its simplicity, it can be effective and

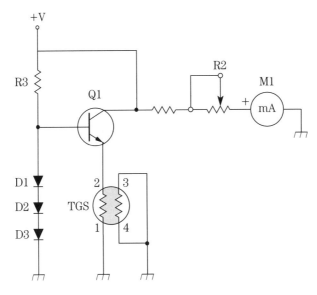

6-2 This is a fairly typical gas meter circuit.

accurate, if high precision components (especially low tolerance resistors) are used throughout the circuit.

In this circuit, only one of the Taguchi gas sensor internal sections is used. The nominal output section (between pins 3 and 4) is deliberately shorted out. Do not omit the connections to pins 3 and 4, however. Although this section of the TGS doesn't appear to be doing anything at all, it is necessary for the correct operation of the sensor. Fortunately, you don't need to go into the technical details of what goes within the Taguchi gas sensor. Treat it as a black box. In effect, the Taguchi gas sensor here functions as a simple two-lead resistor (between pins 1 and 2), whose resistance varies with the concentration of deoxidizing gas in the immediate vicinity. The higher the concentration of deoxidizing gas detected, the lower the resistance between pins 1 and 2 will be. (The resistance between pins 3 and 4 will be similarly lowered, of course, but that is of no practical consequence in this circuit.) Pins 1 and 2 are nonpolarized, which means they can be reversed without altering the operation of the circuit in any way.

Transistor Q1, resistor R3, and diodes D1 through D3 form a simple, but effective voltage regulator circuit. The combined voltage drop across the three series diodes less the voltage drop across the transistor base-emitter junction results in the approximately 1 V needed by the Taguchi gas sensor. The transistor also amplifies and buffers the proportional voltage from the Taguchi gas sensor to the milliammeter (M1). The range of the meter is set by resistors R1 and R2. Notice that R2 is actually a variable potentiometer, and it permits calibration of the circuit. A customized scale, calibrated in ppm, or any other convenient units can be made for the meter. Calibration of this unit is discussed in this chapter.

If the gas meter circuit is intended for frequent use in high concentrations of deoxidizing gases (for example, monitoring the output from an automobile exhaust

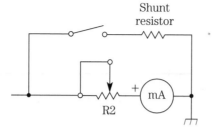

6-3

If the gas meter circuit of Fig. 6-5 is intended for frequent use in high concentrations of deoxidizing gases, desensitize the meter by placing a shunt resistor across it and R2.

pipe), desensitize the meter by placing a shunt resistor across it and R2, as shown in Fig. 6-3.

Because of the way the Taguchi gas sensor detects deoxidizing gases, there is some inherent time delay. When first applying power to this gas meter circuit, it is necessary to wait about 5 to 10 minutes before an accurate reading can be obtained. Similarly, if the Taguchi gas sensor is exposed to a high concentration of gas, it will take several minutes to clear and give accurate results after the deoxidizing gas has been removed from the area.

This circuit can potentially give very accurate results. Unfortunately, accurate calibration can be extremely tricky. For precise calibration, it is necessary to expose the Taguchi gas sensor to exactly known concentrations of deoxidizing gas. In addition to the difficulty and expense of getting precise quantities, there also is the danger of human exposure to the gas samples.

For a crude form of calibration, bring a drop of gasoline near the Taguchi gas sensor. Once the sensor and the circuit stabilize, adjust the meter for a full-scale rating via potentiometer R2. Because the unit is not calibrated to a known quantity, the scale should be marked off in convenient, but vague, units rather than direct ppm readings. A scale divided into three sections labelled SAFE, QUESTIONABLE, and DANGER, as shown in Fig. 6-4, is a practical choice. Keep in mind that the dividing points between these areas is vague and imprecise. Because you have to do some

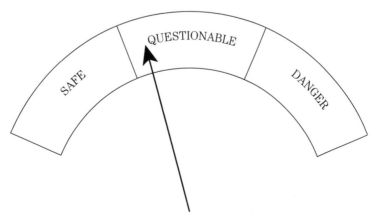

6-4 A convenient scale for a gas meter can be divided into three sections labelled as shown.

guesswork, it's best to err on the conservative side. The safe range should be rather narrow, at the low end of the meter scale, and the questionable area should be large. Begin the danger region at a slightly lower point than you think is truly dangerous. It's much better to be safe than sorry.

In home alarm systems, a calibrated measurement is unlikely to be necessary, or even desirable. You just want a simple yes/no response to trigger the alarm if there is any unusual increase in the concentration of deoxidizing gas in the monitored area. In essence, what you need is a type of gas-operated switch. The Taguchi gas sensor readily adapts to this application as well, and the calibration procedure is much simpler and more reliable.

The first gas alarm circuit, shown in Fig. 6-5, is basically just a simple modification of the gas meter circuit of Fig. 6-2. Instead of driving a meter, the output from the gas-detection circuitry is used as the input to a simple voltage comparator. The reference voltage, and therefore the sensitivity trip-point of the circuit is adjusted via potentiometer R2. Ordinarily, the output of the comparator is LOW, near ground potential. This LOW looks like an open switch to the central control box. When the deoxidizing gas concentration exceeds the preset limit, the comparator output goes HIGH, which the alarm system considers a closed switch. The circuit, in other words, functions as a NO (normally open) sensor in the alarm system.

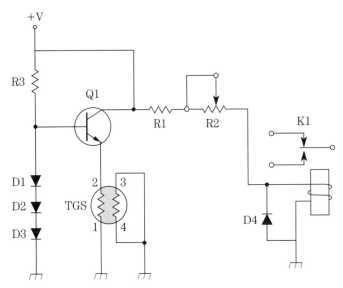

6-5 This gas alarm circuit is basically just a simple modification of the gas meter circuit of Fig. 6-2.

The output voltage of the comparator circuit can be amplified or attenuated, as appropriate, to match the signal levels of the other NO sensors in the alarm system.

Calibration of a gas sensor circuit like this is extremely simple, if you begin with the assumption that the normal air present when the device is installed is safe, but any increase in the detected concentration of deoxidizing gases in the area indicates potential trouble. Adjust the calibration control (R2) for minimum sensitivity, before applying power to the circuit. Wait 5 or 10 minutes to give the Taguchi gas sensor time to stabilize to the atmospheric conditions and to get a meaningful reading. This waiting period is necessary because of the relatively slow response time of the Taguchi gas sensor. A typical resistance versus time graph for a Taguchi gas sensor is shown in Fig. 6-6, illustrating this principle.

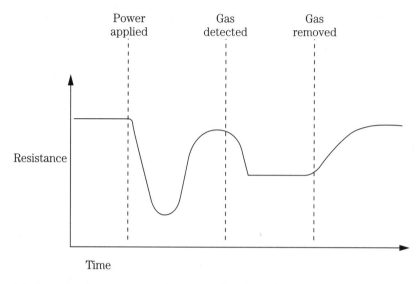

6-6 Typical resistance versus time graph for a Taguchi gas sensor.

Slowly increase the sensitivity until the alarm sounds. Stop increasing the sensitivity immediately and disable the alarm. Decrease the sensitivity control's setting just slightly. Reactivate the alarm to ensure that it won't go off again. That's all there is to it. The gas sensor is calibrated so any increase in deoxidizing gases in the monitored area will trigger the alarm.

A more sophisticated gas sensor alarm circuit is shown in Fig. 6-7. Because this circuit is a bit more complex than the other circuits presented here, a detailed parts list is given in Table 6-1. There is room for variation in most of the component values, but pay careful attention to the following description of circuit operation.

Most of the components in this circuit are devoted to power supply/conditioning functions. The basic sensor circuit could be powered directly by a 1.2 V source, but this is a little inconvenient in most cases. It can actually be more economical and efficient to start with a 12 Vdc (volts, direct current) supply voltage and use this circuit to reduce the power. Of course, a simple resistive voltage-divider string could be used, but the voltage drops across the resistors would necessarily consume more power than the sensor circuit, which is hardly an elegant or economical design approach.

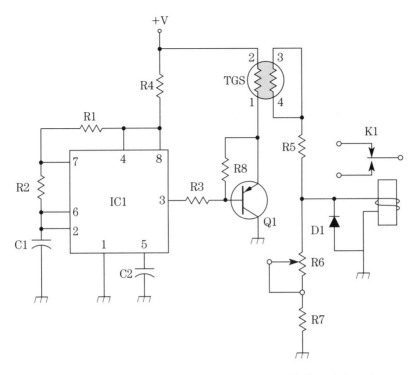

6-7 This gas sensor alarm circuit is somewhat more sophisticated than the one shown in Fig. 6-5.

**Table 6-1. Suggested parts list
for the gas alarm circuit of Fig. 6-7**

TGS	Taguchi gas sensor
IC1	555 timer
Q1	PNP transistor (Radio Shack RS2026 or similar)
D1	1N4001 diode or similar
C1	0.1 μF (microfarad) capacitor
C2	0.01 μF capacitor
K1	Relay
R1	120 kΩ (kilohm) ¼ W (watt) 5% resistor
R2	10 kΩ ¼ W 5% resistor
R3	270 Ω (ohm) ¼ W 5% resistor
R4	120 Ω ¼ W 5% resistor
R5	220 Ω ¼ W 5% resistor
R6	10 kΩ potentiometer
R7	1 kΩ ¼ W 5% resistor
R8	4.7 kΩ ¼ W 5% resistor

IC1 is a standard 555 timer chip, wired in its astable mode, to generate a series of narrow-width pulses, which switch the power transistor (Q1) on and off. The actual pulse width and frequency is determined by the values of resistors R1 and R2, and capacitor C1. There is room for considerable variation, but the component values suggested in the parts list have been selected to give about the maximum possible efficiency.

Capacitor C2 is included in the circuit simply to prevent any instability problems that could conceivably crop up from leaving the chip's unused control voltage input pin (pin 5) floating. Such problems are immediately rather rare in most practical use of the 555 timer, but a simple 0.01 µF disc capacitor is very cheap insurance against any probable aggravation from unusual but always possible stability problems. The exact value of this capacitor is not relevant to circuit operation in any way. The suggested 0.01 µF value is simply the standard recommended value, based primarily on its availability.

Almost any PNP medium-power transistor should work fine for Q1 in this circuit. It might be necessary to do some experimenting with the value of resistor R3 for some specific transistors to get the most efficient power transfer. Again, the differences should be slight, and the recommended value given in the parts list should be close enough, but a perfectionist might find some room for improvement.

Diode D1 provides a little simple voltage regulation for the sensor, to avoid false signals due to any possible supply voltage fluctuations. By using narrow-width pulses to power the sensor, the actual power consumed by the circuit as a whole can be reduced by as much as 80%. This approach is a very efficient way to power the Taguchi gas sensor.

The rest of the circuit is straightforward. Notice that once again pins 3 and 4 are shorted together. Pins 1 and 2 are nonpolarized and interchangeable. (The same is true for pins 3 and 4, of course.)

The output section of the Taguchi gas sensor is part of a voltage divider string. The voltage fed through diode D2 to the relay coil will vary in accordance to the concentration of deoxidizing gas detected by the Taguchi gas sensor and the setting of sensitivity/calibration control R7. When a sufficient current passes through the coil relay, it will be activated. Either the NO or NC switch contacts can be used, to suit the rest of the alarm system.

In some applications, a purely local alarm indication might be appropriate. For this application, the output circuit of this gas sensor can be modified as shown in Fig. 6-8. Here the output control device is an appropriately rated SCR. A sufficient gate signal will turn on the SCR, sounding the alarm. If an SCR is used, a local reset switch must be used to permit the SCR to be turned off (by breaking the cathode-to-anode current flow). Breaking the flow is the only way to stop the alarm from sounding once it has been triggered. Let the Taguchi gas sensor restabilize five to ten minutes after clearing the air before reactivating the alarm, or you might get a quick false alarm indication. Once the Taguchi gas sensor has stabilized, later false alarms are reasonably unlikely.

The calibration procedure for this gas sensor circuit is much the same as for the previous example. Adjust the calibration control (R2) for minimum sensitivity, before applying power to the circuit. Wait 5 or 10 minutes to give the Taguchi gas sen-

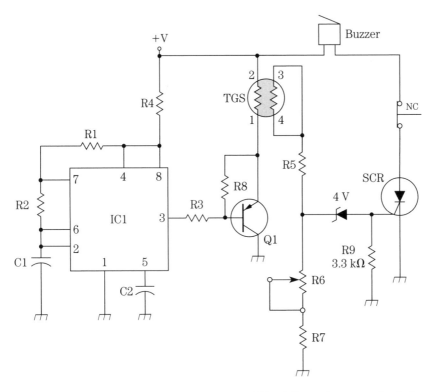

6-8 This modification of the gas alarm circuit of Fig. 6-7 permits a completely locally controlled alarm.

sor time to stabilize to the atmospheric conditions and to get a meaningful reading. Now, slowly increase the sensitivity until the alarm sounds. Stop increasing the sensitivity immediately and disable the alarm. Decrease the sensitivity control setting just slightly. Reactivate the alarm to ensure that it won't go off again. That's all there is to it. The gas sensor is calibrated so any increase in deoxidizing gases in the monitored area will trigger the alarm.

The required and appropriate sensitivity for a gas sensor depends a lot on just what is expected in the protected area. Inside the house, near a gas stove or heater, for example, maximum sensitivity is called for. It is reasonable to consider any deoxidizing gas in the area to be too much. However, in a garage, it would be impossible to avoid all gasoline fumes, especially if there might be periods of poor ventilation. You certainly don't want the alarm to go off just because the garage door has been shut more than a couple of hours. Take such factors into consideration when you calibrate a gas sensor. By all means, the gas sensor should always be calibrated in the actual location where it is to be used to set the normal background level.

In areas where large concentrations of deoxidizing gases might be anticipated, even in the event of an accident, it might be a good idea to add a little automation to the system. In addition to sending an activation signal to the alarm system, the output of the gas sensor also can be used to automatically switch on a ventilation fan or air conditioner to clear the potentially dangerous gas from the area.

Because of the fairly slow response change time of the Taguchi gas sensor, it probably wouldn't be suitable for the gas sensor circuit to turn the automated ventilation fan back off on its own. You could use a timer to shut down the ventilation system after a preset time. Be generous in determining the timer duration. It's much better to let the ventilation fan to run too long than not long enough. Give it enough time to do its job and clear the air in the protected area adequately. For that matter, even if the ventilation fan or air conditioner required a manual switch to shut it down once automatically activated, no real harm would be done, except perhaps a little wasted power and wear and tear on the fan.

7
CHAPTER

Flooding and leakage alarms

The most common types of alarm systems in use today are, by far, intrusion detection alarms, and smoke or fire alarms. Intrusion and fire are probably the most critical emergency situations in the average home. However, an alarm system can be readily expanded to protect against other types of emergencies as well. A good way for an alarm system installer to win good customer loyalty is to provide additional features that offer extra protection.

Many homeowners have experienced a flooded basement. Certainly, a flooded basement is a lesser disaster than a fire, but it can still be very destructive and expensive. Most home basements are used at least partially for storage, often of keepsakes and mementos of great importance to the owner. Items of sentimental importance, such as photographs, letters, projects built by children, etc., have little or no commercial value, and therefore are not covered by homeowner's insurance. Even if it was insurable, what price tag can be put on treasured personal memories?

A flooded basement also can be a risk of structural damage to the house, and can result in expensive repairs.

Obviously, it would be in the interest of the homeowner to be alerted to a flooding condition as soon as possible—preferably before it gets too serious. If the house already has an alarm system, it is easy enough to add a few sensors to detect the presence of water (or other liquids) where it shouldn't be.

Generally, flooding alarms are of less importance or interest in homes without basements, although there can be special cases to consider. For example, a water heater can be located in the back of a walk-in closet, which might be the primary storage area in the apartment. If the water heater should somehow spring a leak, a lot of stored property could be damaged or destroyed. A leak isn't likely, but it is certainly possible, and adding a flooding alarm to a general alarm system costs just a few extra dollars, making it a worthwhile option.

Another potential location for flooding/leakage detectors is in the attic, especially in older houses in rainy climates. You never know when the roof might begin to leak, and because most people don't go into their attics very often, stored items could be damaged or destroyed before someone happens to notice the leak. Again, with time a leak could do some structural damage to the house itself.

How flooding alarms work

Most practical electronic flooding/moisture detection circuits employ the same basic operational principles. Two (or sometimes more) conductive probes are mounted securely some distance apart in the area to be monitored for liquid. A typical arrangement is shown in Fig. 7-1. The mounting supports for the probes are non-conductive, so there is no current path between the two probes. With no current path, the circuit is incomplete or broken.

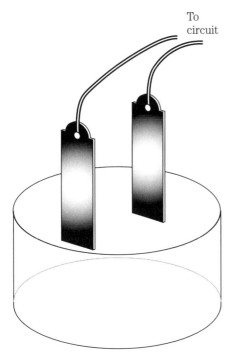

To
circuit

7-1
Typical mounting arrangement for the
probes of a typical electronic flooding
moisture-detection circuit.

Now, if enough liquid floods into the monitored area to simultaneously touch both probes, as shown in Fig. 7-2, the current path between the probes is completed. The resistance of most common liquids is much lower than open air. In effect, the liquid acts like a phantom resistor connected between the two probes, as shown in Fig. 7-3. The completed circuit triggers the alarm or display function, as suits the application.

To
circuit

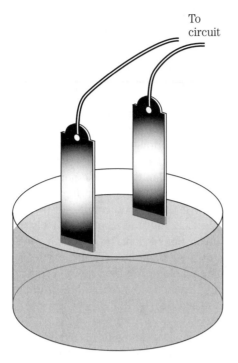

7-2
If enough liquid floods into the
monitored area to simultaneously
touch both probes, the current path
between the probes is completed.

To
circuit

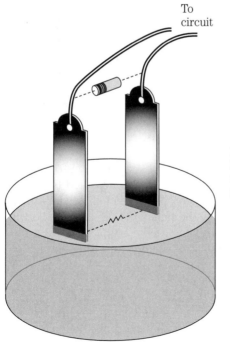

7-3
In a flooding alarm, the liquid between
the two probes acts like a phantom
resistor.

Despite its apparent crudity and low-tech feel, this simple technique works very effectively for most common liquids, though not all. In order for the liquid to be sensed by the probes, it must be ionic. That is, the liquid in question must contain sufficient numbers of ions to conduct a reasonable amount of electric current. Highly purified, de-ionized water, such as used in irons and some other equipment, will not work in this type of circuit. There are too few floating ions, so the pure water acts more like an insulator than a conductor. Its resistance is simply too high to complete the current path between the probes significantly better than open air.

Fortunately, this isn't much of a practical limitation, except perhaps in certain specialized industrial applications. For the purpose of a home alarm, there should be no problem with insufficient ionization. The water flooding a basement is certainly not going to be particularly pure in any sense. It is likely to be carrying plenty of dirt particles and other impurities, which will make it a very good conductor by the time it covers the probes. Even if the source of the flooding started out relatively pure, it is sure to pick up impurity particles from the basement floor. If the flooding is due to a broken pipe, there is likely to be flakes of highly conductive rust particles in it. Flooding water from an over-flowing washing machine can be expected to have detergent and particles from the clothes being washed, to say nothing of impurities that are probably in the standard water mains to begin with. (Who would attempt to wash their clothes with purified bottled water?)

Flooding alarms or moisture detector circuits also can be used to detect spills of almost any liquid. Again, any liquid the average homeowner is likely to be concerned with will be sufficiently ionic for the basic flooding detection trick described here to work.

The specific materials used for the probes and their mounting supports should be selected with the intended type of liquid in mind. If the probes are to monitor a corrosive liquid such as some type of acid, the materials of the probes or their supports should not be a type that is easily or quickly attacked by the corrosive liquid expected. If the probe is eaten away by the liquid it is monitoring, the system can't be expected to work for very long. In home alarm systems, the monitored liquid will usually be water from one source or another. With water, the greatest corrosion concern is rust. Stainless steel or some other strong rust-proof conductor should be used for the probes.

The same basic idea also can be used in the opposite direction to monitor the level of a desired liquid in a tank. The control circuitry is designed to trigger the alarm or other output conductor when the two probes are not shorted by the monitored liquid. The sensing technique is exactly the same. All that's changed is the way the circuitry responds to what is detected by the probes.

For heavy-duty or precision-quality industrial applications, this simple flooding detection technique will not be sufficient, and more sophisticated (and more expensive) moisture detection techniques will be needed. In a home or small business alarm system, there is no real need or point to greater precision than the simple two shorted probes technique offers. Certainly, there is unlikely to be sufficient advantage to justify the greatly added expense. A simple shorted-probe flooding alarm can be built in a few minutes for just a few dollars. A five dollar moisture sensing circuit of this type would be considered moderately expensive. Most other approaches to electronic moisture detection start at prices of several hundred dollars. For home systems, there is no practical reason to even consider alternate approaches to moisture detection.

Flooding alarm circuits

There are very few commercially marketed flooding/moisture detectors. To offer this type of useful extra to your customers, you will almost certainly have to build the sensing circuits yourself. This is no big deal. Anyone who is reasonably handy with a soldering iron should be able to whip up a suitable circuit in only about fifteen minutes or so.

The sensing circuitry really doesn't have to do very much. It simply needs to apply a current source to one probe and monitor the other probe to see if there is any of the current coming back through the other probe, indicating a current path (that is, sufficient liquid) between the two probes. If no flooding condition is detected by the probes, they present an effective open circuit to the sensing circuitry.

The only other thing the sensing circuit needs to do is to convert its output into a form suitable for the rest of the alarm system. Because the circuit only has to simulate a SPST switch, this isn't difficult.

The most direct approach is to design the sensing circuit to simulate a normally open (NO) switch. When there is no liquid between the probes, the "switch" is open. No current flows, just as with an unactivated NO switch. When sufficient liquid shorts the two probes electrically, it effectively closes the switch, permitting current to flow through it.

In most cases, the actual sensing circuitry amounts to little more than a simple buffer stage to prevent undue loading, and to compensate for the relatively high contact resistance when the switch is closed. Water and other liquids are good conductors, but not perfect. The resistance between the probes will typically be several hundred to several thousand ohms, which isn't much, but is not directly comparable to a true closed switch. (The exact resistance will depend on the composition of the specific liquid involved, and any impurities it contains. Also, the farther apart the two probes are, the greater the closed resistance will be.) Without proper buffering, the system could become confused by such an in-between resistance, and erratic operation is likely to result.

One of the simplest self-contained flooding alarm circuits is shown in Fig. 7-4. Only a tiny handful of parts are required. The only active component in this circuit is the SCR. Normally the SCR is held in its off state. Its gate is pulled down to ground through resistor R1, which has a fairly large value (typically 1 MΩ (1,000,000 Ω) or similar). The exact value of this resistor is not at all critical.

When there is no liquid between the probes, they present an open circuit to the SCR. The resistance between them is much larger than pull-down resistor R1. The gate of the SCR is held at ground potential. Because it is off, no current flows through it, or the piezoelectric buzzer (alarm output device) in series with it.

When the liquid level rises sufficiently to create a short between the probes, the resistance between them will be significantly lower than that of pull-down resistor

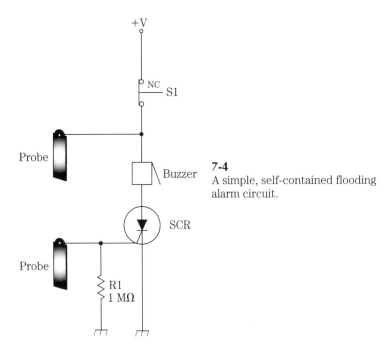

7-4
A simple, self-contained flooding
alarm circuit.

R1. This lower resistance means the positive voltage applied to the far probe is fed
into the gate of the SCR, turning it on. Current now flows through the SCR and the
buzzer, sounding the alarm. This condition will continue until the circuit is manually
reset by briefly opening the normally closed (NC) reset switch (S1). A SCR is turned
off by breaking the flow of current through it. The alarm will not stop sounding on its
own, even if all the liquid has been removed (unless the supply voltage batteries go
dead, of course).

This circuit is simple and effective, but it is really best for self-contained
portable applications, rather than as part of a larger alarm system. One limitation of
this particular circuit is a relatively large supply voltage is required. Some prototypes
have a 27 V power supply (three 9 V batteries in series). This voltage is not likely to
be directly compatible with an existing alarm system.

Also, the output alarm device (the buzzer) is directly part of the circuit. This device can be eliminated, and a separate output signal can be tapped off, although it is
a little inelegant.

One solution that simultaneously takes care of both compatibility problems is
shown in Fig. 7-5. This circuit is the same as Fig. 7-4, except the buzzer has been replaced with a relay, and a current-limiting resistor (R2). This added resistor is very
important. Without this component, the SCR will attempt to draw excessive amounts
of current, risking burning out itself or the relay coil. The exact value of this resistor
isn't too critical. In most cases, a resistor with a value in the 1 kΩ (1000 Ω) to 10 kΩ
(10,000 Ω) would be used. It might be necessary to do some experimentation with
the actual current-limiting resistor value to ensure maximum reliability, depending on
the specifications of the particular SCR used and the coil resistance of the coil used.

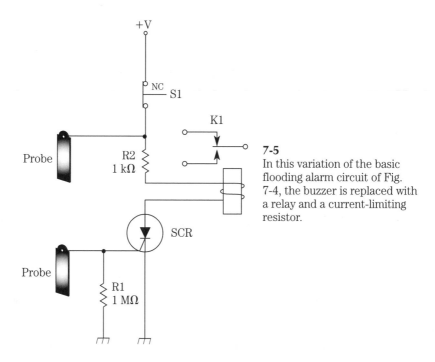

7-5
In this variation of the basic flooding alarm circuit of Fig. 7-4, the buzzer is replaced with a relay and a current-limiting resistor.

The relay coil circuit is electrically independent of its switch contacts, so an output voltage suitable for use throughout the rest of the system can be used. The flooding detector circuit will still require its own relatively large supply voltage. Battery power is very strongly recommended for any flooding/moisture detection circuit. An ac-to-dc power supply might conceivably fail in some way that sends an ac voltage through the probes, which could result in a very dangerous shock hazard. It is best not to take any chances here. The quiescent current drain in a circuit like this is almost nonexistent, so batteries should exhibit almost their full shelf life, unless the alarm is activated frequently or for extended periods.

It might be awkward that the flooding alarm requires local manual resetting, although a little creative circuitry could substitute some sort of electronic switch or system, permitting automation of the reset function.

The circuit shown in Fig. 7-6 has a somewhat higher parts count (although it still doesn't call for much more than a handful of simple components), but it is much more versatile, and can be expected to do a better job pretty much all around. While the approach is somewhat different here, the principle of the circuit operation is essentially the same.

The chief advantage of this circuit is that it is directly designed to drive a relay as its load. This feature makes it easy to use this circuit directly in an alarm system, in exactly the same way as any other switching type sensor.

Nothing is critical in this circuit, because it doesn't have to deal with any precision values. It just serves a simple on/off switching function. Almost any standard low-power NPN transistor should work well for Q1 and Q2, although both transistors

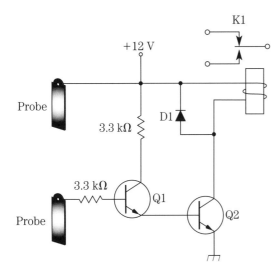

7-6
This is an improved flooding alarm circuit.

should be of the same type number. Diode D1 simply protects the relay coil against possible back-EMF (electromotive force). The values of resistors R1 and R2 aren't critical either. For most transistors resistor values in the 1 kΩ (1000 Ω) to 5 kΩ (5000 Ω) would be suitable. In a breadboarded prototype of this circuit, a pair of 3.3 kΩ (3300 Ω) resistors worked fine.

When any sort of flooding occurs, sufficient for the liquid to come into good contact with both probes, an electrical current path forms between the circuits through a phantom resistor (the liquid). The supply voltage passes through the liquid's phantom resistor, and resistor R2 to the base of switching transistor Q1, turning it on. Transistor Q1 now turns on transistor Q2, which in turn activates the relay. The two-stage transistor switch is recommended in this application to provide enough power to operate the relay properly. When the transistor switches are off, no current can flow through the relay coil, holding it in its deactivated state. When the transistors are switched on, they permit current flow through the relay coil, activating its switch contacts.

Notice that the full supply voltage appears to be fed directly into the relay coil with no current-limiting resistor. In this case, no separate current limiting resistor is required. The internal resistance of transistor Q2 serves the purpose.

As in the preceding circuit, if the liquid level goes down sufficiently to uncover one or both of the probes, the relay will be deactivated.

In addition to, or instead of, sounding an alarm, this circuit could be used to control a pump that will remove the flooding water (or other liquid). The pump will automatically shut off when a sufficient amount of water has been removed.

As with any simple flooding alarm circuit, battery power only is very strongly recommended. Remember this circuit's supply voltage is fed directly through the liquid. If there was a defect in an ac-to-dc converter permitting any ac power to reach the liquid, an extremely dangerous shock hazard would be created. It's not worth the effort. Please don't take any chances. Use only batteries to power this type of circuit.

This circuit is designed to work off a 12 V battery, which is a lot more convenient and practical than the 27 V required by the previous circuit. With some transistors, you might be able to get away with just a standard 9 V transistor battery to power the circuit. You will need to experiment with the circuit on a breadboard to determine if this will work with the transistors you have available, and to determine if the resistor values need to be altered.

A number of other simple flooding alarm circuits have been designed, but the differences are more stylistic than functional. The primary differences generally lie in the specific approach to electronic switching used in any given circuit. The basic operating principles are generally the same as in the two simple circuits examined here.

Any technician with any experience in circuit design at all should have no difficulty in designing customized flooding alarm circuits to meet most circumstances and practical requirements. Even though this type of sensor is not widely manufactured or sold on the commercial level (at least not at the present time), there is no reason why you can't offer this useful, yet inexpensive extra feature to your alarm system customers. Offering special features to your alarm systems can be a big help in making your company stand out over the competition, if those special features actually have practical value and are not merely nifty gadgets and gimmicks.

Installation

There are some special considerations you must keep in mind when adding flood or leakage alarms to a home security system. Water (and other liquids) and electricity do not generally make very good working partners. Many electronic components can be severely damaged or destroyed if they get wet. Excessive moisture can cause many materials to warp or change texture and other characteristics. These physical changes can alter electrical characteristics, often in extremely significant ways. In a few cases, the original characteristics will return once the device is permitted to dry out completely, but in most cases there will be at least some permanent damage. Of course, if the liquid in question is at all acidic, it can be very corrosive, tending to attack certain materials. The plastics used for insulation or adhesive binders on many types of electronic components are particularly susceptible to many types of acids. For example, most technicians are somewhat surprised the first time they see just how much damage cola can do if it is spilled into electronic circuit, especially if the spill is not cleaned up immediately and thoroughly. The acids in the soft drink eat right through many electronic components with remarkable efficiency.

Most liquids (unless highly deionized) also are pretty good conductors, and the physical nature of a liquid causes it to simultaneously touch many (if not all) points in the circuit simultaneously, creating massive short circuits. Because electrical current is diverted to circuit points where it doesn't belong, considerable damage can be done to any sensitive components. Expensive semiconductor devices are extremely sensitive to this type of damage.

The risks of liquids to electronic circuit is bad enough. But the safety risk to any humans (or animals) in the area is even more critical. Again the problem is the natural electrical conductivity of most common liquids, and their tendency to spread and flow everywhere. In all simple flooding alarms, the liquid to be monitored is intentionally made part of the circuit's current path. The sharp decrease in resistance when the liquid is present is what triggers the sensing circuitry. If there is any ac component in the circuit current, there would be a very severe shock hazard. Anyone who touched or stepped into the flooding liquid would receive a very painful shock—if they're lucky. The results could very easily be severe injury or even death.

It should be obvious that an addition to a security system that creates unnecessary dangers of its own is worse than useless; it goes totally against the very intended purpose of any security system—increased safety.

A well thought out and properly installed flooding alarm should present no increased risk. It is extremely vital for the alarm system installer to take the appropriate factors and considerations into account to avoid placing residents of the home at unnecessary risk.

First off, every possible effort must be taken that dc power and dc power **only** be applied to the probes (and hence, the liquid). The shock hazard will come only from an ac power source. The probe circuitry should be powered by batteries **only**. Please do not rely on an ac-to-dc power converter circuit, no matter how fail-safe it might appear to be. There is always the possibility of some unanticipated fault occurring that might feed potentially dangerous ac power through the circuit, creating the possibility of a deadly shock hazard. No matter how slim the chances of this happening might seem, the potential risk is severe enough that it is never worth gambling on. Even a one in a million chance has to come up sometime. Even if you can somehow manage to ignore the moral and possibly even legal ramifications, it certainly wouldn't do your alarm system installation much good if the word gets out that you electrocuted one of your customers.

The possible handiness of using an existing ac-to-dc power supply is simply not worth the potential risk. Ever—not under any circumstances. Only a severely incompetent technician would take such stupid chances.

The other half of the installation problem here is to protect the circuitry. Nothing in the circuit other than the actual probes themselves should be at risk of getting wet during any reasonably predictable flooding situation—that is, the kinds of situations the flooding alarm circuit is intended to guard against. If the circuitry gets wet, it will almost certainly malfunction, and the likelihood of permanent damage is strong. Under some conditions, the erroneous severe short circuit signals might conceivably cause a fire hazard elsewhere in the system.

Of course there can no be any absolute guarantees against unpredictable freak occurrences. In a catastrophic flood like Noah encountered, everything in the house is going to get drenched, and the flooding alarm circuitry would be among the very least of the occupant's worries at that point. By the time the flooding got that severe, it would hardly matter if the alarm system continued to work or not, and a fire is unlikely to break out under water.

More realistically, you can never guarantee that the flooding alarm (or any electronic circuit for that matter) will never get wet in some unpredictable way. Something could get spilled unexpectedly, or a leak can be redirected somehow due to unanticipated circumstances. A simple example is shown in Fig. 7-7. In this example,

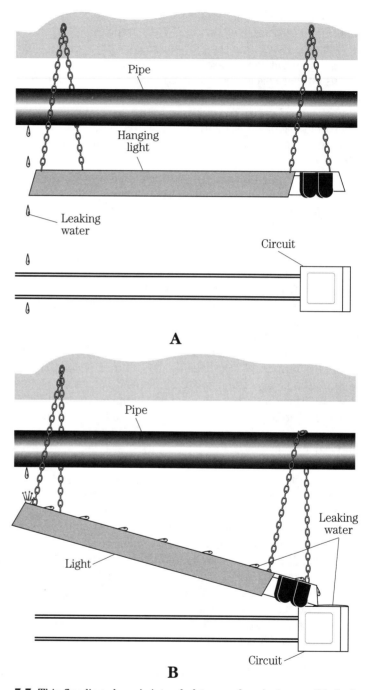

A

B

7-7 This flooding alarm is intended to guard against a possible leak from an overhead pipe (A). If one of the chains on that suspended overhead lighting fixture happened to break just right, the leak could be diverted onto the circuit board (B).

the flooding alarm is intended to guard against a possible leak from an overhead pipe. Ordinarily, as shown in Fig. 7-7(A), if the pipe happens to spring a leak, the water will drop down onto the probes, triggering the alarm, while the rest of the flooding alarm circuit remains some distance away, nice and dry. But what if one of the chains on that suspended overhead lighting fixture happened to break just right to divert the leak onto the circuit board, as shown in Fig. 7-7(B)? No one can reliably predict every freakish possibility, but it is worthwhile for the system installer to take some time to look for as many such possibilities as possible and then take reasonable precautions against them. The best way to correct problems is to prevent them from ever occurring in the first place. Ultimately this is never a completely achievable goal, but it's certainly one worth shooting for. Approach the ideal goal as closely as you can, without being impractically excessive about it. If guarding against a one in a million possible condition would add a couple hundred dollars to the system cost, it probably wouldn't be worthwhile, unless the potential results if the unlikely condition did occur are unusually severe.

Because a flooding alarm circuit, by definition, is likely to be in use in or near an area where flooding might occur, enclosing the circuitry (except the probes themselves, of course) in a relatively water-tight housing would be highly advisable. Use a plastic, rather than metal circuit box, without any loose openings in it. The wires to the probes and to the rest of the system should be passed through grommets that fit as tightly as possible. Leave as little room for water (or other liquids) to pass through as possible.

It might look rather unglamorous, and even a bit unprofessional, but enclosing the entire circuit, plastic housing and all in a plastic bag with its opening tightly taped down around the insulated input and output wires can be very effective at a low cost. This simple but effective technique is shown in Fig. 7-8. This type of water proofing literally costs only pennies. Any alternative of comparable effectiveness would almost certainly cost a lot more. The only real disadvantage is its rather ugly and crude appearance. Fortunately, in most home alarm systems, a flooding alarm circuit is likely to be installed in a location where it is unlikely to be seen much, and even if it is, the appearance is less critical than in most of the home. After all, a flooding alarm will find its greatest use in a storage basement, or a laundry room, which are rarely decorated at all, rather than in a living room.

But even in rare circumstances where the appearance of the flooding alarm might matter, you can still use the inexpensive plastic bag waterproofing trick. Just install the flooding alarm in its actual housing inside the plastic bag as in Fig. 7-8, then enclose the entire thing—bag and all, inside an additional outer case of some sort, as shown in Fig. 7-9. The only purpose of this outer case is aesthetic. It can be designed to look as nice as desired, and to suit any decor. If it is somewhat water proof in itself, great. You can never have too much protection. But even if this outer case isn't water proof at all, it doesn't matter. The circuitry is already protected inside its plastic bag, even if water (or other liquid) gets inside the decorative outer case. For functional purposes, it doesn't matter whether the outer case is there or not, but it might help keep a fussy customer satisfied. Many good technicians get stumped by such problems, and they will go to great effort and expense to try to make the functional elements look good, rather then simply hiding them in a prettier dummy case. When faced with a problem like a customer complaint about a circuit's appearance, it is all too easy to overlook the obvious and easy solution.

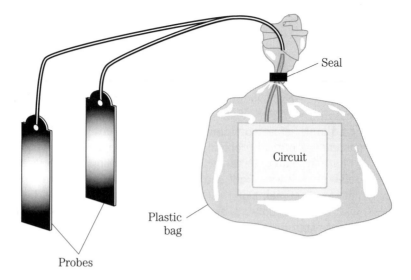

7-8 Enclosing the entire circuit, plastic housing and all in a plastic bag with its opening tightly taped down around the insulated input and output wires can provide very effective and very inexpensive water proofing.

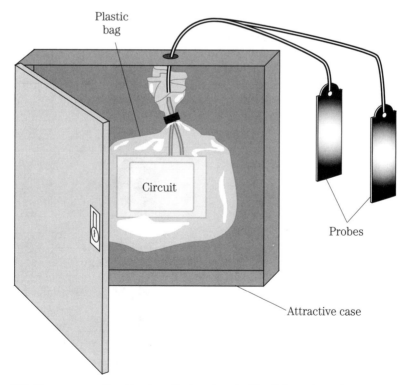

7-9 For a more attractive installation than in Fig. 7-8, enclose the flooding alarm in its actual housing inside the plastic bag; then install this entire assembly inside a more attractive outer case.

Mounting the probes

The most challenging and variable part of installing a flooding alarm is positioning the probes. Positioning will determine the sensitivity and overall effectiveness of the flooding alarm.

Determining the correct positions for a set of flooding probes is really not very difficult. It's just a matter of determining just how much liquid should be permitted into the protected area before sounding the alarm. In some applications, any detected liquid indicates a critical problem, while in other applications, the situation would only be considered an emergency if the monitored liquid exceeds some specific level, for example, if it was about to overflow a storage tank of some sort. Either of these extreme applications, along with everything in between can be achieved quite readily with the same flooding alarm circuit, simply by rearranging the positioning of the probes appropriately.

For most basic home flooding alarm applications, the probes will usually be mounted on an equal level, but this is mostly a matter of neatness and convenience, rather than any technical necessity. The circuitry really doesn't care, and in most cases, an uneven probe placement will not affect the circuit operation in any detectable way. As you should recall, the alarm is sounded when the monitored liquid covers both probes, creating a current path between them. If just one probe is immersed, while the other remains dry, the alarm will not sound. If the probes are not mounted on the same level, the higher probe will determine the flooding alarm's effective trip point, as shown in Fig. 7-10.

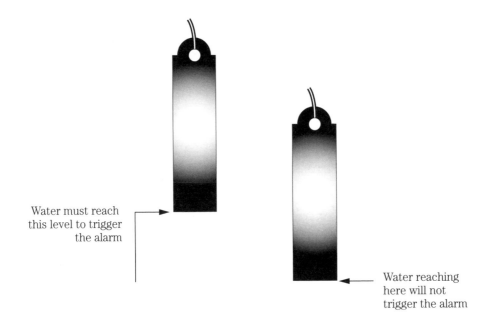

Water must reach this level to trigger the alarm

Water reaching here will not trigger the alarm

7-10 If the probes are not mounted on the same level, the higher probe will determine the flooding alarm's actual trip point.

There is obviously no good reason in a basic flooding alarm application to deliberately mount the probes at differing levels. This mounting wouldn't accomplish much of anything. In most cases, mounting the probes at equal levels will be more aesthetic, and will be less likely to result in any confusion of the actual alarm trip point of the system.

The entire sensing surface of the two probes does not have to be completely covered to trip the alarm, provided enough of each probe is immersed to ensure a solid electrical connection. With a latching alarm system this is not a critical point. Once the sensor circuit is activated, even for just a second or so, the alarm will be turned on, and it will remain on, regardless of what else might happen around the probes. To turn the alarm off, once tripped, the system must be manually (or otherwise) re-set by other means. However, if the alarm is not a latching type, there might be a stability problem if the liquid level is just barely reaching the probes, as shown in Fig. 7-11. If the liquid is totally stationary, with no disturbances, there would be no problem, of course, but in most practical situations, some degree of ebb and flow (or splashing can be expected). At any specific point (including the probe locations), the liquid level can repeatedly rise and fall in a more or less random pattern, as shown in Fig. 7-12. The result would be alarm "chattering." The alarm would be irregularly switched on and off, as indicated in the graph of Fig. 7-13.

7-11
If the alarm is not a latching type, there may be a stability problem if the liquid level is just barely reaching the probes.

For a basic flooding alarm, as part of a complete home security system, this will generally be no more than a technical problem, because the electronic switching circuits in the central control box will almost always be of the latching type. Once the flooding alarm has been triggered, it doesn't matter if the detected liquid splashes around and temporarily uncovers one or the other of the probes from moment to mo-

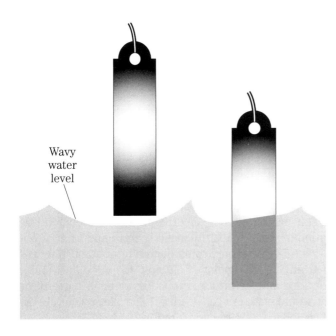

Wavy
water
level

7-12
When the liquid level is
near the threshold point,
the liquid level at any
specific point can
repeatedly rise and fall in a
more or less random
pattern.

On

Off

7-13 Under the conditions shown in Fig. 7-11 and Fig. 7-12, the alarm might "chatter" on and off.

ment. However, it is often useful for a flooding alarm circuit to control some sort of automated "damage control," as well as activate an alarm. For example, if flooding is detected, the circuit could trigger the alarm, and at the same time, activate a sump pump to remove the excess liquid.

The sump pump should not be permitted to run continuously after the problem is corrected. Many types of pumps could be harmed, or at least face premature aging, if permitted to run dry, especially for extended periods of time. So a simple latching type switching circuit would not be so appropriate for this sub-application, even though it is well suited to the actual alarm function.

But, completely unlatched control of the sump pump also can be problematic. If the water bobs about, covering and uncovering the probes (and the action of the pump is likely to contribute to such effects), the pump will be rapidly turned on and off a number of times. This operation is not only very inelegant, and rather annoying, it also would tend to waste power, and place excessive wear and tear on the sump pump motor. Under such abusive operating conditions, many of the pump electro-mechanical parts are liable to wear out much sooner than necessary.

One partial solution is to mount the probes vertically, instead of horizontally, as shown in Fig. 7-14. Horizontal mounting will expose more of the probe's lower sur-

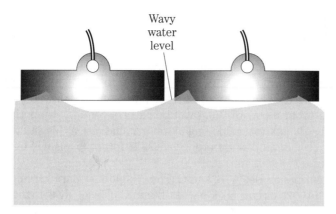

7-14
The bobbing effects of Fig. 7-11 through 7-13 can be reduced by mounting the probes horizontally, instead of vertically.

face to upper edge of the accumulated liquid. But there will still be some inevitable level bobbing, especially with a pump running to remove the liquid, as more liquid is entering the area from whatever leak source.

This sideways mounting of the probes will help, but will scarcely remove the problem altogether. To avoid the possibility of the pump being switched on and off randomly, or running indefinitely, a shutoff timer stage could be added to the system, as shown in Fig. 7-15. This is the same basic idea as the alarm shuoff timer used to automatically silence the alarm after it has been continuously sounding for too long. Once the flooding alarm is triggered, the system alarm will be activated, and the sump pump will be turned on. These two control signal paths are kept separate. The alarm system has its own built-in latch function. The added timer stage only controls the sump pump motor. When flooding is detected by the probes, the timer is triggered, and its output goes HIGH, turning on the sump pump. After a specific predetermined period of time, the timer's output will go LOW again, shutting down the pump motor. If there is still enough liquid to touch both probes, or if flooding resumes at a later time, this timer will be retriggered, activating the sump pump for another timing period.

This solution is a hit-or-miss solution. It's better than nothing, but it's hardly in the high precision class. How long should the timer period be set for? You simply

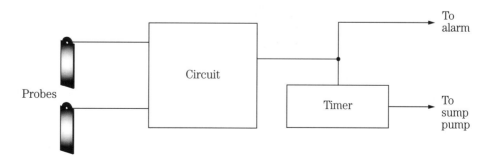

7-15 To avoid the possibility of an automated sump pump being switched on and off randomly, or running indefinitely, a shutoff timer stage could be added to the system.

have to guess. How much liquid do you think the pump will probably have to remove, if its called into action? How can anyone know ahead of time? At least the timer will prevent the potentially on/off oscillations, and the pump won't run dry indefinitely. At worst, the pump won't run longer than the timing period.

A better and more accurate approach would be to use a second flooding alarm circuit, but with this one the output is inverted, to turn the pump off. In this system, there will be a total of three probes. One of them will be used in common by both flooding alarm circuits. Unlike the standard flooding alarm installation, in this situation, the three probes must be mounted at different levels. Different levels will introduce a form a hysteresis into the system.

For convenience, call the three probes A, B, and C. The ON flooding alarm circuit uses probes A and C, while the OFF circuit uses probes B and C. Obviously C is the common probe. The A probe is mounted at a higher level than the B probe, and the C probe is mounted between the other two. A typical probe arrangement is shown in Fig. 7-16.

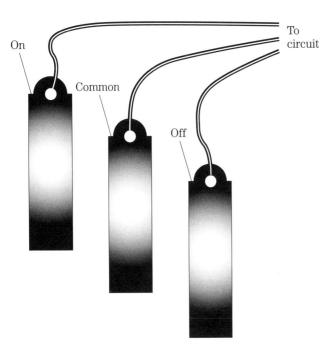

7-16
For a fully automated sump pump controller/flooding alarm, three probes are mounted at unequal levels.

The output of the OFF flooding alarm circuit (probes B and C) drives an electronic switch, which is activated when its trigger signal goes from HIGH to LOW. That is, when this flooding alarm circuit goes from its activated to its deactivated state. A block diagram of the entire multistage flooding alarm system is shown in Fig. 7-17.

Initially, assume the area is dry. The pump is off, and the alarm is silent. Now, let's suppose a leak occurs, and the area starts to fill with water. At first, nothing happens. The water level rises until it creates a current path between probes B and C. The sensing circuitry in the OFF flooding alarm will be activated, but nothing will

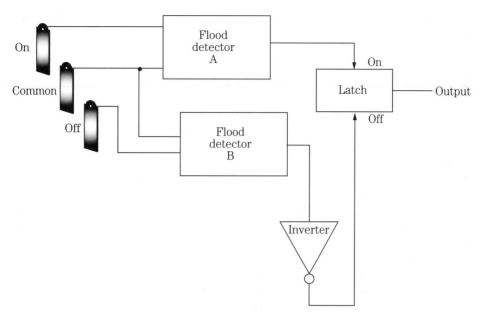

7-17 This is a block diagram for an entire multistage flooding alarm system.

happen, because the output of this circuit goes only to the electronic switch, which ignores anything but a HIGH-to-LOW transition. At this point, there is a LOW-to-HIGH transition, which has no effect.

If the water level then subsides for some reason, without going any higher, the lower flooding alarm circuit will be deactivated, causing a HIGH-to-LOW transition, triggering the electronic switch, which sends a signal out to turn off the pump. Because the pump is already off, there will still be no effect. So far you just have a lot of wasted effort accomplishing nothing in particular.

Now assume the water level in the protected area continues to rise. Probes B and C are already immersed. Eventually, the water level will rise up to probe A, creating a current path between probes A and C, and activating the upper flooding alarm circuit. Now things start to happen. The output signal from this flooding alarm circuit goes to two places. It sends a remote signal out to the main alarm system's central control box to sound the alarm, and it sends out a control signal to turn on the sump pump. The sump pump starts removing water from the flooded area.

What happens if the water level bobs and drops enough to expose all of probe A. There would now be no current path between probes A and C, and this flooding alarm circuit will be deactivated. But this will have no functional effect. The upper flooding alarm circuit can turn on the sump pump, but it can't turn it off. The central control box will have latched itself, so the alarm will continue to sound until the main shut down timer stage times out, or the system is manually reset. Once the flooding alarm system as a unit is triggered, probe A is effectively out of the picture. Whether this probe remains under water or is exposed will make no difference to the sounding alarm or the sump pump once it has done its job of activating the system in the first place.

If the leak is severe and continuing, more water will be coming in as the sump pump is removing it. Hopefully the sump pump will be able to remove water faster than it can flood into the area, but at worst, the sump pump will help hold the flooding level more or less constant, or, at least significantly slow down its rising rate. With luck someone will respond to the alarm and be able to correct the situation before too much damage is done.

Assume the best now for purposes of discussion. Either no more water is coming in, or the new water is coming in much slower than the pump is removing the water already present. In either event, the water level in the protected area has to be going down. Probe A will be completely exposed first, but that won't accomplish anything. When the water level drops below probe C, the lower (OFF) flooding alarm circuit will be deactivated, finally putting out a HIGH-to-LOW transition to trigger the electronic switch. The output from the electronic switch circuit is a signal that turns off the sump pump, now that the water level has been reduced to an acceptable point.

If more water is coming in, the water level will obviously start to rise again, now that the sump pump has been turned off. Everything works just as before. If the water level rises enough to immerse probes B and C, there will be no effect, but if it rises enough to immerse probe A as well, the pump will be turned on again. (The alarm is presumedly still sounding from before, or it can be reactivated if necessary, depending on the timing involved, and the specifics of the main security system.)

As you can see, just a little creative ingenuity can help a home security system not only warn against potentially dangerous problems, but it can even play an active part in correcting such problems as they occur.

For a home flooding alarm, the ideal is a liquid level of zero. Any water in the wrong place is too much. A flooding alarm's probes should be mounted as low as physically possible. Thus far, you have been assuming the probes were always mounted somewhere above the floor, and they often are in practical installations, but that doesn't always have to be the case. In many home installation situations, the probes can be mounted flat on the floor. The closer they are to one another, the more sensitive the alarm will be. If the probes are a couple of feet apart, the flooding alarm will only respond if the leak is sufficient to more or less cover the floor, but if the probes are mounted only an inch or two apart, even a fairly small puddle from a leak could set off the alarm. Of course, this will only work if you can make an accurate guess as to where a leak is likely to be. If you guess wrong, the alarm will not be set off until the puddle grows large enough to make contact with the two probes.

(For the three-probe automated sump pump control system described, probes B and C can be mounted flat on the floor, but probe A must be mounted at a slightly higher level, or the pseudo-hysteresis system will not work properly. This limitation should not be considered a major limitation, because a sump pump won't be of much practical value unless there is at least an inch or two of standing water in the area. It won't be able to accomplish much against minor flooding that just barely gets the floor wet.)

Floor-mounted flooding probes should be as flat as possible, and well secured all around to avoid the possibility of someone tripping over it. Remember, the most likely location for a flooding alarm in most homes is in a storage basement, which is likely to be poorly lit, and it's a good bet that anyone down there might be carrying a load that could obstruct their vision of the floor. Always put safety first.

Many basements include a built-in floor drain, as a crude form of minimal flooding protection. Usually there will be a slight rake to the floor so the drain is at the lowest point, so any standing water will eventually be drawn to and out the drain. In most cases, mounting the flooding alarm probes near such a drain would make good sense. This location is one where any flooding in the basement can be expected to reach, whatever its source. Additional flooding alarms can be mounted at specific high risk locations, such as under a major pipe junction, to offer quicker response to certain flooding conditions.

For most simple home installations, an appropriate choice might be to place one probe on either side of the drain, as shown in Fig. 7-18. A small, inconsequential spill or minor leak will eventually seep to the drain from one side or the other, as shown in Fig. 7-19, but it will not set off the alarm. Only one of the probes will probably get wet under such conditions, and because there is little likelihood of significant or preventable damage, there's no point in setting off the alarm. Anything that was going to be damaged by a minor spill has already gotten wet (and damaged) before the liquid reached the drain and flooding alarm probes. In this arrangement, the flooding alarm will only be activated if the flooding is extensive enough that the built-in drain can't handle it.

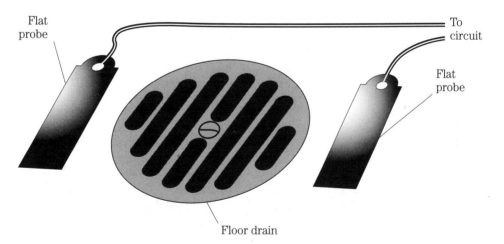

7-18 For most home basement installations, the probes should be mounted on either side of the floor drain.

If critical items are stored in the basement, however, or if the customer is particularly worried about flooding damage for whatever reason, the flooding alarm can be made a bit more sensitive by surrounding the drain with multiple probes wired in parallel, as shown in Fig. 7-20. There is no need for any additional circuitry here. In effect, you are simply breaking each probe into physical subsections, while electrically it continues to function as a whole. The flooding alarm will be set off in this case

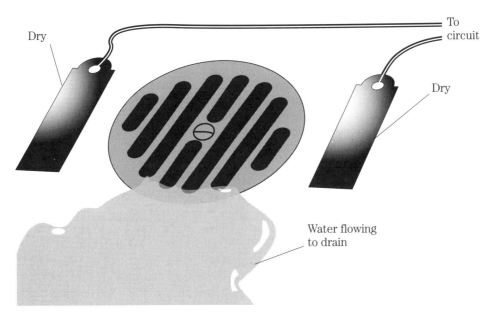

Dry

To circuit

Dry

Water flowing to drain

7-19 A small spill or minor leak will eventually seep to the drain from one side or the other, but it might not set off the alarm.

if any flooding liquid creates a current path between any one or more of the A probes, and any one or more of the B probes.

Almost any conductive material can be used for the probes, but keep in mind that it should not be a material that will be quickly damaged or destroyed by any anticipated liquid it is intended to monitor. For most home alarm system installations, the liquid of interest will be simple (although probably dirty) water, so the probe material should be relatively immune to water-related warpage or rust. Often the cheapest, most convenient, and most reliable choice is strips of copper clad board, like the unetched boards sold for making homemade printed circuit boards.

What kind of alarm is needed?

For an intrusion or fire alarm, it makes good sense to use something loud, and that will be unmistakably heard even some distance away outside. Often it is necessary for a neighbor to summon emergency help (the police or the fire department). A flooded basement is generally a much lesser emergency, so use of the full outdoor alarm would probably be excessive. In some flood-prone older homes, the flooding alarm might be set off with some frequency, which is likely to cause strife among neighbors if a disturbingly loud outdoor alarm is used. Most people are more understanding about a falsely triggered fire or burglar alarm than they would be about even a legitimately triggered flooding alarm, especially if it happens often. After all, if your basement floods, what do you really expect your neighbors to be able to do about it? Call a plumber for you?

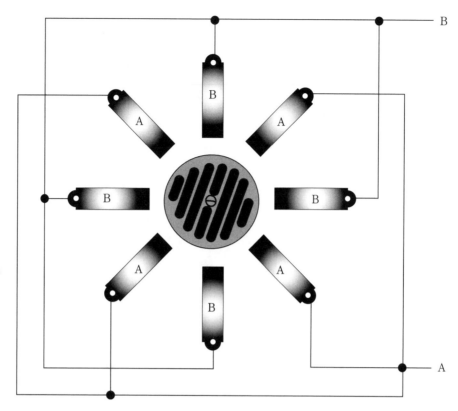

7-20 In critical installations, multiple probes can be mounted around the drain and wired in an alternating parallel fashion.

In this book, it is mentioned that it can be very helpful to use different sounding alarm signals for a detected intrusion than for a detected fire, so the occupants of the home will know what emergency procedures to follow. If the home alarm system is designed to be sophisticated enough to permit different sounding alarms, use a third type of signal for the flooding alarm. Only smaller, indoor output alarm devices or visual alarm indicators should be used in the event of a detected flooding condition. If someone is at home at the time the flooding occurs, they will be alerted to correct the situation, if possible, or at least attempt to retrieve as many stored items from the flooded area as possible before they are damaged by the water. If no one is at home at the time, the alarm won't do much good, but there is unlikely to be much improvement in the actual results, even if the entire neighborhood is forced to listen to the flooding alarm.

A centrally located latching visual indicator or very low-volume audible device, such as a small buzzer or oscillator, would be a good idea for use with a flooding alarm, in addition to the larger general-purpose output alarm devices throughout the house. If someone is home, they will hear and can respond to one of the regular indoor alarm devices. If no one is at home, the alarm system shut down timer will eventually disable the main alarms, but the centrally located latching device should not be automatically reset. This way, when the occupants return home, they can tell right away that flooding has occurred, and probably still needs attention.

8

CHAPTER

Regular maintenance

Any electronic system, and especially one that has electromechanical components, requires periodic preventive maintenance to keep it functioning properly at its peak capabilities and to minimize the need for repairs and troubleshooting problems. Fortunately, most home alarm systems do not require extensive maintenance procedures. You can instruct the customer in regular maintenance, or you can contract to return to the installation periodically for routine maintenance. A six-month or one-year maintenance schedule is sufficient in most cases unless there are special circumstances.

Cleaning

A home alarm system uses a lot of electromechanical devices with small moving parts. Most of the sensors fall into this category. Dirt can be a problem for any such device. Accumulated dust and grime can interfere with the operation of any electromechanical switch. A regular program of periodic cleaning can help minimize the chances for erratic operation or even complete system failure.

Fortunately, most of the electromechanical sensors used in home alarm systems are not too complicated or difficult to clean. Some, such as magnetic reed switches, don't really need to be cleaned. In fact, a magnetic reed switch can't be cleaned, because the switching unit is hermetically sealed. The housing should be wiped clean occasionally with a slightly dampened cloth, just for the sake of appearances. The magnet unit definitely should be cleaned periodically. Too much accumulated gunk, especially metallic gunk, could reduce the effective magnetic field. Obviously, such cleaning of magnetic reed switches is especially important if they are mounted outdoors or in a frequently dirty or smoky environment. Any magnetic reed switch mounted near a fireplace or a coal or gas heating vent will probably require more frequent cleaning. Air conditioning vents or fans can also blow airborne dust particles around, and some will adhere to the magnetic reed switches.

In most cases, such cleaning only needs to be done when the magnetic reed switches start to look dirty. A very visible coating of built-up crud would usually be needed before functional problems would show up. As it happens, commercial magnetic reed switches are white or light colored, making accumulated dirt easily visible.

Periodic cleaning is much more critical for sensors that have some or all of their switching mechanism exposed to air. Dirt can get into the smallest of openings. It can often be difficult to get inside a switching unit to clean it directly. Even if you could manage this, the small parts are often very delicate and easy to bend or break, sometimes even with what seems like an incredibly light and gentle touch. Fortunately, direct scrubbing is almost never called for. If the mechanism is that dirty, the entire device should probably be replaced.

A simple and inexpensive, but effective, cleaning tool for small mechanisms is a rubber or plastic bulb with a small nozzle. Squeezing the bulb forces a burst of air out the nozzle, which can be directed where it is needed to blow the dirt out of the way, as shown in Fig. 8-1. When the bulb is released, the vacuum inside will suck in more air for the next squeeze. Because most of the dirt that gets into such mechanisms started out as airborne dust particles, it is light enough to blow away with a small puff of air unless it has been left long enough to accumulate and cake on. This cleaning just takes a couple of seconds and requires very little effort. It is unlikely to do any damage.

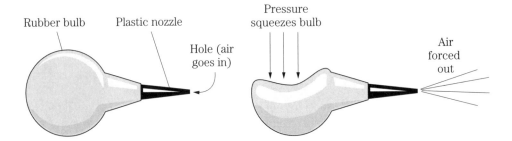

Rubber bulb   Plastic nozzle   Pressure squeezes bulb

Hole (air goes in)   Air forced out

8-1 A rubber or plastic bulb with a small nozzle can be used to blow dirt out of tight spaces.

For more thorough cleaning, use a can of tuner cleaner spray, sold by Radio Shack, many hardware stores, and most electronics distributors. A can of tuner cleaner typically costs only about $1.50 to $2.50, and it should last well over a year, even if it is used on all the electronic equipment throughout the house.

Tuner cleaner is a gentle cleansing compound designed specifically for electronic and electromechanical parts. It comes in an aerosol can, and a thin straw is provided to direct the spray into the small space usually called for. A can of aerosol cleaner is shown in Fig. 8-2.

Batteries

Greatest security can be achieved by an alarm system that uses ac power with battery back-up. If ac power fails or is interrupted for any reason, the batteries take

8-2
Tuner cleaner or contact cleaner comes in aerosol cans. A thin straw is provided to direct the spray into small spaces.

over. It is all too easy to forget about the batteries over time. Forgetting about the batteries can lead to system failure, possibly at the most critical time.

Although battery technology has enjoyed significant improvements in recent years, it is still essential to acknowledge that sooner or later, any battery will need replacement. No practical battery can hold a charge indefinitely. Eventually its stored current will be used up. Even batteries stored on the shelf, with no current drain at all, eventually are depleted. The surrounding air does not have infinite resistance; although it is extremely high, resistance of air is approximately hundreds of megohms. In effect, a battery sitting on the shelf is part of a circuit including a very high phantom resistor, as shown in Fig. 8-3. A small, but real current is constantly drawn from the battery, no matter what you do. Eventually, all of the battery's available current will be used up, leaving a dead and useless battery.

In a home alarm system, the batteries are used only for back-up. So, there is little or no dc (direct current) drain by the circuit itself. The battery will be subjected only to the unavoidable shelf leakage current drain. The back-up battery in a home alarm system should last as long as the same type of battery stored unused. Modern batteries have much better shelf life than earlier devices. Today, the shelf life of most batteries is typically about one to five years. This expected lifespan is not from the date of installation, but from the manufacture of the battery. Many technicians tend to forget this fact. Any time the battery spends stored in a warehouse, on a dealer's shelf, or in your own supply bin, counts as part of the lifespan. Some batteries today are marked with expiration dates, but many aren't. Usually you can only guess the age of an unmarked battery. When in doubt, assume the battery is older.

Remember, a battery's rated expiration date is always just an approximation. There are a great many variables that can affect the actual lifespan of any battery. For example, the resistance of the surrounding air will vary with humidity, tempera-

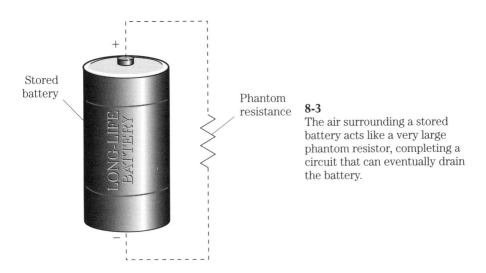

Stored battery

Phantom resistance

8-3
The air surrounding a stored battery acts like a very large phantom resistor, completing a circuit that can eventually drain the battery.

ture, and other climatic factors. Changing the resistance will alter the current drain rate. Also, slight impurities in the active chemicals inside the battery will have an effect on the actual lifespan of each individual battery. In other words, treat a manufacturer's specification date conservatively. Consider it a realistic but optimistic average. For example, assume you have a battery stamped with an expiration date three years and seven months from today. Just to be on the safe side, assume the battery's expiration date is just three years from today's date. It's better to replace a critical battery a little sooner than necessary than to wait until it is too late and the battery actually dies.

An important part of maintenance for a home alarm system is to give the customer a calendar indicating regular dates to check or replace the batteries. Checking the back-up batteries isn't too difficult. Simply remove the ac power and test the system. If it works with ac power disconnected, then the batteries must still be good. For greater accuracy, measure the voltage of each battery. It might be barely functional, still able to put out the minimum voltage, but the battery won't last long. It can be misleading to test a battery without a load. Test it under current drain—that is, while it is actively powering the alarm system. Many customers will be too averse to technology or otherwise unwilling to go through the battery test. Such customers should be advised to simply replace the batteries on the dates shown on the calendar. If the schedule is well thought out, there won't be that much more wasted expense, even if the batteries are replaced more frequently. Despite a little more expense, routinely replacing the back-up batteries even without testing is not at all a bad idea. This practice will give the best system reliability. Any testing will have a certain amount of doubt. The battery might soon go bad after the testing period. Replacing the batteries more frequently would not be a major expense. Of course the system should be designed to use easy-to-find, low-cost batteries whenever possible. Use standard sizes such as AA or D cells or 9 V (volt) transistor batteries unless there is a very compelling reason to use something else. Don't make battery maintenance any more difficult for your customers than it needs to be.

Periodic maintenance calls

Home alarm system installation is a business that more than any other depends on word-of-mouth recommendations. This means customer satisfaction is absolutely vital, and not just in the short term. An alarm system will presumedly be in use for years. Customer dissatisfaction later can be as harmful to your business as dissatisfaction with the initial installation. It is obviously in your professional interest to make sure your customers' systems continue to operate properly long after the installation.

Responding promptly and courteously to service calls is a given. An alarm system installer who doesn't deal with service calls well is unlikely to remain in business for long. Smart alarm system installers will go even further and make arrangements for periodic preventive maintenance calls, hopefully nipping potential problems in the bud.

Preventive maintenance calls should include but should not be limited to the simple cleaning and battery checking procedures discussed in this chapter. The customer can do those things, and they don't require your expertise. Preventive maintenance calls will generally be less frequent than recommended cleaning procedures. For the average home alarm system, a good schedule would be preventive maintenance calls once every six months for the first two years, then once a year, or once every two years (depending on the complexity of the system) after that. The first few preventive maintenance calls should be included as part of the initial installation cost. After that, a contract arrangement with the customer for further preventive maintenance calls can be set up.

With proper planning and organization, a typical preventive maintenance should only take about an hour or two at the most, unless problems requiring significant repairs are found. With good advance planning, you should be able to do about half a dozen such calls in a day. Essentially, the preventive maintenance procedure simply repeats the final system check-out procedures that should have been the last part of the original installation. These check-out procedures are discussed in another chapter.

In addition, the preventive maintenance should include extensive and careful cleaning of all relevant components in the system. The professional technician can open housings and do more delicate and thorough cleanings than can the average customer.

It would be very foolish for you not to check all back-up batteries while you're at it.

As you can see, a typical home alarm system does require some periodic preventive maintenance to ensure reliability and peak performance, but this maintenance need not be difficult or time consuming. The important thing is to schedule appropriate preventive maintenance measures right from the start and make sure they get done. It's the best way to keep your customers happy and recommending your services to their friends, neighbors, and relatives.

9
CHAPTER

Troubleshooting problems

No electronic system is perfect or 100% reliable. Sooner or later, you can expect something to go wrong, and repairs will be needed. To maximize customer satisfaction, it is vital for the home alarm system installer to respond to all service calls as promptly and efficiently as possible. All service calls involving a security system must be regarded as emergencies. Complete security is never a trivial matter, especially to your customers. Carelessness about post-installation servicing is the surest ticket for an alarm installation company to go out of business quickly. Word-of-mouth recommendations are truly the life blood of this business.

In some ways, home alarm systems are among the easiest types of electronics systems to troubleshoot and repair. In other ways, they are among the toughest and most frustrating. Except for computer-based systems (discussed in another chapter), the circuitry in a home alarm system is typically simple and straightforward. There are relatively few things that can go wrong with the circuitry. Even before you begin, you know there are only a very limited number of possible problems you need to look for. On the other hand, a typical home alarm system incorporates a large number of these individually simple circuits, often in a fairly complex, interacting network that is spread out over quite a large area. In a sense, when you are troubleshooting a home alarm system, you are dealing with a circuit the size of a house. It's usually relatively easy to determine and repair the specific cause of the problem, once you've located just where the problem actually is. Locating the problem can sometimes be a little tricky.

Another complication involved in troubleshooting and repairing home alarm systems is that many, if not most, common problems that are likely to occur in such a system are intermittent in nature. A continuous problem is usually relatively easy to find, because it is always there. You know it will be there when you look for it. An intermittent problem comes and goes. It is difficult, if not impossible, to track down the source of the problem when the problem isn't happening while you are looking for it. The troubleshooter has to either wait, keeping fully alert, until the problem shows up then quickly track it down before it disappears again, or stress the system in some way to attempt to force the fault to become permanent. The latter option is not always practical or possible, especially in alarm systems. If you knew where to stress the system, and what stress was needed, you'd probably already have the problem roughly isolated.

This chapter considers a number of issues related to troubleshooting and serving home alarm systems. Because the actual circuitry can vary so much in such systems, it is impossible to cover specifics meaningfully in a book such as this. However, a trained technician should be able to troubleshoot most subcircuits found in home alarm systems down to the component level without much trouble. The emphasis here is on techniques for determining just which subcircuit contains the fault to be repaired.

There are only a handful of basic problems or symptoms that are likely to show up in a typical home alarm system, simplifying the troubleshooting process considerably.

Troubleshooting questions

The first step in troubleshooting any system (electronic or otherwise) is to ask a series of questions to localize the actual problem as much as possible before even touching any test equipment. The basic principles behind the troubleshooting questions in this section apply to any electronics servicing, but the specific questions are focused on the nature of home alarm systems.

The first important question to consider in any troubleshooting process is just what is the problem, exactly. Be as specific as possible. No one can fix what's wrong unless they're absolutely sure about just what is wrong. Consider specifically what part (or parts) of the alarm system are involved. Take the time also to examine what in the system is working correctly. This check might seem like an unnecessary step, but it can be a real time saver, providing important clues for the troubleshooting process. Determining what portions of the system are working correctly almost always eliminates a number of possibilities. Don't waste effort making tests and looking for the source of the problem in a functional portion of the system.

Because a typical home alarm system consists of so many interconnected stages or subcircuits, a block diagram is almost an essential tool for efficient troubleshooting. Without a good block diagram, it's all too easy to miss something, even something that should seem obvious. If you (or your company) originally installed the system, you should have copies of the block diagrams and other paperwork from the system design in your files for that customer. As you can see, it is very important to keep extensive customer files on each system installation you do. Filing a lot of paperwork might not be much fun or interesting work, but it can save a lot of time and expense when later troubleshooting is required.

If the original design paperwork is not available for some reason, you will have to draw up your own troubleshooting block diagram, which will probably include a number of educated guesses. For example, the original installation might have been done by another company that has since gone out of business. Fortunately, most home alarm systems follow pretty standard patterns. Discuss the system features and special functions with the customer as extensively as possible. You should be able to make a reasonable guess of roughly how any given feature was probably implemented in the system. Your after-the-fact block diagram might be wrong on a number of specific details, but if you have a thorough understanding of home security systems you should be able to draw up a crudely accurate representation of the system. At least it can serve as a rough road map to help you narrow down the likely location(s) for the source of the problem.

Consider a fairly typical example, referred to several times throughout this section. A block diagram of the system is shown in Fig. 9-1. In this system, an outdoor keypad is mounted by the front door to permit the legitimate residents to enter a security code to disarm the alarm system so they can open the front door and go inside, without setting off the alarm. The customer's complaint is that the alarm sometimes goes off, even when the security code has been entered. The customer has had to run to the central control box to disarm the system and reset the alarm on several occasions.

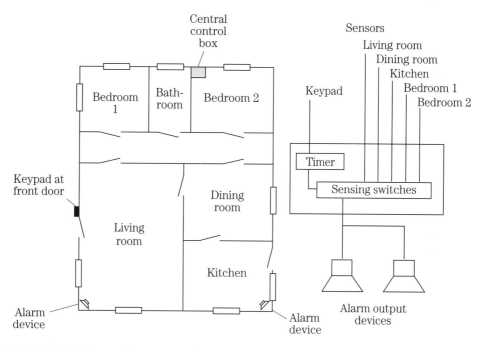

9-1 This typical home alarm system is mentioned in most of the examples in this section.

Obviously, the sensors in the other parts of the house are irrelevant to the problem at hand, and the front door sensor is clearly doing its job, or the alarm wouldn't be set off at all when it is opened. Similarly, you know without question that the output alarm device is working just fine—the alarm definitely sounds off as it should. Looking at the block diagram, you can see three likely possible sources for the problem. The most obvious of these is the decoding circuitry for the security disarm code. It seems clear that this circuit is not responding to the correct security code as it is supposed to do. But just because this seems obvious, that doesn't necessarily mean it is what is actually happening. It is also possible that the decoding circuitry is not receiving the correct security code at all, so the circuitry really is doing its job correctly.

The second suspected subsection of the system is the keypad, and the wires connecting it to the decoding circuit. Assuming a numerical keypad is used, it is possible that (for example) the *2* key is defective, or there is an intermittent break in one of the wires for this key, as shown in Fig. 9-2. If 2 is part of the security code, this signal might not be able to get through to the decoding circuitry at all. As far as the decoding circuitry is concerned, the 2 key was never pressed. The incompletely entered (from the decoding circuit's point of view) registers as an incorrect entry, and the system is not disarmed. The decoding circuitry can't tell the difference.

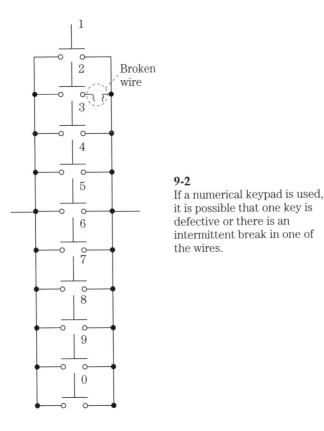

9-2
If a numerical keypad is used, it is possible that one key is defective or there is an intermittent break in one of the wires.

The third possible location for the trouble is not actually shown on the block diagram, but it must always be assumed. The possible trouble is the customer (and any other legitimate resident of the house). It is possible that the security code is not being entered correctly. Perhaps someone is in a hurry and carelessly punching one or more wrong keys. Perhaps they have not remembered the code correctly. In the example problem, an important question to ask the customer is whether the problem seems to affect all members of the household with roughly equal frequency, or does it always seem to happen for one person only?

If the system features a programmable security code (rather than one that is permanently hard wired), it is possible that someone has deliberately or inadvertently reprogrammed the code. In a household with children, little fingers often push buttons if they can reach them. In some circuits, a freakish spike on the power lines might conceivably confuse part of the programmed code, although this is unlikely. Spikes have changed security codes on several actual installations. Such potential problems suggest that a user programmable security code might not be a truly desirable feature in a home alarm system. On the other hand, periodically changing the security code might help offset a breach of security, if some unauthorized person has determined the existing security code. Also some customers might feel safer if even the system installer does not know their security code. Unfortunately, if they forget their code, they can't call the installer for help. Whether the installer should have the code is a judgment call. For most home security systems, a hard-wired security code that can be changed only by a technician with access to the interior of the system's central control box will almost always be the safest and most practical choice. If the security code is inadvertently revealed, or must be changed for some other reason, the customer can call for a service call. If the system is properly designed, this should be just a few minutes of simple, clear-cut work for a technician and should be only a minimal expense.

To return to the example, the block diagram helped isolate the problem to just three likely locations, as shown in Fig. 9-3. Only the relevant stages are shown in this new, simplified block diagram. You can ignore the rest of the system in the troubleshooting process, unless all three of these possible trouble locations are conclusively ruled out during later tests and examination. In that case, the entire system must be reexamined more thoroughly to try to ferret out some other (presumedly less likely) possibility that was overlooked the first time around. Overlooking a problem in a thorough troubleshooting procedure is unlikely, considering the nature of

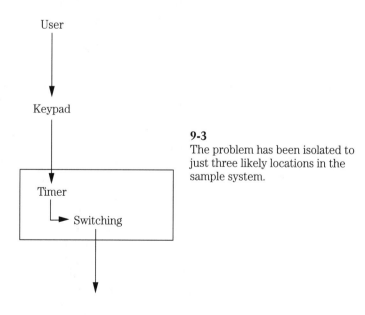

9-3
The problem has been isolated to just three likely locations in the sample system.

home alarm systems and their potential problems. However, you never know when an unpredictable "tough dog" oddity might crop up.

Another vital question to ask near the beginning of the troubleshooting process is whether the problem is continuous or intermittent. That is, is it always there, or does it just show up sometimes? As stated earlier, most problems with home alarm systems are likely to be intermittent. This is because most of the time, most of the subcircuits and system components are idle, just waiting to be activated. The problem is unlikely to be present when the defective component or circuit is in its idle state. Some home alarm system problems can be considered continuous anyway.

To understand the importance of this question, return to the previous example of the system with the malfunctioning disarming code. Does the problem occur every time anyone attempts to enter the security code, or is the code sometimes accepted by the system and other times not? If the security code sometimes works, you can rule out the possibility that the code has somehow been reprogrammed. On the other hand, if the problem occurs only occasionally, careless entering of the code or a defective key on the keypad seem more likely. In a multiperson household, if the problem only occurs when one specific person attempts to enter the code, it seems highly probable that the person is doing something wrong. But even in such a case, don't be too quick to jump to conclusions. Don't be dogmatic about it, or you might alienate your customer. It might still be an electromechanical problem within the system, and the peculiarities of the laws of chance have just made this one person erroneously appear responsible. Remember, the customer will probably call for service after this program occurs just two or three times. The same person entering the code when the defect activates itself is likely according to the laws of probability. This is especially true if the family schedule makes that one person the one most likely to attempt to disarm the system on a day-to-day basis.

With any intermittent problem, the next step is to examine the intermittence for any possible patterns. When does the problem occur, and when does it not occur? Both parts of this question are equally important. What is common or different to these occasions? (You already considered this to some degree in the example problem when you looked at who was attempting to enter the code when the problem occurs.) Does the problem seem to occur at any particular time? What are the environmental conditions when the problem occurs? Is it hot at these times or cold? Does the problem show up during or shortly after rain? Is the problem more likely when the area is well lit or when it is dark? Look for any environmental clues you can find, even if they don't seem to make any sense at first or have any possible connection to the problem that you can imagine just yet. Of course, some of these clues will prove to be red herrings that have nothing to do with the actual problem. But more often than you might expect, there might well be a connecting factor you haven't discovered yet.

Also consider the system conditions when the problem occurs. What else is happening throughout the system at the same time? In the example of the malfunctioning security code, you might find that each time the problem occurred it was later discovered that a window in a rear bedroom had been forgotten and left open a crack. This situation is one where something that seems irrelevant to the problem might or might not be a clue. In this example, it would be a real puzzler. If the window were open enough to set off the alarm, it should set it off anyway. Entering the disarming code and opening the front door wouldn't seem to have anything to do with it. In this case, it is difficult to explain how these two things could be related, but there might be some little oddity in this system that causes this unexpected link.

Don't just focus on the specific problem that prompted the customer to put in a service call. Consider the system. Is there anything else unusual about the way any other portion of the system is functioning? Sometimes a system might operate oddly but in a way that doesn't bother the customer. Things are still working overall, if a little eccentrically. Often the customer might be completely unaware of certain system problems, which by their nature are invisible to the user, unless one specifically looks for them. Such oddities can provide important clues to the source of the main problem you are attempting to service. But again, avoid jumping to conclusions. Sometimes there might be two or more simultaneous, but unrelated defects. The separate symptoms might be just a coincidence. The coincidence isn't terribly likely, but it always must be recognized as a possibility. If you ignore this possibility, you might find yourself wasting a lot of time, running down blind alleys and hopeless dead ends in your troubleshooting attempts.

Ask the customer just when the problem first presented itself. Were there any special circumstances at that time, or a little earlier? For example, if there was a big electrical storm a day or two before the problem was noticed, the possibility of the problem being caused by lightning or a power surge is strongly suggested (though certainly not guaranteed).

Intermittent problems tend to be common in home alarm systems, and by their come-and-go nature, intermittent problems are tricky to troubleshoot and localize precisely. In some cases, an intermittent problem can be forced to occur or somehow simulated. If you know the special conditions that accompany the malfunction you might be able to get the intermittent malfunction to occur "on command," so you can perform the necessary troubleshooting tests.

Some technicians stress an intermittently troublesome circuit by deliberate overheating, or strong mechanical vibrations, or something similar. The idea is to force the intermittent fault into becoming a continuous one, which will be much easier to troubleshoot and localize. When a system or circuit is stressed, its weakest element is very likely to break down and fail first. It is reasonable to assume that an intermittently faulty component will be weaker than a good one. This procedure is somewhat risky, of course. You could end up causing one or more new faults in the circuit or system adding to the repair. But if you know what you're doing, it can be effective in some cases. Unfortunately, this method is rarely applicable to home alarm systems. Still it is worth mentioning, just in case you should happen to encounter a case where it would apply well.

Typical problems and complaints

Usually, there aren't many things that can go wrong with a typical home alarm system. Certain problems can be difficult to localize within a moderate- to large-size system, but the basic symptom category is more or less limited to just a few possibilities.

If you consider just the main function of an alarm system, there are really just two things that can go wrong (ignoring special features and incidental functions). Either the alarm goes off when it should not do so (false alarms), or it does not go off when it should. Either of these broad symptoms might have many possible causes. Defining the problem more specifically will help narrow the field down considerably. The most likely service calls will come from the first category: that is, the alarm goes off at some time when it's not supposed to. This problem isn't more likely to occur but more likely to be noticed. If the alarm is sounded at some unexpected time, and there is no sign of an attempted intrusion, the customer is going to know something is wrong and will almost surely call for repairs. But if the alarm doesn't go off when a given sensor is tripped, this might not be noticed for some time, if at all. The problem might exist for some time before an occasion requiring the alarm to be sounded occurs. Even if such an occasion occurs, it might not be noticed. By definition, there is no alarm to draw attention to it. The only ways the homeowner will discover this problem is by consciously tripping the defective sensor or subcircuit, or if signs of a successful intrusion (presumedly a burglary) are discovered.

If you do get a service call for an alarm system that fails to go off when it should, you can expect the customer to be pretty upset, and understandably so. The feeling of security the system was supposed to provide will have been seriously disturbed by the discovery of the problem.

If a successful intrusion that does not set off the alarm is discovered after the fact, the circumstances must be carefully examined to determine whether the system is truly defective or merely inadequate. That is, does something need to be repaired, or did the intruder find some way to defeat the alarm system that was not considered and blocked by the design of the system? This question is vitally important because the service call will be very different if something is to be repaired, than if the system is to be modified to correct for an original design oversight. Either way, the customer will almost certainly be justifiably upset, so the person who takes the complaint call and the technician who goes out on the service call will have to be very good at customer relations. Be polite and sympathetic and as helpful as possible. Freely answer all of the customer's questions. Do not attempt to bluff. If you don't know the answer to a given question offhand, admit it and promise to do the necessary research and get back to the customer with the answer as soon as possible. Most people will respect the honesty of a technician who admits she or he doesn't know everything immediately and sometimes has to look something up.

Good customer relation techniques are very important in dealing with any service call, but they are vital in a case such as this, where customer relations have already been badly strained by the circumstances before the call requesting service was ever made. Sending out a technician with any attitude problem on such a service call will virtually guarantee bad word-of-mouth publicity for your company, which will surely hurt your business.

Although false alarm and no alarm problems are the only basic problems a home alarm system can be expected to experience, most practical home security systems have a number of extra features and incidental functions that can develop defects. Aside from false alarm problems, the most common service call for home alarm systems involves problems with the entry/exit delay and/or the arming/disarming control. The example from the previous section fits neatly into this category of complaints.

Many home alarm systems feature user programmable entrance/exit delay timers. This feature is often advertised as a highly desirable feature, although just why it might be so desirable never seems to be explained. There are probably no reasonable situations where such programmability would be of any practical value in a home security system. In fact, it could be a significant liability.

The purpose of the entrance/exit delay timer is to give the legitimate occupants of the house time to leave the house after arming the alarm system, or to enter the house and disarm the system before the alarm is set off. The exact time period is not at all critical as long as it is a practical compromise between long enough for legitimate entrances or exits without uncomfortable haste, too short for any unauthorized intruder to get in and defeat the alarm system or get away with valuable property before being caught by the alarm. As discussed in previous chapters, a time period of 30 to 45 seconds will almost always be used for this function in a home alarm system, unless there is some unusual compelling reason to use some other timing period in that system.

Once the time period is set, the timing period should be left alone. What is to be gained by reprogramming in different timing periods? The only possible advantage of such programmability is that it gives the user a feeling of high-tech power over the system. It is too easy to misprogram the timer so it can't do its job properly. Someone might foolishly set an impractical timing period thinking it's a good idea. The misprogramming might occur inadvertently. Perhaps someone doesn't understand how to program it properly, or children with curious fingers have changed it. Either way, the programmable entrance/exit delay can lower the security offered by the system, but it can't increase it.

To add to the foolishness of this feature, many systems proudly advertise that the entrance/exit delay timer can be programmed down to zero—effectively removing it from the system altogether. If that was a useful choice for that system, why include the timer in the first place? Anything under 20 seconds is too short to be practical, and anything more than about 50 seconds is too long to be secure. The 30-second difference within this acceptable range of practicality will be subtle and unlikely to change within any given system. This type of useless programmability is included in systems only because it is nifty and technically possible to do so. That's not a good enough reason. Unnecessary service calls resulting from improperly programmed entrance/exit timers are virtually guaranteed.

At most, the entrance/exit delay timer should be adjustable only with a technician accessible trimpot (trimmer potentiometer) or similar control inside the central control box, requiring removal of the front panel to adjust the setting. There is really little need for even this much controllability. Because this is not a precision function, standard fixed-value components should be close enough.

Assume the system is using a 555 timer circuit for this function (an inexpensive and popular choice). The formula for the timing period for a 555 timer is:

$$T = 1.1\,RC$$

where T is the timing period in seconds, R is the timing resistance in ohms (Ω), and C is the timing capacitance in farads. Typical component values for this purpose might be 100 μF (microfarads) for C and 390 kΩ (kilohms) for R, The nominal timing period (ignoring component tolerances) is:

$$T = 1.1 \times 390000 \times 0.0001$$

$$= 43 \text{ seconds}$$

This time is within the acceptable range. Do you need to compensate for component tolerances? Not really in this application. The component values can be off by quite a bit without making the timing period unacceptable. Assume both components have 10% tolerances. (Modern, quality components usually have tighter tolerances than this.) The actual timing period can be off, at worst ±20%. The worst cases would be a low timing period of 34.3 seconds to a high timing period of 51.5 seconds. Would there really be that much practical difference in this application? Would anyone really notice the difference without a stopwatch? And these are the worst case possibilities. Such extremes are rare in actual practice.

At most, if you want to be a bit more precise, you can temporarily connect the timing resistor to the circuit with clips, then measure the actual timing period with a stop watch. If you don't like the measured timing period for whatever reason, just try a different resistor. Once you find a resistor that gives an acceptable timing value, permanently solder it into the circuit and forget about it. Once a good timing period is found there is no reason to change it. Adjustability or programmability simply are not needed. They can only cause problems, without offering any real-world benefit.

Another common service call for a home alarm system might involve failure of the alarm shutoff timer (which should always be included in every alarm system in any residential area). The most probable complaint would be that the timer fails completely and never shuts the alarm off or shuts it off almost immediately. All of the comments made in the previous sections about entrance/exit delay timers apply here, only more so. The only difference is that the system shutoff timer will be set for a much longer timing period (15 to 30 minutes), and the need for precision is, if anything, even lower here. As long as the alarm sounds long enough to summon help, but doesn't keep going long enough to be a public nuisance and disturbance of the peace, the shutoff timer can be considered to be working properly. A difference of a few minutes one way or the other will be irrelevant in any practical sense. Again, it is ridiculous to make this timing period user programmable. That's just asking for trouble and problems that defeat the entire purpose of including the shutoff timer in the system in the first place.

A seemingly related problem is a chirping or stuttering alarm. In this condition, the alarm periodically emits a brief burst of sound, typically less than a second long. There might be a single chirp, or a string of closely spaced chirps. Usually the problem will come and go, apparently at random and for no identifiable reason. Such a problem probably has nothing to do with the shutoff timer circuit. The most likely causes are an intermittent short somewhere between the output circuitry of the central control box and the output alarm sounding device, or this RF (radio frequency) interference or some other form of power spikes appearing along the connecting wires. If there are multiple alarm sounding devices in the system, it shouldn't be too difficult to localize the problem at least approximately. If only one of several alarm output devices is chirping, the problem must logically be somewhere that can affect only that one unit. On the other hand, if all the alarm devices in the system are chirping, the problem is more likely to be close to or in the central control box.

Interference from RF in the area can be difficult to remove, even if the source can be identified, which isn't always possible. If you can identify the equipment that is creating the interference, you might or might not be able to eliminate or at least reduce the interference at the source, which should take care of the problem. Otherwise, about all you can do in most cases is shield the connecting wires. Remember, any length of wire can act as an RF antenna. You might have to replace some or all of the wiring with shielded cable. Replacement will rarely be necessary, but it could come up, especially in areas with a lot of heavy electrical equipment or radio transmitters.

A less likely, but still possible problem is the alarm system causing RF interference to nearby radio or television receivers. Causing such interference can result in some heavy fines, so such problems must be detected and corrected as soon as possible. Because only low-speed switching is involved in most home alarm systems, RF interference generation is unlikely to be a problem, except in computer-based systems. The high-frequency digital signals in a computer system can create a lot of RF interference unless they are properly shunted to ground and/or shielded. Grounding and shielding is pretty much a standard part of modern electronics, and it would not be practical to go into detail here. It's just important to be aware of the possibility, however unlikely, to avoid potential legal problems.

Of course any electrically powered system can experience power failure for any of a variety of reasons. Complete power failure is relatively unlikely in a home alarm system, because battery back-up is used. If the ac power is interrupted for any reason, the batteries should take over. However, in some systems, this might not be noticed for some time, and it is conceivable that if the condition is caused by a failure in the system power supply circuit, it could last long enough for the batteries to become discharged, leaving a dead system. A well-designed system will have an indicator on the central control panel that lights up when the batteries are being used. Except when the alarm is actually sounding, the current drain of an alarm system will typically be low, so the system should continue to operate on battery power for weeks or even months.

Faults in alarm system power supplies are no different than any other power-supply problems. Look first for blown fuses or popped circuit breakers. Check for short circuits or broken conductors. A voltage regulator IC or a pass transistor could be blown, but this will almost always be caused by a short circuit. Correct short circuits before the damaged component is replaced, or it will quickly be in the same state as the original defective unit.

Many home alarm systems include a trickle charger to make sure the batteries are charged when they are needed. As long as ac power is reaching the system, a small charge is fed into the batteries. If the batteries in such a system are weak or dead when called into use (or when they are periodically tested), there might be something wrong with the trickle charger circuit.

Another power-supply problem is excessive power consumption. Unless the alarm is set off frequently for extended periods, a typical home alarm system should make no noticeable impact on the homeowner's electric bill. In most cases, the power consumed by the system in an entire month probably won't be enough to even show up on the power company's meter. Occasionally, however, a defective alarm system might mysteriously start eating an excessive amount of power. Unusual power consumption should be considered an extra emergency, (even though all alarm system problems should be considered emergencies) because it could be a potentially dangerous condition, which could lead to a fire or a dangerous electrical shock hazard.

Excessive power consumption in a home alarm system is almost certainly due to a short circuit somewhere within the system. It is most likely near the power supply, or in the central control box. It is unlikely to be in any of the sensor loops, because in a normally open loop it would probably set off the alarm, and in a normally closed loop it would probably prevent the alarm from sounding when a sensor in that loop was tripped. It is vaguely possible that a short in a sensor loop might cause excessive power consumption problems under some conditions, but it is very unlikely.

The least critical problem with a home alarm system would be one with a display or indicator defect. Such a problem could be inconvenient and awkward, but in itself it should not get in the way of normal system operation or create any dangerous situation. It should be repaired as soon as possible, of course, but it doesn't need to be treated as an absolute emergency.

Most commonly the problem will be with the indicator device. Indicator lamps can burn out. It is often forgotten, but LEDs can burn out too, although this occurs much less frequently. Excessive current flow can prematurely burn out a lamp or LED, but either type of visual indicator can burn out on its own from age, accumulated fatigue, or a previously unnoticed minor manufacturing defect.

Before replacing an indicator device, check out the immediately surrounding circuitry to determine if there might be an excessive current flow that caused the burn out. Look for shorts or cracked or discolored components. A current-limiting resistor might have shorted out or changed value. If it has opened, the lamp or LED will not light, even though it is not truly burned out. No power can reach it through the opened resistor.

Usually there won't be much circuitry to check out. Often it will be nothing but the current limiting resistor and the connecting wires. Other than that, just make sure the output of the circuit driving the indicator device is putting out an appropriate signal. Again, if this signal is absent or incorrect, the indicator device can't be expected to light when it is supposed to.

Display or indicator defects might not be emergency problems, but they are not trivial and should not be ignored. Such problems should be corrected as soon as possible to avoid the possibility of greater problems in the future. To give an extreme example, remember the accident at the Three Mile Island nuclear plant back in the 1970s. There were multiple causes to this accident, which could have been prevented at several points. According to several reports, the accident could have been caught while still at a fairly minor level if a 50 cent indicator lamp hadn't inopportunely burned out. The main problem was a valve that was stuck. The lamp that indicated whether the valve was open or shut was burned out, so the plant operators did not recognize the problem for what it was, and took inappropriate actions based on their faulty knowledge of what was really going on.

In such a critical operation, each indicator lamp should have been duplicated by a second lamp in parallel and tested on each work shift to catch burn outs as soon as possible. The possible results of defective system indication are certainly less devastating to society in a home alarm system, but they still could be bad enough to the people living in that house. The function of the indicator devices is to clearly indicate what is happening within the system. If this information is incorrect or misleading (which it certainly would be if an indicator lamp or LED doesn't light up when it is supposed to), the full benefits of the system cannot be realized, and the effectiveness of the system might be compromised or even canceled out.

It also is possible though unlikely that an indicator lamp or LED might light when it is not supposed to. If the lamp or LED is lit continuously (as long as power is supplied to that part of the system), or if it acts in unison with something else that it is not supposed to be connected with, the problem is probably a short circuit, permitting an inappropriate signal to erroneously reach the indicator device. If the indicator lights up more erratically, suspect a problem in the control circuitry feeding the signal to that indicator device.

Other types of problems might occasionally turn up in a home alarm system, but they would be exceptional. At least 95% of all the troubleshooting calls you get can be expected to fit into one or more of the general categories discussed in this section. Taking things on a generalized level, there really are just so many things that can go wrong with a home alarm system.

Of course, a computer-based system is much more complex electronically, and many other problems might show up with systems of this type. Computer-based alarm systems are discussed in chapter 10.

A typical simple "tough dog"

Although most problems in alarm systems tend to be relatively simple once they're tracked down, actually tracking them down can often be a bear of a job. Anyone involved with electronics servicing to any degree is familiar with "tough dog" cases. Alarm system tough dogs tend to have a unique bark, but they often don't have as much bite as they appear to have at first. Consider the following example.

These events occurred while I was in college. I was not a technician at the time. Actually, I was a part-time clerk in a small store where the problem occurred. The manager lived more than an hour away from the store. Because I lived closer than any of the other employees, if there was a problem after hours, security would call me.

At one point in the fall, I started getting late-night calls that the alarm system had gone off. I'd rush out to the store only to discover no sign of forced entry or anything out of place. Nothing seemed wrong at all. I'd reset the alarm and go home, after making a careful check of the premises, which never turned up anything.

This occurrence began happening with greater and greater frequency. We had a couple technicians come out and look over the alarm system, but they couldn't find anything wrong. Yet the late night false alarms continued, without any apparent reason. These false alarms always occurred late at night, and it seemed like it always happened on the coldest, worst weather nights. At the time I just thought, "Isn't that always the way?"

Eventually though I realized maybe it wasn't just Murphy's law, but a clue to the problem. Could something in the system somehow be weather dependent? Could a sharp drop in temperature set off the alarm?

Finally, after several months of frustration, we found a hairline crack in the foil tape on one of the front display windows. Most materials expand and contract with changes in temperature. The foil tape didn't expand and contract at the same rate as the glass, so while usually the two pieces of foil tape on either side of the crack were close enough to overlap slightly and make good electrical contact, when the window was very cold, the two pieces of tape would be moved apart, so there was a gap between them, as shown in Fig. 9-4. This gap broke the electrical contact, and the alarm system responded as if the window had been broken.

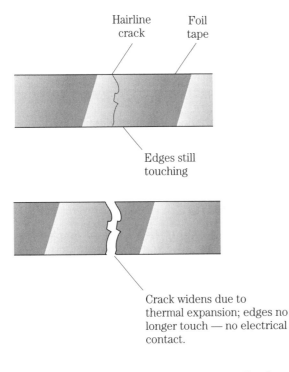

9-4
A hairline crack in foil tape could cause false alarms as the crack is enlarged or reduced due to changes in temperature.

During the day, the crack was too small to be seen with the naked eye, and a continuity check with a *VOM* (volt-ohm-milliammeter) indicated that the foil tape was fine and whole, with no breaks. It wasn't until we realized that the weather connection could be a clue that we could begin to isolate and localize the problem. We had to ask, if the late night cold was causing the false alarms, what part(s) of the system could logically be affected by the cold.

Once the problem was isolated, the repair was ridiculously simple. We just had to replace a couple inches of foil tape on the window, and the false alarms stopped completely.

The circumstances of this story might never occur in your work with alarm systems. The specific problem was unusual. But in many ways, this story is very typical of troubleshooting alarm systems. Simple problems can fool you, and can hide very effectively until you have correctly pieced together all the symptomatic clues.

Test equipment

To proceed with the troubleshooting process, it is usually necessary to make some electronic tests and measurements. Unlike most areas of modern electronics, you generally won't need very much in the way of test equipment for working on home alarm systems, (except, of course, for computer-based systems, which require the same types of test equipment needed for any computer troubleshooting).

All you are likely to need in the way of test equipment for 90% of all home alarm system work is a VOM or *DMM* (digital multimeter) and a small temporary alarm output device (which also was used for the initial testing procedures as part of the original installation process). In some cases, a simple signal generator or signal tracer can be helpful, but rarely mandatory.

Home alarm systems typically use just simple on/off dc voltages, which switch states infrequently. You will almost never have much use for an oscilloscope, a frequency counter, or most other types of expensive test equipment that are considered standard necessities for virtually all other types of modern electronics troubleshooting. If you are specializing in the home alarm system field, you can save a bundle in start-up costs in creating your own business, compared to more typical electronics servicing specialties. Little of the company's assets will need to be tied up in test equipment. Because only simple test equipment is normally used in this field, you also will save on the repair costs (including your own time and trouble) on your test equipment.

Even for the VOM, which will serve as your primary piece of test equipment, there is no need for, or even much purpose to invest in an expensive, high-accuracy, top-of-the-line model. You'll just be making simple, yes/no type tests, such as "Is a voltage present at this point or not?" or "Is there continuity between these two points or not?" Generally speaking, exact values will not be critical in most typical home alarm systems, as long as they are reasonably close. An inexpensive VOM will do as good a job in this application as the most expensive, deluxe instrument on the market.

Of course, if you already have a high-grade multimeter for other electronics work, that's fine. You can certainly use it for your home alarm system troubleshooting work too. On the other hand, it might still make sense to invest in a couple inexpensive VOMs just for the home alarm system work. In any type of field work, the test equipment is likely to get bounced around and possibly roughly treated. It also is much more likely to be lost or stolen than in-shop equipment. Because less expensive equipment will work as well in this type of field work, not risking your best (and most expensive) test equipment might be the best equipment insurance you can have. If a $20 VOM is lost or broken on the job, it won't hurt nearly as much as if it had been a super-deluxe $250 DMM.

In home alarm system work, you can use either an analog or digital meter. In most measurements, the exact values will not be too critical. More often than not, you'll just be looking for either a very low (nominally zero) reading, or a relatively high (preferably near full scale) reading. An analog meter actually has a slight edge here. It's very easy to see at a glance if the pointer is close to the upper or lower end of the scale. You scarcely have to think about it. A digital readout requires a little more mental interpretation of the numbers (although admittedly not very much). Because you generally won't be dealing with continuously changing values, you shouldn't have problems of blurred numerical readings on a DMM.

One additional advantage of analog VOMs over DMMs in this line of work is that generally low end analog VOMs tend to cost a little less. The difference isn't as big as it was a few years ago, but there is still some.

Generally you will be doing just simple voltage tests, and high voltages are almost never involved. You will rarely, if ever, find a voltage exceeding the nominal 120 Vac (volts, alternating current) house current. You also can expect to do a lot of continuity checks with the ohmmeter section. Because you are just checking to see if the resistance is very high, or very low, the scale or range isn't too important for this application.

If you already have a multimeter, of whatever type, or use one in some other type of work, it should work just fine in troubleshooting home alarm systems. If you are buying a multimeter specifically for this purpose, consider a no-frills analog VOM. The most important features you are looking for are low cost, and reasonable durability and sturdiness. For the vast majority of work with home alarm systems, no other feature will be of much practical value and isn't worth paying any extra for, unless the instrument will be doing double duty for some other purpose.

Testing battery voltage

Repeatedly throughout this book, the importance of periodically testing a home alarm system's back-up batteries has been stressed. But there would be little point in bothering to test the batteries if it isn't done correctly and accurately.

Most home alarm systems today use rechargeable batteries for back-up power. A trickle-charger circuit continuously recharges the batteries whenever ac power is present and battery power is not being actively used by the system. Nominally, the batteries should always be at their full nominal voltage, unless ac power is removed from the system for an extended time. But don't make assumptions, or you might be faced with problems.

The trickle-charger circuit might develop a defect so the system back-up batteries are not fully, or even adequately charged when they are needed. A more likely problem is one or more bad batteries. Rechargeable batteries definitely do go bad. They can accept only just so many recharges before they cease to work to peak performance, if at all. A small impurity in the chemicals used within a rechargeable battery could cause it to go prematurely bad, after just a few recharges, or possibly even right out of the package.

Testing rechargeable batteries in a trickle-charged system is every bit as vital as testing regular batteries that can't be recharged.

The easy way to test batteries, the method used by most laymen, and far too many technicians, who should know better, is to remove the batteries from the equipment and test them individually with a voltmeter of some type. This approach to testing batteries is better than nothing, but it is far from a reliable or accurate method. If the battery is really very dead, or badly drained, the voltmeter should indicate it ought to be replaced. But often, a battery's charge will be just borderline, and a weak battery is likely to test as perfectly good. Curiously, an expensive, high-grade voltmeter might give even less reliable results in such a test than a cheaper model.

The problem is that the battery's voltage is being tested without any appreciable load. A no-load test does not resemble the conditions in any functional circuit.

Experienced technicians might be tempted to skip the following explanation as too obvious, but it is all too easy for even experienced and well-trained technicians to forget the obvious in actual field work. There is always the temptation to take the easy way. A periodic refresher of the obvious basics never hurts and can often be of great value.

To greatly simplify, any dc circuit can be represented as a voltage source (the battery) and a resistance (the circuit itself), as shown in Fig. 9-5. In virtually any practical circuit, this resistance is almost certain to vary under different conditions. For the time being, imagine it as a fixed resistance.

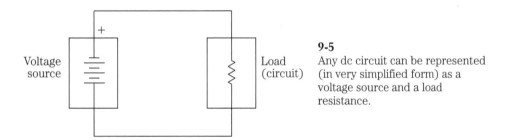

9-5
Any dc circuit can be represented (in very simplified form) as a voltage source and a load resistance.

Voltage source

Load (circuit)

Unless the battery is stored in a total vacuum, there will always be some resistive circuit path between its positive and negative terminals. That is, the resistance will never be truly infinite. Even ordinary air has a finite but very high resistance. The resistance of air can be affected by many variables, including humidity and temperature, among others. For simplicity, just pick a handy high value as a guesstimate, say 100 MΩ (megohms). (A resistance of 100 MΩ equals 100,000,000 Ω.)

According to Ohm's law, the current drain in a simple resistive dc circuit is equal to:

$$I = \frac{E}{R}$$

Obviously, with the high resistance value ($R = 100,000,000$ Ω), the current drain is going to be extremely low. Assume the battery in question is a standard 1.5 V AA cell. The current drain is an almost negligible value of:

$$I = \frac{1.5}{100,000}$$

$$= 0.000000015 \text{ A (amperes)}$$

$$= 0.000015 \text{ mA (milliamperes)}$$

With such a low current drain, the battery can easily put out its full-value voltage with little strain, unless it is in very bad shape. There are actual two resistances in any such circuit—the external resistance (of the circuit or of the open air as in the present example), and the internal resistance of the battery, which is very small, especially in comparison with the very large open-air resistance. (Do not attempt to measure the internal resistance of a battery with an ordinary ohmmeter. The battery's voltage will distort the reading badly and could damage your ohmmeter, which is designed for measurements involving its own internally supplied voltages.) There will be little or no noticeable voltage drop within the battery. Eventually, enough current will be used up by the open-air circuit to cause the battery to become significantly drained, but this will clearly take a long time. The load on the battery under these conditions is minimal, and for most practical purposes it is reasonable to say there is no load on the battery at all. So far, so good.

When you measure a battery voltage out of circuit, you are essentially creating a dc circuit in which the input impedance of the voltmeter serves as the circuit resistance, as shown in Fig. 9-6. Good-quality voltmeters are designed to have as high a possible input impedance to minimize the loading effect when the voltmeter is placed in parallel with a circuit resistance, as shown in Fig. 9-7. The larger the value of the voltmeter input impedance (R_v) in comparison with the actual circuit resistance (R_c), the more accurately the voltage reading will resemble the actual voltage at that point in the circuit when the voltmeter is not connected in parallel (normal operating conditions). The formula for combining these two resistances in parallel is:

$$R_t = \frac{(R_c \times R_v)}{(R_c + R_v)}$$

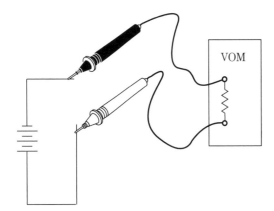

VOM

9-6
When a battery's voltage is measured out of circuit, an effective dc circuit is created in which the input impedance of the voltmeter serves as the circuit resistance.

Assume the total effective circuit resistance works out to 2.5 kΩ (2500 Ω), and the input impedance of the voltmeter is 50 kΩ (50,000 Ω). Putting these two resistances in parallel with each other gives a combined total effective resistance equal to:

$$R_t = \frac{(2500 \times 50,000)}{(2500 + 50,000)}$$

$$= \frac{125,000,000}{52,500}$$

$$= 2381 \ \Omega$$

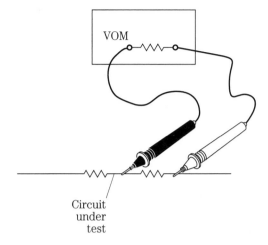

Good-quality voltmeters are designed to have as high a possible input impedance to minimize the loading effect when the voltmeter is placed in parallel with a circuit resistance.

Circuit
under
test

Notice that because the voltmeter impedance (R_v) is so much larger than the circuit resistance (R_c), the total effective resistance (R_t) is reasonably close to the nominal circuit resistance alone, with the voltmeter. This arrangement gives fairly accurate in circuit voltage readings. But out of circuit voltage readings don't work out so well.

Assume the internal resistance of the battery is 20 Ω. When you test this battery out of circuit with a 50 kΩ voltmeter, the voltage is effectively flowing through two very unequal resistances—20 Ω (R_b) and 50 kΩ (R_v). Assume the battery is putting out its full nominal 1.5 V. The current flowing through this test circuit equals:

$$I = \frac{E}{(R_b + R_v)}$$

$$= \frac{1.5}{(20 + 50{,}000)}$$

$$= \frac{1.5}{50{,}020}$$

$$= 0.0000299 \text{ A}$$

$$= 0.0299 \text{ mA}$$

Naturally, virtually all the circuit voltage will be dropped across the external voltmeter resistance. The voltmeter will give a reading of:

$$E = IR_v$$

$$= 0.0000299 \times 50{,}000$$

$$= 1.495 \text{ V}$$

This reading is quite accurate. Unless you are using a very precise digital voltmeter, the odds are you wouldn't be able to distinguish this from an actual 1.500 V reading anyway.

Assume the battery isn't quite up to snuff. Suppose you get a reading of 1.333 V? Is that good enough? Impossible to say. You have no idea what the actual voltage is as seen by the circuit. As a battery goes bad, its voltage changes because its internal resistance has effectively increased. Resistance R_t is effectively larger in comparison with the external resistance.

In the example, a measured voltage of 1.333 V means the current flowing through the internal resistance of the voltmeter (still 50,000 Ω, of course) is:

$$I = \frac{E}{R_v}$$

$$= \frac{1.333}{50,000}$$

$$= 0.0000266 \text{ A}$$

$$= 0.266 \text{ mA}$$

The same current must be flowing through the battery's internal resistance (R_b). The voltage dropped across this internal battery resistance is the missing part of the original 1.5 V, or 0.167 V in the example. This means the battery's internal resistance now has a value of:

$$R_b = \frac{E}{I}$$

$$= \frac{0.167}{0.0000266}$$

$$= 6278 \ \Omega$$

Now, put this exact same worn battery into the circuit (which has a total effective resistance of 2.5 kΩ) and see just how much voltage the circuit is really getting. The battery's internal resistance is the same whether the battery is in circuit or out of circuit, so the total resistance in the circuit works out to:

$$R_t = R_b + R_c$$

$$= 6278 + 2500$$

$$= 8778 \ \Omega$$

The current drain therefore must be equal to:

$$I = \frac{E}{R_t}$$

(Because you are including the battery's internal resistance, E is the battery's full nominal voltage, or 1.5 V):

$$I = \frac{E}{R}$$

$$= \frac{1.5}{8778}$$

$$= 0.0001708 \text{ A}$$

$$= 0.1708 \text{ mA}$$

Notice that this is a much higher current value than you have previously seen in this example. The voltage drop across the external circuit resistance (R^c), and therefore the battery's output voltage as seen by the circuit, works out to a value of:

$$E_c = IR_c$$
$$= 0.0001708 \times 2500$$
$$= 0.427 \text{ V}$$

This result is unquestionably very different than you got when you tested the battery out of circuit (1.333 V). The out of circuit test was virtually meaningless in its results. A battery voltage of 1.333 V might seem passable, but in the circuit, that same battery can only put out less than half a volt. Such a test procedure is functionally useless, and an almost complete waste of time.

If you measure the battery voltage in circuit, however, you can get a reasonably accurate measurement. The total external resistance is the parallel combination of the actual circuit resistance and the voltmeter's input impedance. You have already calculated the value of this combination to be 2381 Ω. The internal resistance of the battery is still 6278 Ω, so the total circuit resistance is now:

$$R_t = 6278 + 2381$$
$$= 8659 \text{ }\Omega$$

The addition of the voltmeter changes the current flowing through the circuit to a value of:

$$I = \frac{1.5}{8659}$$
$$= 0.0001732 \text{ A}$$
$$= 0.1732 \text{ mA}$$

The external voltage drop, and therefore the value displayed by the voltmeter will now be equal to:

$$E_m = 0.0001732 \times 2381$$
$$= 0.412 \text{ V}$$

This value is pretty close to the calculated voltage value seen by the circuit without the voltmeter. This in-circuit test certainly tells you that this battery is no longer up to doing its job and is well past due for replacement, and the out-of-circuit test didn't tell you much of anything at all.

Special battery testers are available, and except for the really inexpensive knock-offs, they can do a fairly good job of testing batteries for most practical purposes. Such a battery tester is nothing more than a stripped down voltmeter (usually with a scale marked only GOOD, BAD, and QUESTIONABLE, or something similar) with a shunt resistance to simulate the effects of a practical circuit. The accuracy of the tests made on such a device will depend on how close the tester's shunt resistance resembles the actual operating resistance of the circuit the battery is to be used in. This is why the scale of most commercial battery testers include a fairly wide questionable range. The battery might or might not still be good enough to be useful, depending on the requirements of the specific application in question. But this is as close as you can expect to come to useful accuracy when testing batteries out of circuit.

When there is any doubt, assume the battery is bad (or soon will be) and replace it anyway, just to be on the safe side.

Of course whenever you test battery voltages in circuit, it is absolutely vital to first make sure that any and all ac power sources are fully disconnected from the circuit under test. Any ac power will not only badly confuse the accuracy of the voltage readings, it will probably be a very dangerous shock hazard and could even result in a fatality. Be careful, and always double check first.

Excessive voltage drop in long wires

In most electronics work, assume the voltage drop across connecting wires is zero, and this is usually a reasonable assumption. Any wire has some finite resistance, but usually it is negligible. The resistance might as well be ignored, because it makes no practical difference in the operation of the circuitry.

However, there are some special conditions where the voltage drop across a connecting wire might become significant enough to cause the circuit to malfunction, or not operate reliably. Such problems are most likely to occur where there are long runs of wire. Home alarm systems normally feature long wire runs from the various sensor areas to the central control box.

In effect, the central control box sends out a small voltage over one wire, and senses whether or not the voltage is returned through the other wire. (This explanation is a crude explanation for illustration purposes. A practical alarm system might not work in exactly the way described here, but the same general principles apply.)

In a normally open loop, as shown in Fig. 9-8, the alarm is triggered if the return voltage is sensed, which can only happen if one or more of the NO sensors in the loop are tripped, completing the circuit.

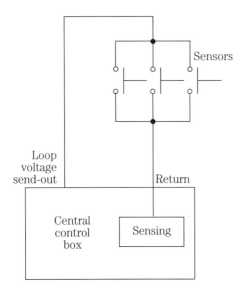

9-8
In a normally open loop, the alarm is triggered if the return voltage is sensed, which can only happen if one or more of the NO sensors in the loop are closed.

A normally closed loop, like the one shown in Fig. 9-9, works in the exact opposite way. Normally the closed sensors create a complete circuit, returning the volt-

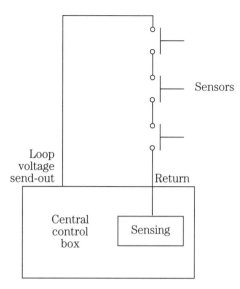

Loop voltage send-out

Return

Sensors

Central control box

Sensing

9-9
In a normally closed loop, the alarm is triggered if the return voltage is interrupted by one or more of the NC sensors in the loop being opened.

age to the central control box, and this voltage keeps the alarm turned off. When one (or more) of the NC sensors is tripped, the loop circuit is broken, and the return voltage disappears. The voltage-sensing circuitry in the control box detects the absence of the return voltage and turns on the alarm.

In either case, it should be apparent that excessive voltage drop along the system's connecting wires can reduce the return voltage to a low enough level that the voltage sensing circuitry in the central control box can't detect it reliably. The alarm system will operate erratically, if at all. If there is excessive voltage drop in a normally open loop, the alarm might not be sounded when a sensor in the loop is tripped. On the other hand, excessive voltage drop in a normally closed loop is likely to cause false alarms. Because the voltage sent out by the central control box is typically very low to begin with (to keep system costs down and safety at a maximum), not much of the return voltage can afford to be dropped without causing problems.

Measuring the resistance of long run of wire is awkward, because even in a very long run, the total resistance will probably be small. The small resistance is difficult to read on most ohmmeters. If you have a deluxe VOM or DMM with a very low resistance range, great. Just measure the resistance. With most practical equipment, however, the measured resistance might be too close to zero to be read clearly (especially on analog meters), even though it might still be high enough to create a sufficiently excessive voltage drop to affect system operation. Excessive voltage drop problems in home alarm systems are not uncommon, but they're hardly common enough to warrant investing in an expensive high-grade VOM or DMM just for this purpose. As discussed previously, a technician working on home alarm systems will usually be as well off with a simple, moderately priced meter.

It is generally easier and more accurate to measure the voltage drop along the wire run directly, on a low voltage scale of your VOM or DMM.

The first step is to measure the voltage the central control box is actually putting out. If you are working on a normally open loop, first disconnect the alarm output device, or replace it with a small indicator device of some type. The voltmeter might complete the loop circuit during the testing procedure, and if the send-out voltage is good, the return voltage will set off the alarm. If you are not sure at this point whether the loop you are working with is normally open or normally closed, assume it is normally open, and disconnect (or replace) the output alarm anyway, just to be safe. It won't hurt anything to do this with a normally closed loop, except waste a couple minutes of your time at worst. A few minutes is cheap insurance.

Now disconnect the external loop and simply measure the voltage between the output (send-out) terminal and ground, as shown in Fig. 9-10. If the central control box is poorly marked and you aren't sure which terminal is which, just try testing the voltage from each terminal. The input (return) terminal should give a reading of zero (or close to it), and the output terminal should give a definite but small voltage measurement. If there is no voltage, or too low a voltage, from the output terminal, the problem is in the central control box.

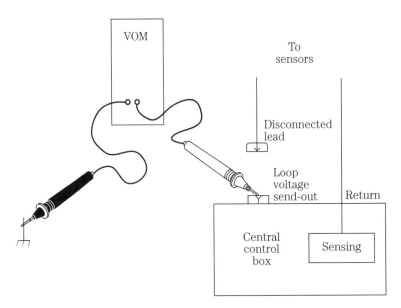

9-10 To determine the system loop voltage, disconnect the external loop from the central control box and simply measure the voltage between the loop output terminal and ground.

How much voltage is enough here? That depends on the specific design of the circuitry used in the system you are working on, of course. If you did the installation, you should know what this voltage should be. Presumedly you are using the same basic control circuitry on all (or most) of the systems you install, so there is no reason for this voltage to change from system to system. But suppose you are attempting to service an unfamiliar system installed by someone else, or it was a special case installation for some reason, and the individual customer records have been lost. How can you find out what the voltage should be?

You can find the voltage easily. If the system has multiple loops, and the other loops are working fine, the same voltage in those loops should work in the problem loop as well. However, many systems use a single output voltage source for all the loops in the system, so if one has an incorrect voltage, they all do. A few systems might use different voltages for different loops for some reason.

It still isn't too hard to find out what the loop voltage should be. Replace the system's normal alarm output device with a visual or a small, low-volume audio-indicator device. Feed the output from a variable voltage generator into the return terminal, as shown in Fig. 9-11.

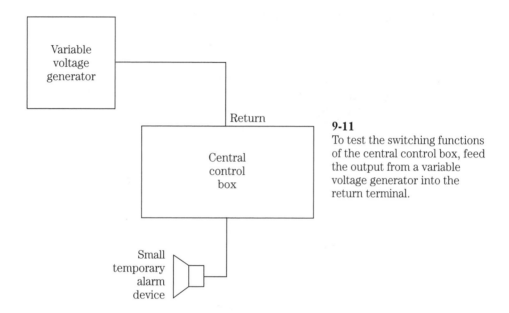

9-11
To test the switching functions of the central control box, feed the output from a variable voltage generator into the return terminal.

For a normally open loop, start the voltage generator at zero volts, and slowly increase the voltage, until the alarm is triggered. The voltage measured at this trip point is the critical voltage. Add a little extra voltage to the measured value to allow for error and variables within the system during practical use.

In a normally closed loop, you must start out with a higher voltage and gradually reduce it until the alarm is triggered, indicating the voltage has dropped below its critical trip-point value. You have to be careful. If the input voltage is too much higher than its desired value, some of the circuitry in the central control box could be damaged or destroyed. If you know the system's supply voltage (which should be easy enough to measure if you don't know it right away), that places an absolute upper limit on the input voltage. The loop voltage must be at least a little less than the system supply voltage. The system supply voltage might still be destructively high, so it's better to start with only about half this voltage.

The safest approach might be to start out with 5 V as an input value. If this triggers the alarm right away (unlikely, but possible), increase the input voltage somewhat, and reset the system to try again. When you find a starting voltage that is high enough not to trigger the alarm, gradually reduce the voltage until the alarm is activated. Now you know the approximate voltage necessary to keep the normally closed loop from triggering the alarm.

If the voltage put out from the central control box seems correct, the problem must be elsewhere in the external sensor loop. An excessive voltage drop is likely. This might be due to a bad sensor, or a poor connection somewhere in the loop. The wire might have been damaged in some way, causing it to increase its resistance. For example, in a stranded wire, one or two strands might break without making a noticeable difference, but if too many strands are broken, the wire can't carry as much current, and the resistance of the wire as a whole will be increased. Rarely, the conductor in a wire might be partially exposed to some form of corrosion, and the chemical change could affect the wire resistance.

Reconnect the external loop. (Keep the temporary test alarm output device connected at this point. Don't risk setting off the main alarm during your tests.) Measure the voltage from the loop output terminal to ground again, as shown in Fig. 9-12. It should be pretty much the same value as you measured before, with the external loop disconnected. If the voltage reading is noticeably reduced, something in the external loop is unduly loading down the control box.

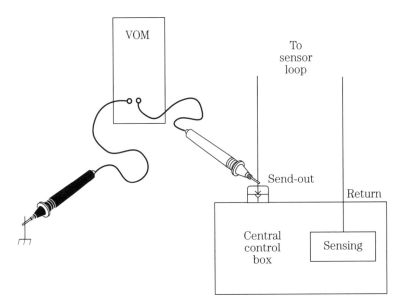

9-12 Measure the voltage from the loop output terminal of the central control box to ground again, with the external loop circuit hooked up again.

If the output voltage seems about right, measure the voltage from the input (return) terminal and ground, as shown in Fig. 9-13. Have your assistant sequentially trip several of the sensors in the loop being tested. Remember, in a normally open loop, the return voltage should normally be at or near zero unless one or more of the sensors are tripped. In a normally closed loop, the full return voltage should be present, unless one or more sensors are tripped, when the return voltage should drop to

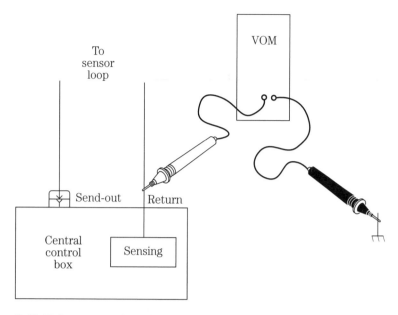

9-13 If the output voltage (from Fig. 9-12) seems about right, measure the voltage from the input terminal and ground.

zero (or close to it). If you don't get this pattern or if the measured full return voltage is too low, there is a problem within the external loop. If the problem only shows up with one or two sensors, the odds are that those sensors are somehow bad, and need to be repaired or replaced. If the problem seems more global in its effects, you probably have excessive voltage drop in the connecting wires.

Temporarily connect a known-good length of wire in parallel with the output wire from the central control box to the sensor location, as shown in Fig. 9-14. If the problem goes away, remove and replace the original wiring. If the problem persists, move the test wire to parallel the return wire. If this does not correct the problem, try replacing both wire runs. If the problem still persists (which is very unlikely, if the testing procedures have been followed as described here), the problem must be somewhere in the sensor wiring, which is shown in Fig. 9-15. If the previous tests have not localized the problem, you will need to replace connecting wires and double check all connections and terminal points one by one.

Admittedly, it can be a hassle to replace the room-to-room wiring in a home alarm system, especially where multiconductor cables are used. If these test procedures indicate one or more wires within a multiconductor cable needs replacement, replace the entire cable. It is better to replace the other wires that are still good than to compromise the entire security system with the one bad wire.

Measuring contact resistance

Sometimes a sensor is obviously bad. You can often see a mechanical fault. A moving part doesn't move where it should, or at all, or it might not hold its physical posi-

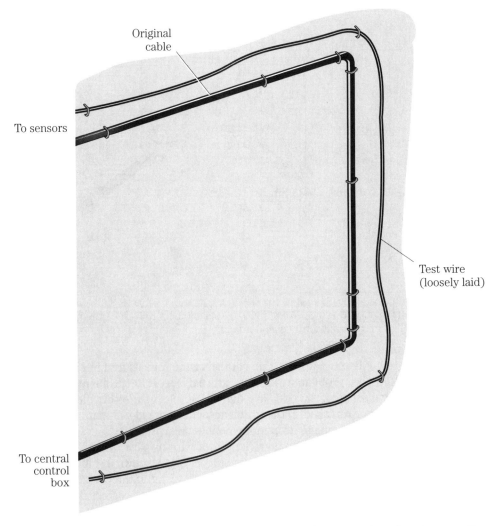

Original
cable

To sensors

Test wire
(loosely laid)

To central
control
box

9-14 To determine if there is an excessive voltage drop in the connecting wires, temporarily connect a known-good length of wire in parallel with the output wire from the central control box to the sensor location.

tion. On the electrical end, it would seem that, like another switching device, a sensor should test either completely open or completely closed, with no in-between values.

However, defective sensors can and do function in-between on and off more often than you might suspect. The culprit is contact resistance. Ideally, the contact resistance should be zero when a sensor (or other switch) is closed and infinite when open. Practical sensors and switches don't quite reach this ideal, of course. In practice, the contact resistance of a good sensor (or switch) will be very low when closed, and very high when open. This less-than-ideal reality should be close enough to do the job.

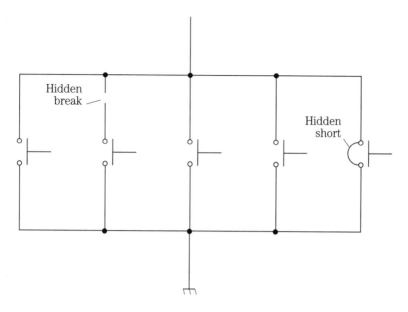

9-15 If the problem still persists after the substitution test of Fig. 9-14, the problem must be somewhere in the actual sensor wiring.

Unfortunately, various defects can cause the closed contact resistance to increase, and\or the open contact resistance to decrease. If the problem is severe enough, the connected circuitry might not be able to reliably determine if the sensor or switch is actually open or closed.

Bad switch contacts are most often caused by accumulated dirt or corrosion. Occasionally a part of the switch might be bent, or a poor solder joint at one of the terminals might be the source of the difficulty. Bad switch contact problems are usually more or less intermittent.

In any application, a bad switch contact is annoying. In an alarm system, such a problem could be very serious, even critical. Remember, a security system is only as good as its weakest link.

The larger the contact resistance of a closed switch, the greater the voltage drop across it. High resistance also increases heat, which might do even more damage. If the closed contact resistance is high enough, the circuitry might not be able to tell that the switch is closed and might interpret it as an open switch. Similarly, though less common, if the contact resistance of an open switch is too low (essentially, the switch is shorted), it might appear to be closed to the circuit. Obviously, such confusion of a sensor switch's state would be disastrous in a security system.

The easiest and most reliable way to check the contact resistance of a sensor or switch is by reading the voltage across it in actual use.

This test, as you might have guessed, is performed with the voltmeter section of a VOM or DMM. High accuracy generally won't be required, but the instrument should have a fairly low voltage range.

The hook-up for this test is certainly simple enough, as shown in Fig. 9-16. Because of the length of the connecting wires in a home alarm system, you might have to determine the polarity by trial and error. This test is so simple and quick, it won't be a hardship to simply reverse the polarity of the voltmeter's test leads if you don't get a good reading on the first attempt. The low voltage involved are unlikely to damage any good-quality meter, even with reversed polarity.

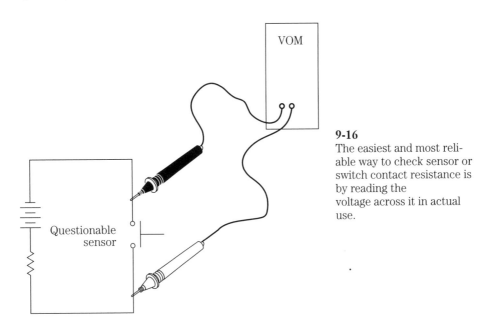

9-16
The easiest and most reliable way to check sensor or switch contact resistance is by reading the voltage across it in actual use.

To avoid confusion with other sensor switches in series or parallel with the device you are testing, disconnect it from the circuit, and temporarily connect a battery between the sensor terminals, as shown in the diagram. The exact voltage of this battery isn't particularly critical. A standard 9 V transistor battery the most convenient for use in such tests, but you can use almost anything you have handy. Just make sure the battery voltage doesn't exceed the maximum contact ratings of the sensor—which is very unlikely, unless you are using an unusually large power battery.

The resistor connected in series with the battery is optional, but strongly advised. This resistor is simply a current-limiting resistor to avoid too quickly draining an otherwise good battery. A fairly small resistance can be used here. Probably something in the 100 to 1000 Ω range would be the best choice.

Set the voltmeter range so it includes the full battery voltage. If possible, this full-battery voltage should be as close to the top of the selected scale as possible. An analog voltmeter will be somewhat easier to read in this test, but a DMM can be used. You'll be able to read an analog voltmeter quicker just by seeing if the pointer is moving up or down the scale, or staying still. With a digital voltmeter, you'll need to be a little more patient and wait for the readout to settle down to a fixed number before you interpret the value.

Operate the sensor like a switch. Determine whether it is a normally open or normally closed device. Open and close the switch contacts several times while watching the voltmeter. When the sensor switch is opened, you should read essentially the full battery voltage across it because the open switch is functioning as a very large resistance. Nominally the resistance between the open contacts can be considered infinite, but remember, even air can conduct some electrical current, so the resistance is actually very high, and not truly infinite. In effect, the circuit is as shown in Fig. 9-17. The resistance between the open switch contacts is by far the largest resistance in the circuit. It will typically be at least several megohms (millions of ohms). Even the resistance of the current limiting resistor will be negligible in comparison. Almost all the voltage in the circuit must be dropped across this phantom resistor between the switch contacts, and this is the voltage you should read on the voltmeter. If the measured voltage seems too low, try replacing the suspected sensor switch with a known good switch in the same test circuit. If the questionable sensor switch had a much lower open voltage than the known good switch, there must be some leakage (a partial short) in the sensor switch. If you cannot locate and repair the problem, you should replace the sensor.

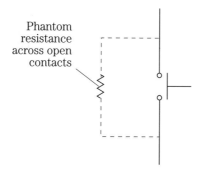

Phantom resistance across open contacts

9-17
Ideally the resistance between the open contacts of a normally open sensor or switch may be considered infinite, but remember, even air can conduct some electrical current, so the resistance is actually very high, and not truly infinite.

When the sensor switch is closed, however, the effective resistance between the switch contacts should be nominally zero (actually very low—no more than a couple of ohms at most). Virtually none of the circuit's voltage should be dropped across the closed switch contacts. (Actually most of the voltage will now be dropped across the current-limiting resistor. The voltmeter should now read zero, or something very, very close to it.

If there is excessive contact resistance, there will be more voltage dropped across this apparent resistor, and you will read a proportionately higher voltage on the voltmeter when the switch contacts are closed. If you get any significant voltage reading across the closed switch contacts (anything higher than one or two tenths of a volt), try cleaning the switch contacts with an appropriate contact cleaning solution. If the contacts are accessible, try buffing them.

Repeat the test procedure. If this cleaning does not get rid of the excessive contact, examine the contacts closely with a magnifying glass for any signs of corrosion, bending, or other damage. If you can't find and correct the problem, replace the questionable sensor.

Of course, some sensor types naturally have different normal contact resistances based on their design principles. It's best to compare readings from several similar devices (preferably units known to be good) to establish a more specific set of guidelines for determining whether a given individual unit is good or bad.

If a questionable sensor switch seems to pass this test okay, try tapping it lightly with a small screwdriver or similar tool while repeating the test (both in the open and closed positions). The tapping will tend to force any intermittent problems to show up more clearly. If the voltage reading jumps noticeably with a light tap (assuming the tap doesn't make you move the hand activating the sensor switch, of course), there might well be an intermittent problem with that device. When in doubt, replace.

Finding breaks in multiconductor cables

Home alarm systems usually have long lengths of multiconductor cables. A single wire in such a multiconductor cable might break from any of a number of potential causes. The result can be erratic or incorrect system operation.

It can be tedious work determining whether or not there really is a break in a multiconductor cable, and if so, which wire (or wires) the break is in. The simple circuit shown in Fig. 9-18 can simplify this job considerably. Any competent technician should be able to build this circuit in just a few minutes, and the parts cost shouldn't be more than two or three dollars, not counting any specialized connectors that might be used to suit the application.

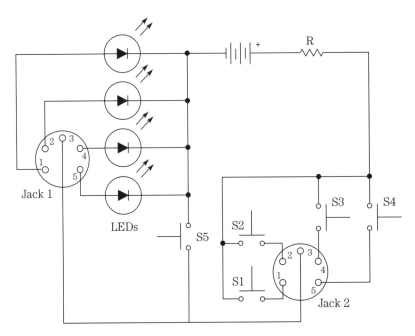

9-18 This simple circuit can simplify the task of finding breaks in multiconductor cables considerably.

This circuit is so simple, there really is no need for a separate parts list. Resistor R1 is simply a current-limiting resistor to protect the LEDs. Any value from 300 to 470 Ω would be suitable.

A standard 9 V transistor battery is used as the power source in this circuit. You could use some other battery voltage, if you prefer, but 9 V will probably be the most convenient, unless there is some special compelling reason to use something else.

The two connector jacks are selected to match the plugs of the cable to be tested. If no plugs are used, you can substitute a pair of appropriate screw-down terminal blocks.

A five-conductor cable is assumed in the schematic, as it is shown here. You can easily increase or decrease the number of LEDs to suit the specific multi-conductor cable you are working with. Except for the ground or common line (or lines), each individual line or conductor gets its own LED on the left-hand side of the diagram, and its own normally open push-button switch on the right-hand side.

In operation, the two ends of the multiconductor cable to be tested are plugged into the two jacks of the test circuit. A known-good extension cable on one end might be helpful for mechanical convenience. Close one of the push-button switches. The appropriate LED should light up. If not, there is probably a break in that wire. If more than one LED lights up when just one button is pressed, there might be a short between two or more of the conductors within the cable. Either result would indicate that the cable is defective and should be replaced. It probably would not be worth the time or cost to attempt to repair a defective cable. A spliced cable won't be as reliable in the long run as will a whole, continuous cable.

The test for the ground connection is slightly different. For this test close switch S5. Nothing should happen. If any of the LEDs light up during this test, there is a short in the cable and it should be replaced.

10
CHAPTER

Computerized systems and high-tech security

To this chapter, this book features fairly low-tech circuitry and devices. There are good reasons for this. For home security systems, low-tech is usually the most appropriate and effective approach. How the system carries out its functions is what counts, not the inclusion of the latest thing.

There's no question that high tech sells and sells big. Certainly no one who chooses to read a book like this needs to be convinced that modern electronics offers many exciting possibilities. But it can be just as important to pull in the reins a bit and consider whether the capabilities of the latest technology is really suitable to the application. All too often, the latest high-tech devices are used for no better reason than they happen to be the latest high-tech devices, and they offer no real advantage beyond the "gee whiz" factor. There is always the disadvantage of added expense, which often can't be justified in any practical terms. More often than you might suspect, the high-tech approach might not even work as well as a simpler, more direct system.

In security systems, recent years have brought many new high-tech inventions and developments. Many of these devices have been invaluable and virtually essential in the modern world, but it is too easy to forget that they were designed for multimillion dollar industries and government agencies, where the stakes are incredibly high, and the motivation for someone trying to get past the security system can be enormously powerful. What is appropriate for a major computer manufacturer or the Central Intelligence Agency is very likely to be gross overkill in the average home security system.

High-tech security obviously carries a hefty price tag. It is necessary to consider whether the added cost is really worth it. In an industrial security system, thousands or even millions dollars are likely to be at stake, but this is unlikely in a home security system. Does it really make sense to invest in a $5000 security system to protect perhaps $3000 of easily stolen property? Perhaps someone who is very wealthy may have enough stealable property in the home to warrant such an expensive alarm system, but this would certainly be the exception rather than the rule.

But what if the security system is being installed not so much to protect material property, as to ensure the personal safety of the homeowner, family members and loved ones? Shouldn't the homeowner get the best security system he or she can possibly afford? How can anyone put a price tag on human lives?

This is a valid point, as far as it goes. But it is necessary to consider how much real extra protection the added expense will truly offer. No burglar alarm will keep a very determined intruder out. Fortunately, most homes are unlikely to be targeted by such a determined intruder. One function of the home alarm system is to scare an attempted burglar off. The other function is to alert any occupants of the house (or the neighbors) of the attempted intrusion, so the police can be summoned. A simple, but well-designed alarm system, like those described throughout this book, will be sufficient to keep out all but the most highly motivated of intruders. Unless there is some very specific and powerful reason for targeting one home, almost any burglar will give up quickly and target another house with little or no security protection. Is there any reason an intruder might be motivated to take the extra effort and risk to get into this specific house? If not, there's no reason why the homeowner should go to the extra expense of special high-tech security.

Often the limited facilities of a small-scale installation might prevent the high-tech security device from doing its job adequately. Inappropriate use of the latest security techniques can actually significantly reduce practical security in the real world.

Lasers for intrusion detection

Take a closer and more specific look at one type of high-tech security device that is very useful for industrial or government use, but wildly impractical and possibly ineffective in a home alarm system.

You have probably heard of the use of laser beams in advanced security systems. The odds are that probably everyone in America has seen such things by now, if only on TV or in movies where there is an impressive crosshatch of laser beams covering the protected areas, as shown in Fig. 10-1. Such portrayals aren't completely realistic. The pattern of laser beams in such systems are similar to those shown in the films, but in real life, infrared lasers are used, with beams that are invisible to the naked eye. Visible laser beams wouldn't be much more than a high-tech version of the decals saying, "These premises are protected by a (high-tech) security system."

To activate the alarm, one or more of the laser beams have to be broken, as the intruder's body passes through them. If the beams are visible, someone could carefully negotiate a path between them. But when infrared lasers are used, the prospective intruder can't see where the beams are, making it impossible to avoid them. The crosshatch pattern makes it highly unlikely that anyone could pass luckily through the protected area without setting off the alarm.

Why do the movies and television so often persist in using visible laser beams? Well, it wouldn't be a very impressive special effect if it couldn't be seen. The concern there is entertaining the audience, not providing realistic security. Whether the

10-1
Some high-tech security
systems use an impressive
crosshatch of laser beams to
provide sophisticated motion
detection, covering the
protected area quite
thoroughly.

intruder successfully gets in or not is the decision of the screenwriter, whose fictional security system will function cooperatively for dramatic purposes.

Basically, the laser beam crosshatch system is similar to the simple broken-beam photosensor systems discussed previously. A simplified version of such a system is illustrated in Fig. 10-2. Normally the light beam (which can be visible light or invisible infrared light) has a direct path from the source to the photosensor. As long as the photosensor is properly illuminated, the alarm is held off. When someone (or some object) passes between the source and the photosensor, the light beam is broken. The photosensor is in shadow, and the alarm is triggered.

Of course, if the intruder knows where the critical light beam is, she or he can find some way to go over, under, or around the beam, and avoid breaking it. This evasive tactic is why light in the visible frequency range is not a good idea for use in security systems. Even with an invisible, infrared beam, a smart intruder might be able to figure out where it is likely to be, either from spotting some of the equipment (the light source, and/or the photosensor) or simply from figuring out the most logical position from the physical aspects of the area. Multiple light beams and photosensors will offer greater protection, of course, because they can cover more area. Ideally, in avoiding breaking one beam, the intruder will be forced to break another, setting off the alarm.

This is precisely the idea behind the crosshatch pattern commonly used in laser security systems. A complex, overlapping pattern of laser beams fills the protected area, making it very difficult if not impossible for anyone to enter or move about within the protected area without breaking at least one of the laser beams, and that's all it takes to set off the alarm.

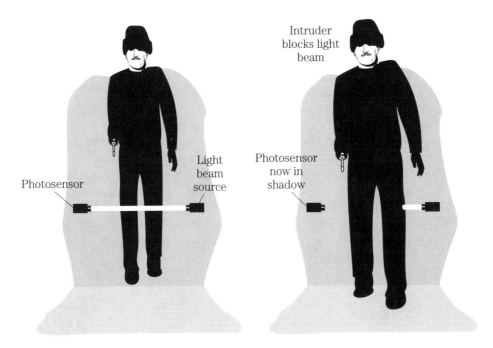

10-2 Basically a laser beam crosshatch system is similar to a simple broken-beam photosensor system.

In essence, crosshatch laser beam coverage in a security system is just a very sophisticated version of motion detection; therefore, it is only suitable for the protection of unoccupied areas. In a typical home alarm system, it would result in frequent false alarms or undue restrictions of legitimate members of the household. In a home with one or more pets, a motion detector of any type would probably be more trouble than it is worth. The motion detector can't tell what is moving. The pet is liable to cause numerous false alarms.

What about setting up the laser system outside the house, as shown in Fig. 10-3, so someone would have to pass through the crosshatch of beams to get to the house. This idea seems to be a good one, but it would rarely be practical. How can you guarantee that birds or animals won't get into the protected yard? The wind could blow in leaves or sheets of paper that could break some of the laser beams and activate the alarm. Unless the house is in a remote area, or the yard is entirely fenced in, there will always be the possibility of someone innocently cutting through the yard. Innocent trespassing can be annoying to many homeowners, but setting off a loud alarm seems disproportionate. In a home alarm system, laser beam coverage might introduce more problems than it protects against.

Of course, the laser beams used in any such system are of a very low power. They certainly aren't dangerous death rays or anything like that. Dangerous booby traps are highly illegal in any security system, and with very good reason. Unexpected circumstances could combine to catch a perfectly innocent person (perhaps

10-3 Setting up a laser crosshatch system outside the house to detect prowlers might seem like a good idea, but it would almost certainly be plagued with numerous false alarms and other problems.

even a loved one) against all predictions. Even in the case of a real intruder, no one legitimately has the right to act as judge, jury, and executioner. Either everyone (including the obviously guilty) has the right of trial by jury, or no one is safe from mistakes or abuses of the legal system. If an unarmed intruder who breaks in only with the intent to steal is killed or injured by a booby trap, whoever controls the area, or whoever set the booby trap is probably subject to criminal charges. The person setting the trap exceeded reasonable bounds of legitimate self-defense.

So you can see why only very low-power lasers are ever used in security systems. Each laser beam is made only strong enough to do its job, which is just reaching a detector on the far side of the protected area from the laser beam source. These security lasers typically have power ratings of just a tiny fraction of a watt.

Anyone can walk through such laser beams without suffering any physical harm. The only risk the laser beams subject the intruder to is the risk of setting off the alarm.

There is one potential risk that occurs whenever lasers are used. If someone stares directly into a laser beam source for an extended time, their eyes could be damaged. How long is too long is directly dependent on the power of the laser involved. With such low-power lasers for security systems, someone would have to stare at the beam source for a very long time before they suffer any ill effects. The eyes would feel discomfort before permanent injury was done. The chances of someone being injured in this way are highly unlikely, especially if the laser beam sources are well placed to begin with.

The laser beams do not really do anything at all to keep anyone out of the protected area. Instead, they are highly sensitive motion-detector sensors used to set off the alarm if someone enters the protected area while the system is armed.

Why would anyone want to bother with using laser beams in such an application at all? It's not just because they look so nifty—an especially moot point when infrared beams are used. Laser light is used because it is more efficient and can be more specifically aimed and detected than any ordinary light source. Ordinary light does not really make a very good beam, at least not for security devices. The light beam tends to spread out and diffuse as it moves further away from its source, as illustrated in Fig. 10-4. Eventually the light becomes completely diffused, and the beam, as such, ceases to exist.

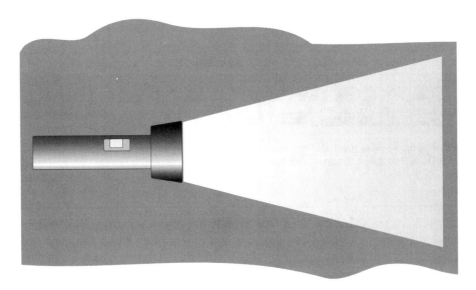

10-4 An ordinary light beam tends to spread out and diffuse as it moves further away from its source.

A laser beam, on the other hand, is naturally very tightly focused and unidirectional. As shown in Fig. 10-5, a laser beam spreads out very little as it moves away from its source. Even if you directed a laser beam toward the moon, it would still

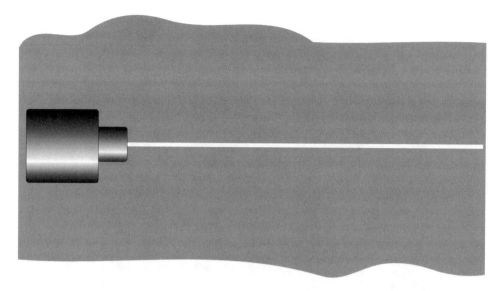

10-5 A laser beam is naturally very tightly focused and unidirectional.

hold its beam-like shape by the time it got there. The beam would be somewhat wider after travelling that much distance, but it would still be a remarkably tight and concise beam.

Since a laser beam is comprised of just a single specific light frequency, it is unlikely that a tuned sensor will be fooled by light from any other source. The old burglar's trick of shining a flashlight onto the photosensor while crossing through the protective light beam is unlikely to work in a laser system.

Laser light is efficient and economical in power consumption and effectiveness, but laser sources tend to be expensive, certainly far more expensive than ordinary light sources. It would not be economically feasible to use a separate, independent laser source for each individual beam in a security crosshatch pattern. In most such systems, one or just a few actual laser devices produce all the beams needed by the system. Reflectors split the original beam into multiple paths throughout the protected area. A simplified example of this is shown in Fig. 10-6. Each reflected beam is aimed at its own individual sensor. The tight beams of laser light make this possible. If you tried this approach with ordinary light sources, you would not get a crosshatch pattern of beams at all, but simply a well-lit room. Even if one of the reflected "beams" were broken, the photosensor would probably still be well illuminated by bleed-over light from other nearby beams.

A laser beam crosshatch pattern is best suited to protecting relatively large, open areas that are unoccupied while the alarm system is activated. A warehouse or long office hallway would be good choices. In a home, most areas are really too small to gain much practical advantage of the crosshatch pattern. Equal security can be achieved by simpler, less expensive means. Couple this with the high cost of the necessary equipment and its installation, and the inherent problems of everyday stray motions

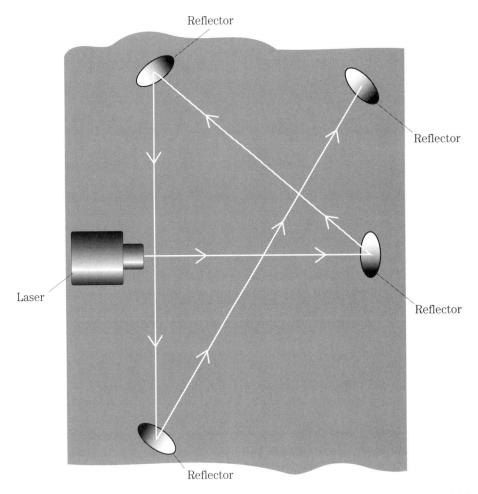

10-6 In practical systems, reflectors are used to split the original laser beam into multiple paths throughout the protected area.

causing false alarms, and it becomes clear that it is inappropriate to apply such technology to most home alarm systems, except under the most unusual circumstances.

Advantages of computer-based security systems

A high-tech device more commonly used than lasers in many home alarm systems is the computer, which is showing up in almost every application imaginable. These days *digital* is a hot sales buzzword, whether it has any relevance to the application at hand or not. Everything is being computerized it seems. In many cases, use of a computer offers many advantages, but in other applications, it doesn't really add much, and a computer might not be able to do some jobs as well as simpler analog circuits.

In effect, the computer takes the place of the central control box, permitting more flexible and powerfully switching functions within the system.

Does it make sense to use a computer in a home alarm system? Well, maybe yes, and maybe no. There are advantages and disadvantages, and individual circumstances will determine which outweighs the other. For the time being, concentrate on the advantages.

The chief advantages of using a computer in a home alarm system are pretty much the same as using a computer in most other common applications—more detailed conditional control, automated record keeping and analysis, and programmability.

A computer can address each sensor or group of sensors independently, and in any desired combination. This feature might be used to reduce false alarms. For example, it was explained in a previous chapter that motion detectors and sound detectors can both be useful, but either can easily be fooled, often resulting in excessive false alarms. A sound detector might be triggered by a loud noise outdoors that happens to have the right frequency characteristics. A motion detector can be triggered by a blowing drape or even a passing shadow. If there really is an intruder in the area, the odds are good that a sound would be accompanied by motion. In a computerized alarm system, these two sensors can be ANDed together. (With an AND gate, both inputs must be positive to produce a positive output.) If just the sound detector or just the motion detector is briefly triggered, the computer will ignore it and the alarm will not be sounded. Only if both sensors are activated together, or within a predetermined time of one another will the alarm be set off. The computer also might be programmed to set off the alarm if either the sound detector or the motion detector is triggered for a suspiciously long time, or repeatedly within a specific time span. For instance, three or four triggering sounds within a period of one or two minutes would be suspicious and warrant investigation.

The computerized alarm system also can utilize multiple outputs. Some events might trigger the alarm. Others might turn on selected lights somewhere in the house. A small "investigate" alarm might be installed in the master bedroom, that is sounded when the system detects something suspicious, that should be checked out, but doesn't really justify setting off the full alarm. For example, if a sound detector is repeatedly triggered, but no other sensor in the system has been tripped, the situation really calls for human judgment.

Under computer control, selected portions of the alarm system can be activated, while leaving other sensors inactive. This feature makes it easier to turn on outside and entrance sensors while people are at home, without risking setting off the alarm by accidentally tripping an inside sensor. The sensors in one part of the house can be deactivated, while the rest of the system is on guard. For example, after everyone goes to bed, sensors (including perhaps motion detectors) can be turned on in the living room, kitchen and basement, while the bedrooms and bathroom area systems are shut down, so no one in the household will inadvertently set off the alarm by sleepily making a trip to the bathroom in the middle of the night.

Such interconnections are made in software rather than hardware. They are in the computer rather than in the circuits. Switching between one combination and another is simply a matter of telling the computer which program it should respond to. Changes and modifications in any program can be made relatively easily. There's no need for a bunch of workers to come trooping in with their tools to rearrange the wiring, which is often a tedious process.

A computer also can store information collected from the various sensors in the system, either in its own memory or on an external device such as a printer. If the alarm is set off by an intruder, how far he or she got, and his or her motions through the protected area can be effectively and precisely tracked. The tracking occurs by keeping a record of what sensors were tripped, in what sequence, and the timing between them. The records will make it easier to inventory anything that was stolen. It also will give the police good information on where to look for possible clues such as fingerprints or footprints.

Sometimes a homeowner might want to keep track of the usage of various rooms, perhaps for energy conservation. A computerized home alarm system could be programmed to perform extra duties. For example, when the family is home, the computer can keep track of what rooms are occupied, and which have been left empty for an extended period, and can turn on and off lights and/or heating/cooling equipment appropriately. The same sensors (especially motion detectors) can be used for tasks other than alarms. The only difference is in how the computer has been programmed to respond when the various sensors are tripped. Does it turn on the alarm when motion is detected, or does it turn off the lights if no motion is detected for a half hour or so?

As you can see, a computer-based home alarm system can be very flexible and powerful.

Disadvantages of computer-based security systems

A computer-based home alarm system also can be very expensive and complex. It requires considerably more skill and experience to install and program properly and reliably.

Generally it would be most practical to use a dedicated computer circuit designed specifically for the purpose. To use a commercial, general-purpose personal computer to control an alarm system would be impractical in the vast majority of cases. The computer would be tied up and could not be used for other purposes without shutting down the alarm system. To use the computer as a general-purpose personal computer would be even more wasteful. You'd be paying for a lot of features and functions that would go unused in this application. A typical home alarm system computer needs just a *CPU* (central processing unit) and a few kilobytes of memory. Even with detailed record-keeping functions programmed in, this is not a memory-intensive application. A full keyboard isn't really needed either. Programming and operational commands can be entered via a smaller and less expensive hexadecimal keypad. A full monitor is probably overkill as well. LED or LCD (liquid-crystal display) readouts can give sufficient output information for the purposes of most alarm systems. A full printer might be required for permanent hard-copy records, however. This printer would not be frequently used by the alarm system computer, and could easily be shared with a regular personal computer system.

Another major disadvantage of using a standard full-function personal computer to control a home alarm system, is it would be difficult to conceal it and make it inaccessible to a potential intruder. Remember, it is important to protect the central control box. Even if the alarm has already been set off, if an intruder can shut it down fairly quickly (perhaps even by smashing the central control box or computer) the neighbors are likely to assume it was just a false alarm and will ignore it. A dedicated computer circuit can be built into the same kind of protective housing we discussed for regular analog central control boxes.

Computer circuitry is obviously much more complex than the analog circuitry used in standard alarm systems. This complexity means there is much more that can go wrong with such a system. Yes, a computer system will be mostly purely electronic in nature, with fewer electromechanical components. As a rule of thumb, purely electronic components are more reliable over time than moving parts, but the total parts count is much higher in the typical computerized system, counteracting the presumed electronic reliability factor. Moreover, in an alarm system, many of the same electromechanical devices (mostly the sensors) still need to be used, even if the system is under computer control. So, a computerized home alarm system is subject to most of the same potential faults as a typical analog home alarm system, plus there are additional potential problems within the computer or in its programming. Troubleshooting can often be complicated from difficulty in determining whether a functional problem is due to a programming bug or an actual fault in the hardware circuitry.

It is beyond the scope of this book to discuss troubleshooting computer faults. Many other books on this subject are available. A computer controlling an alarm system is not fundamentally any different from any other type of computer, so it can be serviced in the same manner.

So is it worthwhile to use computer control for a home alarm system? As you can see, this is an individual judgment call that depends heavily on the specific circumstances. As a rule of thumb, it would probably be unnecessarily overdoing it in most home systems. There would be little to be gained beyond the "gee whiz" factor, which hardly justifies the added cost, bother of programming, and increase in potential problems. On the other hand, in a large house with a lot of valuable (and easily stolen) property that is likely to attract burglars, it might offer enough extra protection and special features to make economic sense. This decision can only be determined on a case-by-case basis.

Appendix
Alarm sensors and their functions

Here is a summary of some sensors that you can use in security and alarm systems. They are categorized by type of sensor and whether they are normally open (NO) or normally closed (NC).

Switching sensors

- **Acoustic sensor (usually NO)** Also known as a *sound sensor*. Detects audio-frequency vibrations either in the air or on a surface (such as a pane of glass). Usually tuned to respond to a specific limited frequency range. Often has sensitivity and reliability problems. Most frequently encountered in the form of a glass-break detector.
- **Compression switch (NO or NC)** A specially designed push-button switch, designed so that its plunger will be pushed in when a monitored door or window is closed (or sometimes when opened), activating the switch. Somewhat unreliable due to the possibility of accumulated dirt within the mechanical mechanism.
- **Flooding alarm (NO)** Also called a *moisture detector or alarm*. Activated when a liquid creates a short-circuit current path between a pair of probes.
- **Foil tape (NC)** Placed around parameter of a window. If the window is broken, so is the foil tape, opening up the connection. Often considered unattractive.
- **Glass-break detector (usually NO)** A specialized acoustic sensor designed to respond specifically to the sound of breaking glass. It can detect the sound vibrations in the air or directly from the glass surface itself. Often has sensitivity and reliability problems.
- **Heat sensor (NO or NC)** Also called a *temperature sensor*. Any temperature-sensitive device. Switching-type heat sensors are activated

when the detected temperature exceeds a specific preset limit (usually designed into the device by the manufacturer and not adjustable). Used in fire alarms. Also can be a continuous-range sensor.

- **Magnetic reed switch (NO or NC)** A two-part device. One part is a small permanent magnet, and the other is a reed switch that is activated when the magnet section is brought close enough. One of the most commonly used sensors in home alarm systems. Used primarily to monitor doors or windows for unauthorized opening or closing.
- **Mercury switch (NO)** Also called a *tilt switch*. Detects physical motion of an attached object by a globule of mercury rolling into place over the switch contacts.
- **Moisture detector (NO)** Also called a *flood detector* or *flood alarm*. Activated when a liquid creates a short circuit current path between a pair of probes.
- **Motion detector (NO)** Any of a broad class of devices that respond to physical motion within the protected area. The two most common methods of motion detection use broken light beams (usually infrared), or ultrasonic echo patterns. Called an *active alarm system*, because it actively sends out a test signal (optical or ultrasonic). Often subject to false alarms.
- **Panic button (usually NO)** An emergency switch strategically placed so that a legitimate occupant of the house can press it and sound the alarm in an emergency, even if the system is presently disarmed.
- **Pressure mat or pressure switch** (usually NO) A small flat mat, that activates an internal switch when it is compressed by external pressure placed on it. Often placed so an intruder is likely to step on it, without knowing it is there.
- **Proximity detector** (NO or NC) Senses the presence of a person, usually via natural body capacitance. Usually only reliable if the person moves very close to the device.
- **Pull-trap switch (usually NO)** A type of sensor that is activated when a small tab is pulled out of place. Often considered unattractive.
- **Roller switch (NO or NC)** Incorporates a small rolling ball in the body of the switch (somewhat like a computer mouse) that makes contact with a window or door as it closes. Somewhat unreliable due to the possibility of accumulated dirt within the mechanical workings.
- **Smoke detector (usually NO)** A small, usually self-contained fire alarm that is activated by smoke. Can work by optical or chemical means. Can be a lifesaver, but it is often prone to false alarms. Might not respond to certain types of fires until it is too late. Best when used with heat sensors (which are also inadequate by themselves).
- **Snap-action switch (NO or NC)** A push-button switch with a lightweight extension arm or lever over its plunger. Can be activated by a very light pressure. Very sensitive. Reliable but somewhat fragile.
- **Sound sensor (usually NO)** Also known as an *acoustic sensor*. Detects audio-frequency vibrations either in the air or on a surface (such as a pane of glass). Usually tuned to respond to a specific limited frequency range.

Often has sensitivity and reliability problems. Most frequently encountered in the form of a glass-break detector.

- **Temperature sensor (NO or NC)** Also called a *heat sensor*. Any temperature-sensitive device. Switching-type heat sensors are activated when the detected temperature exceeds a specific preset limit (usually designed into the device by the manufacturer and not adjustable). Used in fire alarms. Also can be a continuous-range sensor.
- **Thermal switch (usually NO)** A heat-activated switch. Activated when the detected temperature exceeds a specific preset limit (usually designed into the device by the manufacturer and not adjustable). Used in fire alarms.
- **Tilt switch (NO)** Alternate name for a mercury switch
- **Vibration switch (usually NO)** A device that can be mounted to some surface or object. If the object is moved, it will cause vibration, activating the device. Tends to be rather bulky and expensive. Often subject to false alarms.

Continuous-range sensors

- **Gas detector** Detects the presence and concentration of dangerous deoxidizing gasses in the atmosphere surrounding the device.
- **Heat sensor** Also can be a switching sensor. See the section on switching sensors.
- **Infrared detector** An optical sensor tuned to respond only to light in the infrared range, which is invisible to the human eye. Usually very reliable. Used for motion detection and broken-beam detection.
- **Optical sensor** Also called a *photosensor*. Any of a broad class of devices which respond to the presence or absence of light, whether visible or infrared. Some typical examples include photodiodes, photoresistors, photovoltaic cells, phototransistors, and LASCRS (light-activated SCRs).
- **Photoresistor** An optical sensor that varies its resistance in proportion to the amount of light striking its sensing surface.
- **Photosensor** Also called an *optical sensor*. Any of a broad class of devices which respond to the presence or absence of light, whether visible or infrared. Some typical examples include photodiodes, photoresistors, photovoltaic cells, phototransistors, and LASCRS (light-activated SCRs).
- **Taguchi gas sensor (TGS)** The most common type of gas detector. Detects the presence and concentration of dangerous deoxidizing gasses in the atmosphere surrounding the device. Very sensitive and operational over an extremely wide range.
- **Temperature sensor** Also can be a switching sensor. See the section on switching sensors.
- **Thermistor** A temperature-dependent resistor. The resistance varies proportionally with the detected temperature. Can be used in fire alarms, although thermal switches are generally more directly appropriate for fire alarms.

Glossary

AND gate A circuit or device, usually digital that deals with just two input and output levels—HIGH and LOW. An AND gate always has at least two inputs. The output level is HIGH if and only if all inputs are HIGH. If any one or more of the inputs is LOW, then the output will be LOW.

access code A secret number which must be entered to permit access to the operation of a secured circuit or function.

acoustic sensor A device that produces an electrical response when it detects vibrations corresponding to sounds. It might respond to any sound of sufficient intensity, or it might be tuned to respond only to sounds containing specific frequency components.

activate To turn on or engage a function. To cause a device or circuit to go to its non-normal state. For example, a normally open switch is closed when activated, and a normally closed switch is open when activated.

active alarm system A type of intrusion system that bathes the protected area with some sort of signal beam(s) (usually infrared or ultrasonic). It monitors the returned beam(s) for disturbances that indicate an intrusion. Broadly speaking, a motion detector.

alarm 1) A warning sound or other automatically initiated indication of some detected emergency situation (typically an intrusion or a fire). 2) An electronic or electromechanical device that generates such a warning sound, such a bell, buzzer, or siren.

arm To activate an alarm system so it will monitor and respond to any disturbances of its sensor devices.

auto-dial alarm A type of alarm system that automatically dials a preprogrammed emergency number when triggered and plays a prerecorded tape to summon help.

automated lighting Indoor or outdoor lighting that is turned on electronically in response to any of three types of triggering conditions:
- Preset time intervals
- Monitored ambient light levels

- Tripped sensor(s) indicating a possible intrusion into a protected area

   Such lighting tends to discourage intruders, and make it more difficult for them to hide or escape without being spotted.

automatic reset A subcircuit that determines if the area is secure (no sensors tripped) after a shut-down timer silences the alarm. If all is secure, the system is reactivated to monitor for any additional intrusions.

beam emitter A device in an active alarm system that generates the test signal (usually ultrasonic or infrared beams). A dedicated sensor recovers this transmitted signal at another location and checks it for disturbances, interruptions, or distortions indicating a possible intrusion.

bell An electromechanical device often used as an alarm output device. A clapper is moved electromechanically to strike the bell and produce a loud ringing sound.

bipolar transistor A three-part semiconductor "sandwich" with sections of oppositely polarization. This device is often used as an electronic switch, via saturation biasing.

black box A concept of convenience—a circuit or system with unknown or unspecified details that accepts certain input signals and produces specific, predictable output signals. Specifically how the input signals are processed to create the output signals is dismissed as irrelevant for purposes of the discussion at hand.

block diagram A design or diagnostic tool in which a complex circuit or system is drawn as a series of functional blocks or units without bothering with specific details of the actual circuitry. A block diagram can be very useful in troubleshooting because it makes it easy to roughly isolate the section or section(s) responsible for the problematic function or function(s).

buffer A simple subcircuit used to match up input and output signals correctly, and/or to prevent an output from being excessively loaded by an input or vice versa.

buzzer An electromagnetic device often used as a low to moderate volume alarm output device. Usually the buzzing sound is generated by forcing a piece of piezoelectric material into vibration. Very high-volume sound output is usually not possible with this type of device.

cable A length of insulated wire, usually though not always, with multiple conductors that are electrically insulated from each other to permit the simultaneous conduction of independent signals. Cables can be shielded or unshielded. A shielded cable includes a metallic mesh coating surrounding the actual signal conductor(s) that helps prevent possible RFI (radio-frequency interference) pick up. Shielded cables usually are not needed in most home alarm systems.

callback A repeat service call, usually to correct a problem or oversight from a prior installation or service call. The technician is called back to a job that was thought to be completed.

central control box The "brains" of a home alarm system. This is the main switching circuitry that decides when and how the output alarm device(s) will respond to the various sensors. The primary means for arming and disarming the system are also normally part of the central control box.

closed circuit A complete current path.

coaxial cable A specific type of shielded cable used primarily with RF (radio frequency) signals. It is rarely needed in home alarm systems, and its use would merely add unnecessary bulk and expense.

code A meaningful pattern without corresponding surface meaning. In alarm systems, a code is a specific pattern of switch closures required for an attempted user to gain access to critical system functions, such as arming and disarming the alarm.

color code A system of assigning functional meaning to specific colors of wire insulation to aid in troubleshooting and circuit tracing. For example, an orange wire would carry signal type A, and a green wire carries signal type B. A technician can tell at a glance which is which.

commercially monitored alarm system An alarm system featuring an autodial alarm or some other form of remote monitoring that contacts a contracted company when a potential emergency situation is detected and they send out personnel to check out and cope with the situation. Such a system tends to be rather expensive on a continuous basis, and false alarms can be especially troublesome.

common wire A wire or line in common with two or more circuits or subcircuits. Usually, but not always, the common wire is at ground potential. In alarm systems, a common wire is one that is part of multiple sensor loops, minimizing the total number of wires connected directly to the central control box.

comparator A circuit that compares two (occasionally more) voltages (or other electrical signals) and produces an output indicating which of the inputs has the higher value at that moment. Usually one of the inputs is given a fixed reference value.

computer-based security system An alarm system that uses a computer as a "smart" central control box to permit programmability, automated record-keeping, and generally more versatility in the system functions. For most home alarm systems, it is unlikely that the advantages of a computer-based security system will justify the greatly increased system cost and complexity.

conduit A hollow, semiflattened tube housing used for running lengths of wire without risks of being pulled out of place or causing accidents.

contact block A small unit that makes contact with one end of a strip of foil tape and permitting a wire to be attached for connection with the alarm system.

contact resistance The dc resistance between switch terminals. Usually the term *contact resistance* implies the resistance when the switch is closed (the minimum possible resistance for that unit), but in some cases it is useful to refer to the open contact resistance (the maximum possible resistance for that unit).

continuous-range sensor A sensor with an output that can vary over an analog range, rather than the usual simple on/off, yes/no type response of a switching sensor.

continuous-tone siren An electronic circuit used as an alarm output device, which produces a loud, unvarying tone when activated.

control circuitry Circuitry that routes and processes signals, converting the input signal(s) to the appropriate output signal(s).

crosshatch A pattern of beams (usually infrared and almost always of the laser type) that covers a large two- or three-dimensional area (as opposed to a simple straight line). Multiple sensors monitor the various beams of the crosshatch pattern. If an object (or person) breaks any element of the crosshatch, the motion is sensed and the alarm is activated.

current drain rate A measure of how rapidly a battery is discharged by its load. On the shelf, the surrounding air creates a very high-resistance load for the slowest possible current drain rate for that particular battery.

customer files Detailed (and confidential) information on each individual alarm system installed or serviced by a company, kept in secured files at the company's office. The specific information in the customer files can be vital in dealing with later callbacks and service calls for that system.

deactivate The opposite of activate. To turn off or disable a circuit or system. When an alarm system is deactivated, it ignores the states of its various sensors, and the alarm will not be sounded, even if one or more sensors are tripped.

dead bolt A mechanical lock in which a solid bolt passes directly into the door frame, preventing the door from being opened by force.

decoding circuit A circuit that examines a security code entered by a potential user and determines if that code is correct or not, providing or blocking access to the protected function as appropriate.

deoxidizing gas A gas that chemically binds with oxygen, making it very poisonous because it "steals" the oxygen the body needs. Typical deoxidizing gases include carbon monoxide, hydrogen, methane, propane, and vapors from gasoline or alcohol.

diac A bidirectional trigger diode often used to control a triac in a switching circuit.

digital gate A simple circuit (today almost always in IC form) that deals only with binary or digital signals, which can only be either LOW or HIGH, with no intermediate values recognized. The output state is determined by the specific combination of input states. The most common types of digital gates are as follows:

- Buffer—one input, one output; output state same as input state
- Inverter—one input, one output; output state opposite of input state
- AND gate—two or more inputs, one output; output HIGH if and only if all inputs HIGH
- OR gate—two or more inputs, one output; output HIGH if any one or more inputs HIGH
- X-OR gate—two inputs, one output; output HIGH if either input HIGH, but not both

disarm Deactivate. To disable an alarm system and reset it if necessary. To turn off a sounding alarm.

DMM Digital multimeter. A device for measuring voltage, resistance, or current, with its output in the form of directly displayed numbers rather than an analog meter and pointer. Very useful in some applications, but in some applications, an analog VOM will do a better job.

double locking Two separate locks on a single door. Often one is automatically latching, engaging whenever the door is closed (unless mechanically disabled beforehand), while the other must be manually locked when desired.

DPDT Double-pole, double-throw. A basic switching pattern. Two separate circuits are simultaneously switched, each with a common contact that can be switched to either of two possible contact points.

DPST Double-pole, single-throw. A basic (but relatively uncommon) switching pattern. Two separate circuits are simultaneously switched, with each circuit being opened or closed in unison.

duct pipe An often ignored security risk. A large duct pipe (used for heating and cooling) might provide an entryway for an intruder to crawl through. An adequate alarm system must secure the vents of any large duct pipes.

electronic switch A circuit that electronically and automatically simulates the action of a mechanical switch in response to an appropriate electrical input signal.

entrance/exit delay A short-duration timer (usually with a time period less than one minute) that gives legitimate occupants time to go out and shut the door after arming the alarm system, or to come in and disarm the system before the alarm sounds upon returning.

false alarm A frequent potential problem with any alarm system, in which the alarm is erroneously sounded when no actual emergency situation exists. False alarms can be kept to a minimum, but can never be eliminated entirely.

FET Field-effect transistor. A special semiconductor device that more or less simulates the operational characteristics of a vacuum tube. It is often used in high-speed switching circuits, although its advantages are usually minimal in most practical home alarm systems.

fire alarm A circuit that detects the possible presence of a fire and sounds an alarm to alert any occupants who might be endangered. Most practical fire alarms work by detecting either excessive temperatures, or the presence of smoke.

555 timer IC A popular, easy-to-use device that is very well suited to the various timing and delay functions throughout a full-featured home alarm system.

flow chart A very useful design and troubleshooting tool, illustrating the functional stages in a system or process, indicating every significant step and choice or option. If you know the system is doing everything it should up to point X, you're well on the way to locating and isolating the source of the problem.

foil tape An adhesive-backed strip of a thin conductive material. It is usually is placed on windows. Breaking the window will also break the foil tape, opening up the current path through it, functioning like a normally closed sensor.

flooding alarm A circuit that responds and sets off an alarm when the level of some liquid is detected above some specific point, usually by creating a short circuit current path between a pair of simple probes.

gas detector A special sensor that detects the presence of specific dangerous chemicals in the air, usually in the form deoxidizing gases.

glass-break detector A special sensor designed to be tripped specifically by the breaking of glass. Most glass-break detectors are specialized acoustic sensors or vibration sensors. Either type can subject to false alarms.

hard wired A function that is a built-in part of a physical circuit (as opposed to functions that are provided by software or programmable functions). The function can not be changed without making physical changes to the circuit itself, which is usually not feasible or convenient.

heat sensor A temperature-sensitive device that can be used to activate an alarm if the ambient temperature exceeds a specific level. Heat sensors are useful in fire alarms.

hook and eye A simple form of mechanical latch for holding two things together. The eye (an open loop) is mounted on one object, and a hinged hook is mounted on the other. To hold them together, the hook is fitted into the eye loop. A hook and eye provides only minimal security, because it usually can be forced without too much effort.

horn-type speaker A metallic speaker that is well suited for outdoor use. It is relatively weather-proof, and can produce a very loud sound from a fairly small unit.

infrared beam A beam of light that is outside the visible spectrum. In alarm systems it can be used to detect motion. If an object (such as an intruder's body) passes between the beam source and a sensor, the alarm will be sounded. Since the infrared beam is invisible to the naked eye, it is harder for the intruder to know it is there and to avoid it.

infrared detector A specialized photosensor designed to respond only to light beams within the infrared range, which is outside the visible spectrum. An infrared detector is used to determine the presence (or absence) of this type of invisible light.

integrated circuit (IC) A monolithic equivalent for tens to thousands of discrete components (transistors, resistors, capacitors, etc.) etched onto a tiny semiconductor slab to perform some specific circuit function.

inverter A "reversing" circuit, that exchanges HIGH for LOW, and vice versa. Both analog and digital inverter circuits exist. A digital inverter is one of the simplest types of digital gate, with just a single input and a single output, which are always at opposite states.

keypad A set of push-button switches, usually numbered for entry of security codes and other types of data. (Generally, only security codes are used in most home alarm systems.)

key switch A locking switch that requires a key to be opened or closed. In most cases only a simple, minimal lock is used, which can be picked without much difficulty. Most key switches offer only a moderate amount of security. Also called a lock switch or locking switch.

kick plate A metal plate that is used to strengthen a door and spread out any applied force to minimize its effect. Kick plates are also known as *strike plates*.

laser beam A highly focused beam of light at a single frequency. Because of its tight focus, a laser can make very efficient use of its supply power, and it can be very precisely aimed. Laser light can be visible (usually, but not necessarily red) or invisible to the human eye (infrared).

laser crosshatch A pattern of laser beams (usually infrared) that covers a large two- or three-dimensional area (as opposed to a simple straight line). Multiple sensors monitor the various beams of the crosshatch pattern. If an object (or person) breaks any element of the crosshatch, the motion is sensed and the alarm is activated.

latch Something that holds something else. Mechanically, a latch is a simple form of keyless lock, useful mostly to prevent accidentally opening. In electronics a latch is a circuit that holds some specific electric value or condition, even if the causative input signal is removed. The latch circuit must be reset by some other means, usually manually.

latching switch The opposite of a momentary-action switch. Once it is moved from open to closed, it will stay closed until it is physically moved back to the open position, or vice versa.

latching relay A special relay that can hold its activated state. All relays are activated by a current passing through the coil. In most relays, the switch contacts are automatically deactivated when the current flow through the coil stops. A latching relay will remain activated, even if the current flow through the coil stops. The relay can only be deactivated by a separate reset signal or manual button.

lighting protection Good lighting reduces the risk of intrusion, because an intruder will usually want to avoid being seen. In an home security system lighting protection consists of one or more of the following:
- Preset time intervals
- Monitored ambient light levels
- Tripped sensor(s) indicating a possible intrusion into a protected area

load A resistance in a current path, which consumes power. The larger the resistance, the greater the load (and the more power consumed).

lock switch A special security switch that requires a key to be opened or closed. In most cases only a simple, minimal lock is used, which can be picked without much difficulty. Most key switches offer only a moderate amount of security. Also called a key switch or locking switch.

loop A complete current path. In alarm systems, a group of sensors treated as a single unit by the central control box. Loops using normally closed sensors are in series, while loops using normally open sensors are in parallel.

magnetic reed switch A two-unit device, consisting of a small permanent magnet (with no electrical connections) and a magnetically sensitive reed switch, which is physically wired into the circuit. The reed switch is activated whenever the magnet is brought close enough to it. Moving the magnet further away deactivates the switch. Magnetic reed switches are widely used to electronically monitor doors and windows. This is one of the most frequently used type of sensors used in most home alarm systems.

main control panel The primary operating controls of a system. In an alarm system, the main control panel is normally part of the central control box, and must be secured in some way against unauthorized use, or an intruder can defeat the purpose of the alarm system.

manufacturer's warranties Manufacturers of alarm system components often respect warranties only if the device in question is properly installed. An installer can be held liable for the cost of any repairs or replacements if the necessary warranty documentation is not properly kept on file.

mercury switch A simple type of motion sensor. A mercury switch consists of a small globule of mercury enclosed in a glass tube. When at the correct angle, the mercury shorts the two terminals together, closing the switch. If the mercury switch is moved from this position, the mercury will roll away from one or both of the internal terminals, opening the switch. Mercury switches also are known as *tilt switches*.

modular alarm system A simple, more or less self-contained alarm system that requires little or no installation. Some form of motion detection is normally used. For a number of reasons, the actual security provided by such a device is limited.

moisture alarm A circuit that responds and sets off an alarm when the level of some liquid is detected above some specific point, usually by creating a short circuit current path between a pair of simple probes.

momentary-action switch A switch with a "preferred" position, either open or closed. It holds this preferred position until acted upon by some outside force or signal, which activates the switch into its momentary (nonpreferred) state. When the activating force or signal is removed, the switch immediately reverts to its normal preferred state. A momentary action switch can be either of two types:
- Normally open—Preferred position is open; activated position is closed
- Normally closed—Proffered position is closed; activated position is open

monitored alarm system An alarm system featuring an auto-dial alarm or some other form of remote monitoring that contacts a contracted company when a potential emergency situation is detected and they send out personnel to check out and cope with the situation. Such a system tends to be expensive on a continuous basis, and false alarms can be especially troublesome.

motion detector An active alarm system. Rather than switch-type sensors, a motion detector puts out some sort of signal (usually ultrasonic or infrared light beams) into the protected area, then the system picks up and senses the signals after they have passed through the room. Any detected changes indicate something in the signal path has moved, altering the pattern of reflections. This is used to set off the alarm, under the assumption that the unauthorized motion is some form of intrusion. Motion detectors are almost always subject to frequent false alarms.

multiconductor cable A set of multiple wires, insulated from one another, each carrying its own independent signal. The wires are grouped together into a single cable for convenience in physically running the wiring in a system. All of the individual wires in the cable are bundled together within a collective insulating jacket. The cable as a whole can be either shielded or unshielded. (There is rarely much reason to use shielded cable in most home alarm systems.)

multitone siren An electronic alarm output device that periodically varies its pitch to make a more distinctive and ear-catching sound than a continuous tone. The frequency can switch instantly between specific, discrete values, or it can sweep through a range of values.

normally closed (NC) A type of momentary-action switch in which the contacts are closed when the switch is not activated, and are opened only when the switch is activated by some outside force or signal.

normally open (NO) A type of momentary-action switch in which the contacts are open when the switch is not activated, and are closed only when the switch is activated by some outside force or signal.

NOT gate A digital inverter. A digital gate with a single input and a single output, which is always at the opposite state as the input. If the input state is HIGH, the output state is LOW (or not HIGH), and if the input state is LOW, the output state is HIGH (or not LOW).

open circuit A broken or incomplete current path. There is some sort of interruption or blockage in the path the current needs to follow.

OR gate A circuit or device, usually digital in design, which deals with just two input and output levels—HIGH and LOW. An AND gate always has at least two inputs. The output level is LOW if and only if all inputs are LOW. If any one or more of the inputs is HIGH, then the output will be HIGH.

output alarm device The part of an alarm system that actual alerts the user(s) to a detected problem or possible emergency condition. Usually the output alarm device will generate a loud sound, but in some cases, a visual indicator might be useful in addition to, or even instead of an audible alarm. An auto-dialer or some similar automated system also can be used as an output alarm device.

panic button An emergency switch strategically placed so that a legitimate occupant of the house can press it and sound the alarm, if necessary, even if the system is currently disarmed.

parallel circuit A circuit in which the elements are connected side-by-side, with all "top" ends wired in unison and all "bottom" ends similarly shorted together. Normally open sensors must be wired in parallel within a loop.

passive alarm system An alarm system that does not send out a signal directly into the protected area, but uses a number of switch-like sensors that can be manually activated when someone enters the protected area or moves something (such as opening a door). Most home alarm systems are primarily passive. Curiously, a passive alarm system alone actually tends to provide greater overall security than an active alarm system alone in most cases.

password A security code. The specific sequence of numbers, letters, or other keystrokes that must be entered to gain access to the protected function(s). An unauthorized person presumedly would not know the password, and would therefore be denied access. A password is often used to disarm an alarm system, or to permit operation of its main control panel.

periodic maintenance calls Regularly scheduled preventive service calls to prevent and catch any possible problems before they interfere with the operation of the system. Any failure of a security system can have dire consequences.

phantom resistor The resistance of an open circuit, usually just plain air. A true open circuit is not possible except in a vacuum. Normally open air resistance is extremely high—approximately several hundred megohms. Under some circumstances there can be an unforeseen current path with a resistance low enough to affect circuit operation. The effect is the same as connecting a physical resistor of a comparable value across the supposedly open circuit.

photoresistor A continuous-range sensor that responds to light. The resistance of this device varies proportionately to the amount of light striking its sensing surface.

photosensitive controller A circuit using some sort of photosensor to operate some other circuit or device in specific ways, dependent on the detected light levels.

photosensor A type of sensor that responds to light from some outside source striking its surface. Photosensors can be continuous range or switching. Common photosensors include, but are not limited to, photodiodes, photoresistors, photovoltaic cells, phototransistors, and LASCRs (light-activated SCRs).

power-failure sensing circuit A circuit that monitors the system ac power source. If the ac power is interrupted, or drops below the required levels for any reason, the power failure sensing circuit automatically switches the system over to back-up battery power. In some cases, this circuit can also activate a small audible alarm, or a visual indicator of some sort to draw attention to the power failure problem, so it can be corrected before the back-up batteries are discharged.

pressure mat A small, flat mat that closes an internal switch when pressure is placed on it, usually by someone stepping on or leaning against the mat. To be effective in a security system, a pressure mat must be strategically placed and concealed from view. A pressure mat also is called a *pressure switch.*

programmable A function that can be created, selected, or modified without making any physical changes in the circuitry itself. The programmable instructions or data are usually entered via a keyboard or keypad of some sort, but some simple types of programmability can use a group of ordinary switches, whose desired positions are "remembered" by the programmed system.

protected area The vicinity actually within the protective range of an alarm system or sensor.

pull-trap switch A type of NO sensor that is closed when a small tab is physically pulled out of place.

push-on/push-off switch A latching push-button switch. Most push-button switches are momentary-action type. A push-on/push-off switch can hold either state indefinitely. If it is open, pushing the button once will close the switch. Pushing the button a second time will open the switch again.

recessed mounting A form of installation in which a hole is drilled or cut out to hold the installed unit snugly so it is flush with the original mounting surface rather than jutting out on top of the mounting surface. Recessed mounting is generally neater and more secure than comparable surface mounting, although it requires greater effort and expense.

relay An electromechanical switching device with electrically isolated input and output circuits. When an input current flows through the relay coil, the switch contacts in the output circuit are pulled into their activated positions.

reset switch A switch that shuts down the alarm when sounding and rearms the system to monitor for additional indications of intrusion (or other emergency condition). For normal security system use, the reset switch should always be secured (with a key switch or a security code password of some sort) to prevent unauthorized use. For testing purposes, a temporary, easy-to-use reset switch can make the job a lot faster and more convenient.

return line The wire(s) that brings the loop signal back into the central control box to determine if any of the sensors in that loop have been tripped (also called *signal return*).

RFI Radio-frequency interference. Home alarm systems rarely transmit any RFI, but in some cases, erratic control problems could be caused by RFI pick up, especially in long wire runs.

SCR Silicon-controlled rectifier. An electrically switchable diode. Current can not flow through the device until an appropriate trigger signal is applied to the gate terminal. Once triggered, an SCR will conduct current in one direction like an ordinary diode unless the external flow of current is cut off or reverses direction, resetting the SCR.

security code A specific pattern of numbers, letters, or key presses used to activate a secured function, such as disarming an alarm system. Also known as a password.

security system An electronic system designed for monitoring a number of electromechanical sensors to guard and warn against potentially dangerous emergency situations, most commonly intrusion and/or fire, but protection against other potential problems may also be included in a security system. Loosely speaking, a security system is the same as an alarm system, but technically speaking, *security system* has more generalized implications. All alarm systems can be called security systems, but some security systems mat not actually qualify as alarm systems.

security switch A hidden or otherwise protected switch on a central control box that must be used to permit access to the control of critical functions.

security timer An electric timer that can be used to turn lights (or other electrical devices) on and off at preset times, which is often used to create the illusion of someone at home in an unoccupied house. This trick is generally effective only against casual, impulse intruders, and can alert a more experienced and observant burglar that the house is unoccupied at certain times.

sensitivity A measure of how strong a signal or force must be to activate a given function or reaction.

sensor An electromechanical device that gives an electrical indication of some non-electronic environmental condition, such as light, temperature, or pressure, among many others. Sensors can be switching or continuous range, depending on the specific application.

series circuit A circuit in which the components are connected sequentially, end-to-end. A normally closed sensor loop must be a series circuit.

shielded cable A type of cable with a metallic mesh shield between the individually insulated internal conductors, and the cable collective outside insulation jacket. The purpose of the shield is usually to prevent RFI pick up or transmission.

short circuit A direct electrical connection, with little or no load resistance. Usually the term is used for an undesired fault condition, rather than a desired electrical connection. A short circuit permits some or all of an electrical system to get in some part of the circuit or system where it doesn't belong. A short circuit can also cause excessive current draw because of the minimal resistance. Besides wasting power, this can damage or destroy sensitive components and possibly even cause a fire.

shut-off timer A timer circuit that automatically turns off a sounding alarm after a preset time. This is an essential part of any serious alarm system. A long-term continuously sounding alarm is a violation of the rights of neighbors and loudly advertises the fact that the home is now unprotected.

signal return Same as return line. The wire(s) that brings the loop signal back into the central control box to determine if any of the sensors in that loop have been tripped.

silent alarm A nonlocal alarm that does not alert an intruder that it has been activated. Instead an audible or visual indicator at some other location summons help, presumedly to come and catch the intruder in the act. This type of alarm is generally not appropriate in home security systems.

siren An electronic output alarm device, designed to produce a very loud, hard to ignore sound when activated. Sirens can be continuous tone or multitone.

smoke alarm A simple localized fire alarm, that responds to the presence of smoke, rather than the fire or heat. A smoke alarm can sense the smoke chemically or optically. Certainly better than nothing, but a smoke detector alone can not detect all fires in time.

snap-action switch A push-button switch with a lightweight extension arm over its plunger, which can be activated with a very light pressure.

sound sensor A sensor that responds to acoustic vibrations in the air. Some can respond to any sound of a sufficient volume, and others are tuned to specific frequencies (also known as an acoustic sensor).

sounding (alarm) An activated alarm, emitting some sort of loud, ear-catching noise.

SPDT Single-pole, double-throw. A basic switching function in which a single common line can be connected to either one of two optional circuits, depending on the switch position.

spring-loaded lock A simple and inexpensive type of mechanical lock, which is notoriously easy to defeat. This is the type of lock that can often be opened by jiggling a credit card between the door and the frame.

SPST Single-pole, single-throw. The most basic and common switching function. A single circuit can be either opened or closed, depending on the switch position.

status light/indicator A visual device used to inform a user of some particular system condition, such as an activated function.

strike plate A metal plate placed over part of a door to make it more difficult for someone to break through it. The plate spreads out the force of impact over a larger area, lessening its effect (also called a kick plate).

surface mounting A type of installation in which the installed unit is affixed directly over the wall or other surface. The mounted unit necessarily projects outward from the surface. Less expensive and time consuming than recess mounting, but not as neat or secure.

switching device An electrical or mechanical unit that performs some switching function.

Taguchi gas sensor (TGS) A continuous-range semiconductor sensor that can detect and measure very low or very high concentrations of deoxidizing gases.

temperature sensor An electromechanical device that produces a switched or continuous-range response to the ambient temperature of its immediate environment. Temperature sensors can be useful in fire alarms.

temporary test-alarm device A small, low-volume (or visual) indication device temporarily used in place of the system main (loud) output alarm devices during test procedures to avoid creating unnecessary disturbances from repeatedly triggering the alarm.

TGS See Taguchi gas sensor.

thermal switch A heat-sensitive switching sensor that is activated when the sensed temperature exceeds a specific level. The trip temperature is usually designed into the thermal switch and is not adjustable.

thermistor A type of continuous-range temperature sensor, which varies its resistance proportionately with the sensed temperature.

tilt switch Alternate name for a mercury switch.

time delay A circuit designed to introduce a pause of a preset length before the system responds to some triggering condition.

timer A circuit that is activated when triggered, and remains activated for a specific preset period of time and then automatically deactivates itself. Also called a timing circuit. Often (though not necessarily) used interchangeably with the term *time delay*.

timing circuit A circuit that is activated when triggered and remains activated for a specific preset period of time, and then automatically deactivates itself. Also called a timer. Often (though not necessarily) used interchangeably with the term *time delay*.

transistor switch An electronic switch circuit built around one or more saturated transistors.

trickle charger A type of battery recharger circuit designed to apply a continuous low current charge to back-up batteries as long as ac power is available. If the ac power is interrupted or significantly reduced for any reason, the back-up batteries are switched in to power the system until normal ac power is restored. The trickle charge counteracts the normal, inevitable shelf discharge of the batteries, ensuring that they will be fully charged whenever they are needed.

triac A bidirectional SCR. Similar to a SCR in all ways, except when triggered it permits the current to flow in either direction. The external current flow must be interrupted to deactivate a triac.

trigger diode A special diode designed to provide an optimum gating signal for a SCR, triac, or similar device.

triggering Activating or turning on a function in response to some external stimulus.

troubleshooting The process of logically analyzing a circuit or system to localize the source of some fault or problem, so it can be repaired or replaced.

tuner cleaner spray A chemical used to clean electrical switch contacts, potentiometers, and similar devices.

ultrasonic wave A sound wave with a frequency that is too high for the human ear to detect. Often used in motion detectors. Receiving sensors recover the transmitted ultrasonic waves and analyze their echo patterns to determine if there has been any disturbing motion.

U-nail A curved, double-pronged nail (also called a staple) designed to hold a wire or cable against a wall or other surface, under the curved center of the nail.

VCO Voltage-controlled oscillator. The frequency of the output signal is determined by the level of some external control voltage. Often used in whooper alarms.

vibration sensor A device that can be mounted to some surface or object, which if moved, will trigger the vibration sensor.

voltage regulator A circuit designed to hold an input voltage to a specific value, despite varying external conditions (such as a variable load).

VOM Volt-ohm-milliammeter. The basic piece of test equipment, good for most troubleshooting of most standard home alarm system. A VOM can measure voltage, resistance, or current. Usually an analog meter is implied by the term *VOM* but sometimes considered functionally interchangeable with a *DMM* (digital multimeter).

warning decal A sticker that warns that the premises are protected by some specific type of alarm system. Ultimately good primarily for advertising purposes. A warning decal is unlikely to frighten off a serious intruder, especially since often the decals are used where there is no actual alarm system backing them up.

weatherproofing A method for limiting corrosive or damaging effects of outdoor environmental conditions, such as rain, high winds, wide temperature extremes, etc.

wire tag Small labels on one end of a long wire in a group of such wires, identifying the function of the wire or the location of its far end.

"whooper" siren A type of electronic output alarm device with a very distinctive and ear-catching "whoop-whoop" sound, usually achieved with some sort of VCO circuit. One of the hardest type of alarms sounds to ignore or mask with other sounds.

X-OR gate A type of digital gate with two inputs and a single output. It is a specialized variation of the basic OR gate. In an X-OR gate, the output is HIGH if and only if one and only one of the inputs is HIGH. If both inputs are LOW, or if both inputs are HIGH, the output is LOW. Also known as a *difference detector* or *difference gate*.

Index

Other Related Bestsellers of Interest

Computer Technician's Handbook, 3rd Edition
Art Margolis
A step-by-step guide to the troubleshooting and repair of any kind of computer.
Previous edition sold 20,000 copies. For technicians and advanced hobbyists.
ISBN 0-8306-3279-4, #157547-2 $26.95 Paperback

Radar for Technicians: Installation, Maintenance, and Repair
Frederick L. Gould
The professional electronics technician's practical guide to understanding the installation, maintenance, and repair of modern radar systems.
ISBN 0-07-024062-0 $45.00 Hardcover

How to Order

Call 1-800-822-8158
24 hours a day,
7 days a week
in U.S. and Canada

Mail this coupon to:
McGraw-Hill, Inc.
P.O. Box 182067
Columbus, OH 43218-2607

Fax your order to:
614-759-3644

EMAIL
70007.1531@COMPUSERVE.COM
COMPUSERVE: GO MH

Shipping and Handling Charges

Order Amount	Within U.S.	Outside U.S.
Less than $15	$3.50	$5.50
$15.00 - $24.99	$4.00	$6.00
$25.00 - $49.99	$5.00	$7.00
$50.00 - $74.49	$6.00	$8.00
$75.00 - and up	$7.00	$9.00

EASY ORDER FORM— SATISFACTION GUARANTEED

Ship to:

Name _____

Address _____

City/State/Zip _____

Daytime Telephone No. _____

Thank you for your order!

ITEM NO.	QUANTITY	AMT.

Method of Payment:

☐ Check or money order enclosed (payable to McGraw-Hill)

	Shipping & Handling charge from chart below	
	Subtotal	
	Please add applicable state & local sales tax	
	TOTAL	

☐ **VISA**   ☐ DISCOVER

☐ AMERICAN EXPRESS Cards   ☐ MasterCard

Account No. ☐☐☐☐☐☐☐☐☐☐☐☐☐☐☐☐☐☐☐

Signature _____ Exp. Date _____
   Order invalid without signature

In a hurry? Call 1-800-822-8158 anytime, day or night, or visit your local bookstore.

Code = BC15ZZA